In Defense of Civility

In Defense of Civility

How Religion Can Unite America on Seven Moral Issues That Divide Us

James Calvin Davis

WJK WESTMINSTER JOHN KNOX PRESS
LOUISVILLE • KENTUCKY

First edition
Published by Westminster John Knox Press
Louisville, Kentucky

10 11 12 13 14 15 16 17 18 19—10 9 8 7 6 5 4 3 2 1

Book design by Drew Stevens
Cover design by designpointinc.com
Cover art © iStockphoto.com

Library of Congress Cataloging-in-Publication Data

Davis, James Calvin.
In defense of civility : how religion can unite America on seven moral issues that divide us / James Calvin Davis.—1st ed.
p. cm.
Includes bibliographical references and index.
ISBN 978-0-664-23544-4 (alk. paper)
1. Christian ethics—United States. 2. Ethical problems. 3. Courtesy. I. Title.
BJ1251.D275 2010
205.0973—dc22

2010017884

PRINTED IN THE UNITED STATES OF AMERICA

∞ The paper used in this publication meets the minimum requirements of the American National Standard for Information Sciences—Permanence of Paper for Printed Library Materials, ANSI Z39.48-1992.

Westminster John Knox Press advocates the responsible use of our natural resources. The text paper of this book is made from at least 30% postconsumer waste.

For my family of faith,

First Presbyterian Church of Hudson Falls, New York

Contents

Preface ix

Acknowledgments xiii

Part One: Public Religion and the American Moral Tradition

1. At War over Values (Allegedly) 3
2. Aren't We a Christian Nation? 21
3. But What about the Separation of Church and State? 37
4. Isn't Religion a Conversation Stopper? 55

Part Two: Rethinking the Big Four

5. Abortion and Stem Cells 75
6. The End of Marriage as We Know It? 89
7. Living and Dying Well 103

Part Three: Beyond the Big Four

8. War *Is* a Moral Issue 117
9. Tree Huggers and Bible-Thumpers Unite! 131
10. It's the Economy (Again), Stupid! 143
11. In Defense of Civility 155

Notes 171

Index 189

Preface

> I firmly believe that the selection of a president should begin with a recommitment to traditional moral values and beliefs. Those include the sanctity of human life, the institution of marriage, and other inviolable pro-family principles.[1]
>
> —James C. Dobson, Focus on the Family

> If your reason for supporting a particular policy is based on a Bible verse, you ought to be a minister rather than a politician.[2]
>
> —Barry W. Lynn, Americans United for Separation of Church and State

Homosexuality, abortion, euthanasia, embryonic stem-cell and fetal research—the debate over these issues represents nothing less than a referendum on the importance of moral values in American society. At least that is what the political rhetoric surrounding these debates has been suggesting for nearly thirty years. From the Moral Majority in 1980 to James Dobson's "Values Voters" in 2008, conservative voices in American politics have been assuming (and telling us) that a vote for moral values means a vote against euthanasia and gay marriage, and for the protection of embryos and fetuses.

While Christian conservative leaders like Dobson rally like-minded voters under the banner of a "values vote," many of his political opponents attack his position in such a way as to grant the assumption that to be for "moral values" requires that one be socially conservative, religious, or (ideally) both. In fact, among secular liberals, the preferred solution to the moral values debate often is to rid politics of religious contributions entirely. Accepting the premise that moral values are synonymous with conservative religious priorities, secular liberals insist that all this talk of morality in public debate and political campaigns represents a violation of the "separation of church and state." As a result, the public debate over "moral values" has dissolved into a "culture war" between two extremes: spokespersons for the Religious Right who assume they have a monopoly on moral priorities, and liberal secularists who dismiss the entire debate as an inappropriate invasion of private religion into the realm of politics.

With this book, I hope to bring some clarity to the current American debate over moral issues by addressing two questions:

1. What really count as "moral values"?
2. Is it good or bad for public debate that some of us weigh in on them from a religious point of view?

From one end, this book challenges that widely held assumption that moral values are the exclusive domain of conservatives. In my view, the community of "values voters" includes not only those who oppose abortion and gay marriage, but also those who support reproductive rights and the freedom to marry. It also includes those who believe our public discourse is dominated by the wrong issues altogether, those who consider war or poverty or the environment to be at least as pressing moral challenges as abortion. What distinguishes people on one side of these issues from those on the other is not that one side is morally motivated and the other side is not, but that each side is informed and inspired by different moral ideals and commitments. This book, then, explores what it means to hold moral values, in order to uncover the shared concerns that lie beneath some of our most intractable differences. In doing so, I hope to suggest a better way for Americans to engage in conversation about the issues that most perplex us.

I also believe that religion can participate—perhaps even lead—in the rejuvenation of healthier public conversation, so the role of religion in American political debate is the other focus of this book. Considering the question both historically and philosophically, I reject the claim that public religion violates the spirit of the First Amendment. Instead, when citizens of faith offer religious reasons in public discussion, they are exercising the freedoms the First Amendment means to protect. I also am not persuaded by the assertion that public religion introduces an inherently divisive element into American politics. To the contrary, throughout our history religious figures and communities have made essential contributions to the development of an American moral tradition. Sometimes religious language has brought special insight to seemingly unending debate, and occasionally, from the mouths of our most eloquent and respected leaders, it has given expression to moral norms that appeal to a wide spectrum of Americans. Similarly, I believe thoughtful religious perspectives can broaden our understanding of the ethical issues in today's contentious climate, and the second part of this book considers some of those contributions to debates over abortion, homosexuality, environmentalism, and other divisive issues. Most of my examples have to do with the Jewish and Christian traditions with which I am most familiar, but when they engage conversation productively, all sorts of religious communities have the potential to improve our discourse by reminding us of the virtue of civility and by providing us with models of moral discourse.

Because Americans have been wrestling with the relationship between religion and politics since the seventeenth century, it is no surprise that so much has been written on the subject. The philosophical literature on religion in public discourse is vast and deep, and the number of good historical studies of religion's impact on American politics has grown considerably in the last several years. Professional scholars familiar with this material may object that my distillation ignores some of the nuance in both the historical record and contemporary philosophy. To these scholars I can only respectfully reply: this book was not written for you. Instead, I have written this book for the general reader, the lay person who is not familiar with the philosophy of John Rawls or the nuances in Thomas Jefferson's theology but who finds herself dissatisfied with the current state of political discourse. For such a reader, this book is an introduction to contemporary debates over religion in public moral debate, understood in the context of religion's complicated historical relationship with the American moral tradition. To the concerned citizen who yearns for a starting place for more careful thinking about the role of religion in public moral debate, past and present, this book is for you.

Acknowledgments

Among the debts I incurred while writing this book are those to my home institution, Middlebury College, which granted me a sabbatical that allowed me to begin, as well as a Mellon-funded course release, student researchers, and other support necessary to finish. One of those student researchers, Celia Cohen, was invaluable, not just for her dedication to digging up newspaper articles, but for her willingness to serve as a sounding board in the beginning stages; it is no exaggeration to wonder if this book would ever have taken shape without her help. To John Melanson of Carol's Hungry Mind Café and Kristin, Peggy, and Mary Ann at Wilson Café, two Middlebury establishments where most of this book was written, I am grateful for reliable offers of caffeine and friendly banter. My editor at Westminster John Knox, Jana Riess, helped me to reimagine this book in ways that made it more interesting and accessible, and a tighter read. Colleagues who read or thought through portions with me include Hal Breitenberg, Elizabeth Hinson-Hasty, David True, Tom James, Burke Rochford, and "Dean" Scott Needham of Elderly Services in Middlebury, Vermont. Similarly, I thank the extraordinary Middlebury students who took my course on evangelicalism in the fall of 2006 for reading through earlier versions of some of this material. My good friends Larry Yarbrough and Karen Northrup deserve special thanks for reading through the entire manuscript, as does my wife Elizabeth, whose editorial skills and (more importantly) loving support were essential in a writing process that stole more summers than it was originally allowed. Our older son, Jae, worked hard to maintain balance in his father's life during the busyness of writing, by sharing his enduring preoccupation with monster trucks and NASCAR. (Our younger son, Kisung, showed up as this book went into production, presumably as a reward to his father for work well done.) Finally, this book is dedicated to my friends at First Presbyterian Church in Hudson Falls (New York), for their abiding interest in the work of their "resident theologian," and for the model of civility they consistently display.

PART ONE

Public Religion and the American Moral Tradition

1
At War over Values (Allegedly)

Modern Americans have been disagreeing about the political importance of "moral values" for at least four presidents. Back in the late 1970s, the term used in public debate was sometimes "moral values" and sometimes "family values," and the issues put on the table included abortion, fetal-tissue research, and homosexuality. A "moral majority" emerged as a political player in 1980, and the votes of Americans concerned with the moral direction of the country helped end Jimmy Carter's presidency and usher in the era of Ronald Reagan. During the Clinton years, political references to "moral values" often came with the suggestion that the president did not have any, and the test case for that theory emerged in the Monica Lewinsky affair. In many ways, the impeachment trial of President Clinton was more a referendum on the political importance of morality than it was an investigation into questions of perjury. The political use of the language of "moral values" hit an apex in the 2000 and 2004 presidential elections, when it came to stand specifically for opposition to abortion, euthanasia, embryonic stem-cell research, and gay marriage—what I call the "big four" of American moral conservatism. George W. Bush's success in those two campaigns allegedly depended on his ability to persuade average Americans that he was more in touch with their moral convictions than his opponents were. By 2008, both the meaning of "moral values" and the Bush administration's commitment to them were open to debate again, and many have viewed the election of Barack Obama as a signal that most Americans are no longer as preoccupied with the "big four" as they are with economic issues. In spite of radical changes in the political and moral climates, the concept of "moral values" has played a formidable role in American presidential politics for the better part of three decades.

But what exactly are "moral values," and are Americans as deeply divided over them as recent national elections would suggest? Are we, as numerous pundits have claimed, in the midst of a "culture war" between the defenders of morality and those who wish to rid our American society of its moral bearings? Who are "values voters"? What counts as a "moral value"? Oddly enough, as prevalent as this language has been in recent American politics, it has rarely been critically parsed. No better illustration of the problems that result from careless use of this language can be found than the reelection of President George W. Bush in 2004.

LESSONS FROM THE 2004 ELECTION

Immediately after it was over, the news media declared that the 2004 presidential election was in fact decided by "values voters." Political analyst David R. Jones, covering the election for CBSNews.com, proclaimed that President George Bush's reelection was due primarily to his successful emphasis of so-called moral issues, particularly opposition to gay marriage, which offset any gains Senator John Kerry might have made in emphasizing the downturn in the economy and the unsettled situation in Iraq.[1] Tucker Carlson, cohost of CNN's now-defunct *Crossfire*, also declared that it was "the issue of what we're calling moral values that drove President Bush and other Republicans to victory," and *USA Today* went so far as to call the election "a referendum on moral values."[2] Joe Klein of *Time* similarly assumed that "moral values" helped President Bush, but to him "moral values" represented an aura of self-confidence and moral certitude as much as any particular position on a specific issue.[3] Across the political spectrum, pundits agreed that the "values gap" had done in Kerry's campaign.

How did the media come to this conclusion? The projections of most major media outlets relied on a single exit poll, the National Election Pool Exit Poll. In the NEP Exit Poll, voters were given a list of public issues related to the campaign and asked which issue was the most important to them. For 22 percent of voters polled, "moral values" represented the most important issue, giving this choice more first-place votes than taxes, education, the economy, health care, terrorism, or even the situation in Iraq. Furthermore, of those voters who picked moral values as the primary issue of the campaign, the vast majority (80 percent) voted for President Bush.[4] Thus, the polling data to which all of the major media outlets had access seemed to suggest a straightforward connection between this hot-button issue and the Republican victory.

In the weeks following the election, the fallout from this "moral values" victory was as clear as the evidence for it seemed to be. For the most part, both political parties played along. Republicans touted their facility with the language of morality, celebrated the apparent confirmation of the GOP as the moral-values party, and thanked those religious and moral organizations that assisted them in the cause. In contrast, the Democrats conceded the battle over moral values and lamented their party's inability to speak to those issues. During the inaugural celebrations in Washington the following January, three conservative organizations—the Family Research Council, American Values, and James Dobson's Focus on the Family—sponsored a "Values Victory Dinner," at which they congratulated themselves for the electoral victory and reaffirmed their opposition to issues such as gay marriage and abortion.

Some conservatives also warned the GOP that they would expect compensation for their role in delivering the election, in the form of renewed attention to certain "moral values" measures. Conservative commentator William Bennett, for instance, called the Republican victory "a mandate to affect policy that will promote a more decent society," and politely reminded the president that his values voters considered his reelection "the time to begin our long, national cultural renewal."[5] James Dobson appeared on ABC's *This Week* shortly after the election and warned that "the president has two years—or more broadly the Republican party has two years—to implement those [moral values] policies . . . or I believe they'll pay a price in the next election." When pressed for specifics on what issues he expected the president to give priority, he singled out abortion and the defense of traditional marriage. Given the results of the midterm elections in 2006, when Republicans lost control of both houses of Congress, it may be that Dobson and his fellow "moral values" defenders made good on their threat. At least that is how Dobson interpreted the midterm results. After the 2006 elections, he issued a statement in which he claimed that "in 2004, conservative voters handed [the Republican Party] a 10-seat majority in the Senate and a 29-seat edge in the House.

And what did they do with their power? Very little that Values Voters care about." As a result, argued Dobson, "many of the Values Voters of '04 simply stayed at home this year," and consequently the GOP lost control of Congress.[6]

But what exactly are "moral values"? What does it mean that nearly a quarter of voters thought they were the most important issue of the 2004 campaign? The answers are not immediately clear. According to CBS producer Brian Healy, folks in his newsroom watched the effect of the values vote on poll numbers throughout election evening, but it wasn't until 4:00 a.m. that someone bothered to ask what the term meant—to which no one had a response.[7] The problem was that the NEP and other polls asked voters to choose the issue most important to their vote from a list that included "moral values," but they never provided a definition or specific examples of the values the polls had in mind. The exit polls treated the term as if its meaning were straightforward and universally accepted. Political commentators quickly assumed that "moral values" stood for opposition to one or more hot-button conservative issues—abortion, embryonic stem-cell research, euthanasia, and gay marriage—and there was some basis for this assumption. Long before 2004, "moral values" served as popular code within conservative circles for their stances on the big four issues, and election analysts simply picked up this usage when they interpreted the polls. Values voters were seen as conservative, "a group of people . . . who want to live and do live in what we would call an old-fashioned life," a kind of *Father Knows Best* social perspective.[8] If the polls did not specify what was meant by the term, many of those interpreting the polls, as well as those celebrating the values vote afterward, seemed certain that "moral values" means support for the convictions of American conservatives.

But is this the only way to understand the term, as a commitment to conservative positions on these four specific issues? Can we assume that everyone who selected "moral values" as the most important concern of the 2004 election understood the term this way? Gary Langer and Jon Cohen, directors of polling for ABC News, have argued that the NEP Poll—on which so much of this moral values talk in 2004 was based—was faulty. They cite a survey conducted by the Pew Research Center after the election that found widely different interpretations of the term "moral values." More than half of the respondents said the term brought to mind either gay marriage or abortion, but another third thought it referred to religion, personal qualities like honesty, or "other policy issues." In fact, 2 percent of those surveyed thought moral values referred to "what's on TV"![9] Given the open-endedness of the term, can we know for sure what it means that 22 percent of voters selected it as the most important issue in the 2004 presidential election?

BROADENING OUR SENSE OF THE MORAL

It's difficult to know what we were supposed to make of those post-election polls in 2004, since the polling itself was done so poorly. But all the hubbub then and since signals the importance of asking, once for all, what it means to have, cherish, and protect moral values. In contrast to the way the term is almost universally used, I want to suggest that we need a much broader understanding, one that includes but goes beyond the priorities of conservative religious persons, to recognize that the convictions of their ideological opponents are often themselves rooted in a moral vision for America. Moral values need not be conservative—nor religious, for that matter—and exclusively equating moral values with conservative religion causes us to misunderstand the nature of our public disagreements. To ignore this fact is to misconstrue recent presidential elections as battles between moralists and hedonists, or (in William Raspberry's words) "believers" and "pragmatists."[10] In fact, believers can be found all over the ideological spectrum—at the liberal end as well as on the conservative end—and nonbelievers are as committed to moral worldviews as religious people. Contrary to what much political rhetoric implies, the social conflicts that preoccupy us are not a contest between religious people and atheists. They are not a battle between those who cherish moral values and those who do not. Instead, our collective disagreements are usually over *which* moral values should hold sway. Conservatives, moderates, and liberals, religious believers, skeptics, and atheists all contribute to our public debates over abortion, gay marriage, war, and health care from particular moral visions for America, so that the "moral values debate" is really a debate *between* moral agendas, not for or against them.

We need, then, to rescue the concept of moral values from the constricted way we talk about them now to a broader recognition that all citizens make political choices, vote, speak out, and support candidates from the perspective of a moral worldview. There is more to moral values, in other words, than just *conservative evangelical* moral values. To be clear, though, I am not trying to reclaim the term because I harbor a natural hostility toward conservative religious values; there is too much evangelicalism in my family for that to be a possibility. Certainly my aim is not to rescue American politics from the influence of religion. Quite the contrary: it is only when we acknowledge that conservatives, liberals, and moderates alike derive their positions from moral worldviews that we can be free to appreciate the diverse ways in which religion can enrich our public debates over moral values.

In suggesting that religion can make a positive contribution to our debates over moral values, though, I do not mean to imply that *only* religious persons can converse in the language of morality. The assumptions of pundits like William Raspberry and some friends of the GOP notwithstanding, any of us with agnostic or atheist friends knows that you do not have to be religious to be a moral person. Plenty of Americans conduct their lives along an admirable moral compass without the assistance of a religious creed. (I say this as a believer myself.) Not only is the possibility of nonreligious moral values verifiable through experience; it also makes sense from a religious point of view. All of the major religious traditions in the United States recognize that persons with no religion (or a different religion) can be moral, and all of these traditions have been able to make sense of this fact theologically. For instance, most schools of thought within the Christian tradition acknowledge a human capacity for morality that is endowed by God, shared across religious boundaries, and identified alternatively as reason, conscience, or the natural law.[11] Judaism similarly recognizes a natural capacity for moral achievement beyond the influence of halakic law; as one rabbi put it, "If Torah had not been given, we could have learned modesty from the cat, aversion to robbery from the ant, chastity from the dove and sexual mores from the rooster."[12] And while the relationship between moral reasoning and God's decrees is a kind of chicken-and-egg debate in Islamic thought, the need to explain non-Muslim morality itself implies the recognition of this universal capability.[13] The capacity for being moral and acting ethically is, in general, a characteristic of being human, so that the ability to hold moral values cannot simply depend on religious influence, but rather must be a sensitivity to good and bad, right and wrong that is available to persons within and outside a specific religion.

But while experientially and theologically it does not make much sense to imply that only Christians, Jews, or Muslims are capable of moral values, I still contend that members of religious traditions may have something important to contribute to our debates over them. Many critics of religion in politics argue the opposite point, charging that faith-based arguments are part of the problem with our public moral discourse. They point to the political activity of some religious conservatives as evidence that faith makes one intolerant, closed-minded, and disrespectful. Furthermore, they argue that religion cannot make a substantial contribution to public reasoning in our pluralistic society because faith-based perspectives are not persuasive to those outside a particular religious tradition. Finally, they argue that religion in political discourse violates the long-standing American tradition of the "separation of church and state."

Such a position is an uncharitable characterization of religious conservatives, many of whom contribute with great sophistication to public debate. It also represents an unfair assumption about the persuasive power of religious reasoning (even to those who do not share the commitment to religion) and a selective reading of the American tradition of "church and state." In the rest of this book, I make the case not only that religious arguments in public moral debate are appropriate, but that they also make a significant contribution to a healthier public discourse. There is both philosophical justification and rich historical precedent for welcoming religious perspectives into our most important public conversations, though care should be taken to avoid too close cooperation between the *institutions* of religion and the state. But beyond what is simply *permitted*, I argue that the contributions of religious perspectives *enrich* our public discourse. Religious perspectives contribute substantially by offering powerful arguments on all sides of the many debates that preoccupy us. Religious reasons and the communities that nurture them also, at their best, remind us how to engage in collective reasoning, contributing to our common life traditions of civility and patterns for moral discourse. But religion's contributions cannot be fully appreciated until we correct our notions of what count as "moral values."

Certainly the vagueness of the term made the 2004 poll question on moral values bad political science, but it also illustrated a deeper problem with our public debates. As we have noted, absent a definition by the polls themselves, many Americans assumed that support for "moral values" referred specifically to opposition to abortion, embryonic stem-cell research, euthanasia, and gay marriage. This implies that defending abortion rights, stem-cell research, gay marriage, or a right to die is not and cannot be grounded in a moral perspective. In reality, however, many Americans support abortion rights, embryonic stem-cell research, a right to die, or civil rights for gays and lesbians as *moral* commitments. For instance, many Americans support abortion rights out of an ethical commitment to the protection of women. Citizens who petition for embryonic stem-cell research often do so because they place a moral priority on fighting disease and helping the sick. Some Americans support a so-called "right to die" as an expression of the moral importance of human dignity. For those who insist on the civil recognition of gay and lesbian partnerships, that concern usually comes from a moral dedication to civil rights. To many Americans, therefore, being good moral citizens requires *support* for these issues. Our political rhetoric, however, in the debates over abortion, stem-cell research, euthanasia, and gay marriage implies strongly that those who oppose these four issues are concerned with moral values, while those who support them are not.

Furthermore, by positioning "moral values" against issues like taxes, education, war, health care, and the economy, we ignore the fact that these other issues themselves raise moral questions and concerns. In other words, abortion, euthanasia, gay marriage, and stem-cell research are not the only measures of a commitment to moral values. For instance, many of those who indicated that the economy was the most important issue in the 2008 election may have done so because they considered joblessness and irresponsibility in the financial sector the greatest *moral* crisis facing our nation today. Certainly it has become increasingly evident that many of us look at the situations in Iraq and Afghanistan as failures on moral as well as strategic grounds. And the "health care crisis" is referred to as such not just because it represents a looming threat to the U.S. economy, but because to many it symbolizes a monumental moral failure of our social covenant with the disadvantaged.

I am suggesting, therefore, that we need to expand our definition beyond simple opposition to the "big four" conservative issues. What *are* moral values? Perhaps we should back up a step and ask what it means to be moral in the first place. At its most elementary, being moral means doing what we ought to do and being the persons we ought to be, as individuals and as communities (local or national). But how do we define the "ought"? The convictions by which we judge what is good and right in ourselves, our neighbors, and our world derive from our *worldviews*. A worldview is a moral reading of the universe. It is an interpretation of the events that surround us, the choices that confront us, and the responsibilities that obligate us—all in relation to a particular understanding of the "meaning of life." A worldview is the philosophical or theological lens through which we understand the circumstances we find ourselves in, and through which we interpret the significance of our choices and actions, other people's choices and actions, and the things and people that act upon us. A worldview is the perspective by which we discern moral meaning in our lives.

Admittedly, this is a vague definition of a worldview, so perhaps an example will better illustrate the idea. A committed Christian, by virtue of the teachings of her faith, might understand world history as the stage on which God fulfills God's intentions for the world (and, in particular, human beings). The source for what she knows about God's intentions is the message and ministry of Jesus Christ. Christian doctrine tells her that Christ is the distinct revelation of God; he was (as the tradition has put it) the very incarnation of God. As such, Christ's priorities tell our committed Christian something about God's priorities for human beings and the larger creation. Specifying what were Christ's priorities is subject to interpretation, but how our committed Christian understands the significance of the life, ministry, and death of Christ will give rise to some assumptions about what God wants (and does not want) for the world. In turn, her understanding of the significance of life and history—her worldview—will suggest to her (consciously or otherwise) which moral values she ought to prioritize.

Let's suppose that our Christian friend reads the Gospel of Luke and concludes that what was most distinctive about the ministry of Christ was the solidarity he displayed with the poor and the oppressed in his society. This might lead her to conclude that such a priority for the needs of marginalized human beings is a reflection of God's most fundamental sympathies. This in turn might give rise to a moral worldview in which she too places priority on the needs of the poor and the oppressed, in an attempt to fulfill the Christian obligation of *imitatio Christi*, to live in imitation of Christ. Placing a priority on the needs of the oppressed, our Christian friend will interpret the events of the world and the choices that confront her through this moral sensitivity. She will find that her belief in a God who comes down consistently on the side of the poor compels her to interpret the events of her life and her world through a set of moral values that includes an emphasis on justice and economic well-being. She will evaluate personal decisions on the basis of their impact on the disadvantaged, and she will support public policies that seem consistent with her moral commitment to justice. Her moral values originate in but also affect the way she reads the world. They derive from, but also influence, her worldview.[14]

Moral values, then, are convictions about what we ought to do and be, as persons and communities. They emerge out of our understanding of the "meaning of life," out of our worldviews. In our example, the principal influence on the committed Christian's worldview is her religion, but a moral worldview does not have to be religious, nor does it not have to be altruistic—hedonism is a moral worldview, as is a commitment to the "survival of the fittest," a kind of economic natural selection. Religious or not, other regarding or not, all people operate from some kind of worldview, some kind of interpretive framework that suggests to them what is good, right, and worthy in the world—in short, that suggests to them moral values they ought to pursue.

THE MANY FACES OF "MORAL VALUES"

But what do these concepts look like? Some religious people insist that moral values are dictated by God, that whether in holy scripture or through religious tradition or by more intuitive means, God tells us what is right and good for us to pursue. Others (including some of a religious persuasion) argue that our moral values come from our reason; that is, we rationally understand certain principles as good to live by because they resonate with our sense of what it means to be human, make us more productive people, lead to happiness (however we define it), or contribute to a greater good. Still others argue that moral values are determined by social convention, that morality ultimately means conforming and contributing to the habits and customs of a community (whether local, ethnic, or national) for its greater good. There is a lot of debate within and among theologies and philosophies regarding the source and nature of the moral obligation that governs and guides our lives; the question of who we ought to be and what we ought to do can be answered in an infinite number of ways. But whatever your particular theological or philosophical background, the bequest of that "ought" is a set of convictions you consider important to guide your character and behavior. These are the "moral values" of your religion, philosophy, or creed—and everyone has them.

Contrary to popular assumption, these convictions do not have to be absolutes in order to be moral values. Some people hold absolute moral convictions; for instance, a strict pacifist might believe that killing is always wrong, in every situation. Roman Catholics who hold to the official teachings of their church believe that the intentional abortion of a fetus is always wrong, regardless of the tragic circumstances (like rape) that might have led to the pregnancy. But others of us hold moral convictions that we believe are authoritative and binding but nonetheless have exceptions. A person may believe that killing is *normally* wrong but is justified in cases of self-defense, or that lying is wrong except when to do so would save someone's life. Philosophers call this kind of moral conviction a prima facie (literally, "at first glance") norm. Prima facie norms are more than simply advice, for in most cases they oblige us to do or not do something. But these kinds of convictions are also flexible enough to allow for exceptions in cases where other moral concerns are at stake.

The temptation may be to see prima facie norms as more wishy-washy than absolutes, but flexibility does not have to mean wishy-washy; it can mean strong, yet realistic. A prima facie ethical outlook acknowledges that many life circumstances require us to choose between moral values. And prima facie norms are not preferred only by liberals. While we tend to assume that conservatives and only conservatives love absolutes, plenty of conservative viewpoints exhibit the flexibility and room for exceptions of prima facie norms. For instance, many conservatives oppose abortion but allow for exceptions in cases of rape, incest, or risk of physical harm to the woman. On the other hand, despite the popular characterization of liberals as relativists, some self-identifying liberals nonetheless subscribe to absolutes, like many of the radical pacifists in my home state of Vermont, who entertain no exceptions—not even self-defense—to the prohibition of killing that informs their opposition to war. Moral values can be absolute or a little less than absolute, and both ways of thinking about moral values show up in the convictions of conservatives and liberals.

In addition, moral values may take the form of rules—"thou shalt not kill," for instance—but they do not have to be rules. There is a long tradition in both religion and philosophy of imagining moral values as virtues, like courage or compassion or peacefulness. Aristotle thought of morality this way, as did the great Catholic theologian Thomas Aquinas, the Jewish philosopher Moses Maimonides, and much of the Buddhist tradition. From this perspective, defending moral values is not simply about following or enforcing rules so much as it is about encouraging the development of moral *character* in people. Again, neither one of these ways of thinking about moral norms is more characteristic of conservative or progressive stances. Conservative pundit William Bennett is as comfortable with the language of virtues as progressive religious activist Jim Wallis is with invoking a moral rule against poverty. But it is helpful to remember that appeals to moral values can take more varied forms than just the invocation of biblical law.

Moral norms also do not have to be restrictive; they can just as well describe what a person is morally permitted, obliged, or encouraged to do. In other words, there is more to having a moral worldview than subscribing to a bunch of "thou shalt nots." Certainly a healthy sense of moral direction requires some moral restrictions; it is important to define what is off limits in a morally acceptable life. Besides signaling what it is morally important to *avoid*, an ethical perspective probably should indicate what it is morally necessary or commendable to *do*. In this way, a healthy moral perspective includes not just "thou shalt nots," but also "thou shalts" and "thou shoulds." For instance, the following is an important restrictive norm: "you should not take the life of another person (unless you have a morally grave reason to do so)." Now we can debate how to interpret this norm—who counts as a person (do embryos and/or fetuses?) and what (if anything) should be considered a "morally grave reason" to violate the prohibition against killing. But in its basic form, this moral rule is restrictive; it describes an action that is (normally) off limits. By contrast, consider the following rule: "you may (or should) protect the life of an innocent person with lethal force, if necessary." Again, we might disagree over the definition of "innocent" and what represents a "necessary" turn to lethal force. We could debate the scope of this norm, whether a rule like this applies only to those who stand for the authority of government (i.e., police officers and the military) or whether private citizens reserve this right (or obligation) to kill predators in order to protect the life of innocent victims. But the basic form of the moral norm is positive; it tells us not what we may *not* do, but what we *may* (or should) do.[15]

Finally, contrary to popular opinion, moral values are not simply private in scope. How often do we hear someone chime in the abortion or gay marriage debates, for instance, that the government should not interfere with the "private moral choices" a person makes, as if to suggest that morality is a private issue, to be distinguished from public issues that are more social or political? This private-public distinction was implied in that 2004 NEP poll as well, where "moral values" were set up against "public" issues, both domestic and international. But if we take as our starting point the definition for morality that I suggested above, we see that the quest to "be and do what we ought to be and do" cannot be confined to the realm of our so-called private lives. Being moral speaks as much to doing what we ought to do in the workplace as it does to what we do in the bedroom. Being moral dictates as much the kind of persons we collectively are in relation to the poor in our society as it does how we relate to each other in our families. Defining morality as "being and doing what we ought to be and do" places within morality's parameters both the so-called private issues and the apparently public ones.

Even the issues commonly referred to as "private" have very public dimensions. For instance, abortion may center on an individual choice by a particular woman, but that choice (right or wrong) implicates a larger medical public on whom she depends to act on her choice. Her choice is also made in the context of a political culture that dictates the extent of her freedom to make the choice and the restrictions on that choice. Similarly, gay marriage may seem like an obviously private act between two people, but the real crux of the debate lies in whether or not society should recognize such unions as legitimate family forms with all the civil rights and privileges enjoyed by more traditional family units. As soon as the conflict over gay marriage becomes about social rights and privileges, it becomes a public issue. Euthanasia may appear to some to be a private decision one person makes about the termination of his or her own life, but a person who wants to "die with dignity" requires the cooperation of health-care professionals, loved ones, and social regulations in order to follow through with this seemingly private decision. So only the most naive reading can claim that issues like abortion, gay marriage, and euthanasia are simply private matters.

Our definition of morality suggests that "moral values" can mean something beyond the invocation of absolute rules, something beyond conservative positions on so-called private issues. As the convictions that guide us to "do what we ought to do and be who we ought to be," moral values can be conservative or progressive, rules or character traits, absolute or a bit more pliable, negative but also positive, private but also public in scope. From this vantage point, it seems that a proper understanding of the term "moral values" means much more than what it is often assumed to mean in American politics. "Moral values" represent those convictions that lead many Americans to oppose abortion, embryonic stem-cell research, euthanasia, and gay marriage, but the term also captures those deeply held convictions that compel other Americans to support abortion rights, stem-cell research, gay marriage, and a right to die. And contrary to much of our political rhetoric, "moral values" may also underwrite many Americans' views on war, education, the environment, health care, poverty, and our national economic priorities.

GETTING BEYOND THE CULTURE WARS

You may ask, however: why should we care that election polls and political rhetoric are so narrow in their understanding of "moral values"? What do we gain from rethinking the meaning of the term? To my mind, understanding moral values in the broader sense that I have outlined here promises to get us past the seemingly intractable differences over issues that currently dominate American politics and paralyze our public discourse—the "culture war" that dominates modern American politics. At the 1992 Republican National Convention, conservative icon Pat Buchanan famously proclaimed to the audience that "there is a religious war going on in this country, a cultural war as critical to the kind of nation we shall be as the Cold War itself." He called this ideological conflict a "war for the soul of America," and he rallied his audience to "take back our cities, and take back our culture, and take back our country."[16] In the past couple of elections, political pundits have grown increasingly fond of talking about the United States as divided between red states, populated by religious Americans dedicated to the preservation of conservative values, and blue states, inhabited by progressive secularists suspicious of the influence of traditional religion on politics. One political cartoon even characterized these red states and blue states as separate countries, Jesusland and the United States of Canada! From the evidence assembled on the Internet and the plethora of cable TV "news" shows dedicated to offering up verbal battles between the far right and the far left, the depiction of our political climate as a "culture war" seems apt.

At the same time, a number of political observers insist that the culture war is being waged exclusively between political elites, and that ordinary Americans are not as fundamentally polarized as the "culture war thesis" makes us out to be.[17] If this is true, then it would seem that the trick to rejuvenating our political discourse lies in empowering the sizable moderate middle to reclaim the public agenda in this country and to change the language with which we talk about our differences. A revitalized notion of moral values and the widespread recognition that citizens across the political spectrum are engaged in the same project we are—the development of a moral vision for America—are significant accomplishments that hold some promise for improving the health of our public dialogue. Recovering an expansive and sophisticated understanding of moral values—what they are, who holds them, and how my opponents' are both similar to and different from my own—may neutralize some of the simplistic "us against them" rhetoric so pervasive in the current battles between ultraconservatives and radical liberals in American politics. For recognizing that a defense of "moral values" is at work in our opponents' position undermines the temptation to demonize them as amoral or immoral, and instead encourages us to approach the "moral values" debate as a shared responsibility to embrace meaningful dialogue.

A more robust understanding of moral values also promises to make the conversation more inclusive. By defining moral values so restrictively, current political rhetoric in this country essentially disqualifies many Americans from the conversation. The debate (such as it is) now rages only between those who consider themselves the exclusive defenders of morality and those who insist that "private" notions of morality have no place in politics. As a result, political "discourse" has become a shouting match to which only the extremes are invited and, increasingly, to which only the extremes want to be witness—a culture war between radical factions, with the rest of us suffering as noncombatant casualties.

To understand moral values expansively, however, is to rethink the idea of "public debate." It is to acknowledge that the conversation over issues as different as abortion and climate change is itself a moral endeavor, in which every American has a responsibility to participate. And every American's contribution to thinking about these issues is a defense of moral values, whether our dominant priorities are a respect for fetal life or a concern for women's health, whether we are more concerned with humanity's effect on the environment or the impact of environmental regulations on families' ability to feed their children. Expanding our understanding of moral values takes the power to define the conversation away from the extremes and energizes the moderate majority to see their contributions to public debate as important. It says to average Americans that our public debate can be different. It can have a more civil tone, it can welcome complicated viewpoints, it can be patient with nuance and complexity and uncertainty and messiness, and it can welcome pragmatic compromises instead of always insisting on unconditional ideological surrender. To understand moral values this way does not guarantee an end to the deep disagreements we harbor over the issues that preoccupy us. But it does offer to return us to a more civilized debate, to make a place at the proverbial table for those of us whose views do not fit exactly with the radical left or right, and to put an end to the "culture war" mentality that now frustrates any attempt at serious public conversation.

Yes, mutual disparagement is a habit deeply rooted in American politics, as any historical study of presidential elections reminds us. Still, our expansion of the concept of moral values encourages us to see the moral commitment and integrity of those involved on all sides of our public moral debates. So-called "conservatives" might recognize that their progressive or liberal counterparts normally are not conscience-deprived hedonists seeking to sabotage the moral fabric of American society at every turn, but instead are equally committed to a vision of a moral society. It just happens that they differ from conservatives over the moral principles that they think should form the foundation of that society. And liberals should recognize that conservatives are not closed-minded zealots just because they campaign for a moral foundation to our common public life. Liberals are often reluctant to admit it, but they make claims for the moral foundation of American culture too—just different moral values. At least implicitly, liberals insist on an America based on moral values like tolerance for diversity and respect for individual choice, and in doing so they are engaging in the very same exercise as conservatives when the latter call for a society that "protects the family." Both conservatives and liberals push for a "moral America," just different visions of that moral society, and to do so is an entirely appropriate extension of the American moral tradition. For the idea of a morally neutral culture is an absurd myth. All culture is based on moral presuppositions and priorities, so that no civil society that enjoys any kind of collective identity exists without some moral foundation. Liberals would do well to acknowledge this fact and admit that they too are in the business of commending a certain public morality. For their part, conservatives might also entertain the possibility that they are not the only ones with a moral vision for American society.

With this recognition that many of the participants in public moral debate are trying to do the same thing—that is, effect a moral culture—perhaps some real dialogue can take place. Understanding what is going on across the table from us might allow us to get past simple political positioning and engage in deeper philosophical conversation about the competing moral visions at stake in our debates. Instead of sound bites and superficial mischaracterizations, perhaps we can get to more substantial dialogue over how our vision for American society and of the American moral tradition differs from that of those who oppose us. At least we would be talking the same language, that of moral discourse. With this recognition that we are all engaged in the same enterprise, is it beyond the realm of possibility that we might discover some grounds for tentative consensus, even if we cannot eliminate all the reasons for deep disagreement? Might we find some moments of concurrence, even if only on penultimate matters?

In these measures toward an improved political culture I believe religion can make a profound contribution. To the extent that religion has contributed to the *disintegration* of political discourse, it has been because religious communities have too zealously incorporated the worst strategies and values from our current political environment, not because of some fundamental incompatibility between religion and public life. To the contrary, religious perspectives at their best provide necessary correction to our downward slide. Critics of religion in politics may be unconvinced, given the media's apparent preference to cover religion only when it is polarizing, so it remains for us to demonstrate the substantial contributions religious perspectives can and do make to our consideration of the "big four" and other moral issues, across the spectrum of political positions. That is our task in later chapters of this book.

Many critics may also remain skeptical out of fear that inviting religious persons to bring their views into our public debate puts at risk that cherished "separation of church and state," so vital to the American tradition. Public religion, say its cultured despisers, is not only naturally divisive; it is also a violation of a fundamental American political virtue rooted in the First Amendment of the Constitution. Our next task, then, is to take up the debate usually fought between "strict separationists" and those who believe that the United States ought to aspire to be a "Christian nation"—that is, the disagreement over religion's role in shaping the moral character of our nation.

2
Aren't We a Christian Nation?

In the debate over moral values, some Americans clamor for a return to our country's Christian roots. They argue that the founders' "original intent" was to establish the United States of America on biblical principles and reserve a place for religion as the moral compass of the new nation. The current crisis over moral values, they say, is a result of our departure from the Christian underpinnings of American democracy. In response, critics of this reading of a "Christian America" deny that the founders intended to give religion a prominent social role in the new United States. Many of the founders were only nominally religious themselves, and they explicitly constructed their new government in such a way as to protect American democracy from religion's divisiveness and thirst for power. So who is correct? Did the founders intend the United States to be a "Christian nation," or did they mean to relegate religion to the "private" sphere with no public role in the American experiment? What does our answer to this question say about the proper role of religion, if any, in our current debates over moral values?

DETERMINING "ORIGINAL INTENT"

Some prominent leaders of conservative evangelicalism routinely claim that the United States has been and ought always to be a "Christian nation." The late Jerry Falwell, for instance, insisted that biblical principles were the philosophical backbone of the American experiment. In *Listen, America!* the 1980 book that essentially launched the Moral Majority movement, Falwell argued that

> our Founding Fathers established America's laws and precepts on the principles recorded in the laws of God, including the Ten Commandments. God has blessed this nation because in its early days she sought to honor God and the Bible, the inerrant Word of the living God. Any diligent student of American history finds that our great nation was founded by godly men upon godly principles to be a Christian nation. . . . They developed a nation predicated on Holy Writ. The religious foundations of America find their roots in the Bible.[1]

Similarly, religious broadcaster and former presidential candidate Pat Robertson has insisted that "the original intent of the founders can be read on every page of the history they give us. They left us a clear prescription for national success."[2] According to Robertson, most of the founders were deeply committed Christians whose religious belief inspired them to give priority to two great American virtues, freedom and respect for law. Their "original intent," then, was to construct a nation whose reverence for liberty and law was rooted in Christian belief, and their "prescription" for our collective future was for us to maintain those Christian values as the foundation for our moral and political culture.[3]

Despite the American tradition of "separation of church and state," Falwell denied that the founders had any intention to ostracize religion from directing American public life. With a nimble survey of early American history, he highlighted example after example of religion's prominence in the formation of the early republic. The Puritans, he noted, populated New England not to get away from religion but to form a society guided by right religion: "One has only to research all the early documents of American history," wrote Falwell, "to find that, time and again, our Puritan Pilgrim heritage was centered around advancing the Kingdom of God."[4] Colonial charters from Connecticut to Virginia acknowledged God as both the source of the colonies' good fortune and the ultimate judge of their endeavors. The journals of the Continental Congress are filled with appeals to God to justify a defense of basic liberties. George Washington, commander-in-chief of the Continental Army and first U.S. president, insisted publicly that "it is impossible to rightly govern the world without God and the Bible." Falwell pointed out that on the very day it adopted the First

Amendment's protection of religious freedom, the U.S. Congress also approved Washington's call for a national day of prayer. Although the Constitution's Bill of Rights separated the institutions of church and state *in function*, Falwell insisted that the historical prominence of faith in the early years of the republic makes clear that "our Founding Fathers most certainly did not intend the separation of God and government."[5] In fact, Falwell argued, "The goal of the framers of our Constitution was to govern the United States of America under God's laws."[6]

Given their religious fervor, Robertson believes that the founders could not have had any other aim except to make America from its inception "a Christian nation, inspired by the dreams of the early settlers who came here to tame a continent for the glory of God and His Son, Jesus Christ."[7] They bequeathed to us a nation centered on the concepts of "individual liberty given by God and protected by the rule of law," a nation that "has served as a standard to the entire world, primarily because of near-universal acknowledgement of the importance of the Christian faith, the Ten Commandments, and the Sermon on the Mount" to its collective identity.[8] Religion drove their political experiment, and the founders assumed that religion would remain a significant influence on the future of the United States. Biblical principles provided the values of our Constitution and our legal system, and religious teachings continue to cultivate a sense of public morality in a healthy republic. This public presence for Christianity is, in Robertson's words, "the legitimate heritage of the American people."[9]

According to the advocates of a Christian America, that "legitimate heritage" is under assault in our times. They believe that the United States has drifted from the biblical principles on which it was established, and they insist that the health of American society depends on a return to honoring "God and the Bible" as the founders intended. Evangelical leaders like the late D. James Kennedy insist that "our nation's truly Christian heritage" has been "virtually expunged by the secular revisionists."[10] As a result, the Coral Ridge Presbyterian Church where he served as pastor regularly hosts a national conference aimed at "reclaiming America for Christ." The purpose of the conference is to energize evangelical Americans to "take back the portals of power," to reassert biblical norms for American government, and to make the United States (in Kennedy's words) "a Christian nation that should be governed by Christians." Secular liberals are in the process of stripping American culture of its religious roots, and it is the responsibility of Christians to fight back by reclaiming "every aspect and institution of human society."[11]

Robertson is a die-hard believer in the American culture war, and he insists that liberals' refusal to heed the biblical underpinnings of American identity lies at the heart of this conflict. In a passage alarming enough to quote at length, Robertson insists that recent presidential elections have revealed a "gaping chasm" between the Christian traditionalists of the "red states" and the revolutionary liberals of the "blue states"—or as he puts it, between "two Americas":

> We are in danger of becoming two Americas, not one. On one side are those who reject biblical norms and Christian values in favor of abortion-on-demand, radical feminism, intrusive central government, homosexual rights (including homosexual marriage), pornography and sexual license, weakened military defense, an ever-increasing role for nonelected judges, and the removal of our historic affirmation of faith from the public arena.
>
> On the other side are those who believe that biblical standards are truly the glue that holds society together. They are men and women who respect human life at every stage, who stand for the sanctity of marriage, who want limited government and lower taxes, and who do not wish to give veto power over public actions to tiny, radical minorities. We believe in free enterprise and a strong defense, and we want the judges who serve in our courts to decide cases on the basis of established law rather than trying to rewrite the law to suit their own whims.[12]

According to Robertson, Falwell, and like-minded advocates of the return to a Christian nation, the culture war in the United States is real. It pits God-fearing defenders of the country's Christian heritage against secular revisionists set on obliterating our nation's religious foundations. What the "Christian nation" advocates believe is in play is nothing less than the future of American democracy, whose health will be guaranteed only when we return the United States to the "original intent" of its founders—as a nation whose law and sense of social morality are guided by Christian principles.[13]

RELIGION AMONG THE FOUNDERS

So is this reading of early American history correct? Were the founders Bible-believing Christians who sought to create a society that reflected and protected Christian moral principles? Or were they, as detractors of the Religious Right vigorously insist, devotees of the Enlightenment, dedicated to governance by reason and inherently suspicious of religion's influence on a pluralistic society? Does the historical evidence support or refute the idea of America as a "Christian nation"?

With due respect to Revs. Falwell and Robertson, I think that what a "diligent student of American history" finds is a picture more complicated than what "Christian America" advocates see. To a certain degree they are right. Strict separationists misread (and misuse) the historical record when they ignore the important motivational, rhetorical, political, and philosophical roles religion clearly played in the formation of the new republic. Most of the founders considered themselves Christians, and many of them saw theological significance in their struggle for independence. They signed on as a group to the Declaration that all human beings "are endowed by their Creator with certain unalienable Rights" and committed themselves to defending those rights "with a firm reliance on the Protection of divine Providence."

At the same time, many of the most prominent men responsible for the new government professed beliefs that hardly resembled traditional Christianity. Many of the founders tended not to share with their latter-day evangelical admirers belief in traditional Christian doctrines, and given their loose relationship with the Bible, they never would have dreamed of explicitly establishing the new nation on scriptural authority. Especially when it comes to the religious convictions of men like Washington, Adams, Jefferson, and Franklin, advocates for a return to a "Christian nation" tend to read their own religious commitments back into history, for the evangelical Christianity they assume they share with the founders looks nothing like the belief systems of these eighteenth-century political fathers.

George Washington, for instance, is a favorite of contemporary "Christian America" defenders, for his public pronouncements were replete with references to God—how the success of the American experiment was indebted to God's oversight and how attention to religion was important to maintaining public morality in the new nation. In his First Inaugural Address, Washington considered it appropriate to offer from the executive office "fervent supplications to that Almighty Being who rules over the universe, who presides in the councils of nations, and whose providential aids can supply every human defect." In "tendering this homage to the Great Author of every public and private good" and asking for God's continued providential care, Washington assumed that every member of his immediate audience (the Congress) and indeed every American would concur. For those who assume the founders were sympathetic to the vision of America as a Christian nation, Washington appears to be an important historical ally, except that Washington's public invocations of religion never included the specific doctrines that might align him with evangelicals, then or now.

Washington never publicly espoused belief in the Trinity, the divinity of Christ, or the authority of the Bible. In fact, for all his public talk about religion, Washington had little to say about his private beliefs. Instead, his public references to God were always in the vague theological language of what we might call "rational theism." Rational theism depended less on confession of specific Christian doctrines than on a belief in a broadly conceived heavenly governor, a moral code that was more rational than revealed, and an afterlife that offered people an incentive to moral striving. This theism was the religion of choice for several prominent leaders of the new nation, including John Adams, Ben Franklin, Washington, and (most infamously) Thomas Jefferson.

So Washington could publicly pray to the "benign Parent of the Human Race" and he could give thanks for "providential agency," but he would not invoke the "Lord and Savior Jesus Christ," and he did not intend the establishment of a Bible-based theocracy. In fact, the connections he famously drew between religion and morality in his public addresses made so much sense to him because, for Washington, religion was little more than a metaphysically underwritten moral code. Religion *was* moral tradition, and little more than that, which (along with the limited religious pluralism in the eighteenth century) made it relatively easy to assume that public morality would need religion. Rather than advocating a public commitment to Christian evangelicalism, Washington prescribed a theistic moralism that, while not resembling the religion of today's evangelicals, was a popular interpretation of religion in a time so influenced by the Enlightenment.

Furthermore, as open as Washington seemed to be in his public appeals to a generally religious culture, he was at least equally concerned to avoid endorsing a particular religious tradition in the name of the nation. As president he went to great pains to assure both domestic and international inquirers that religious freedom, and not Christianity, was the mantra of the new United States. To the Hebrew Congregation of Newport, Rhode Island, Washington wrote that

> it is now no more that toleration is spoken of, as if it were by the indulgence of one class of people, that another enjoyed the exercise of their inherent natural rights. For, happily, the Government of the

> United States, which gives to bigotry no sanction, to persecution no assistance, requires only that they who live under its protection should demean themselves as good citizens, in giving it on all occasions their effectual support.[14]

By eschewing the language of toleration for that of religious liberty, Washington assured the Jewish congregation of Newport that their freedom to practice their religion was not granted at the whim of a benevolent Christian government, but was instead guaranteed by the institutional separation of religion and government on which the United States was built. Similarly, in a peace treaty with the Muslim nation of Tripoli of Barbary, first negotiated under Washington's administration (and concluded at the beginning of Adams's), cooperation between the two nations is predicated on the declaration that "the government of the United States of America is not in any sense founded on the Christian Religion." Despite his occasional references to the public importance of religion, Washington seems to have been far from imagining the United States as a "Christian nation."

Like the president he succeeded, John Adams is also invoked frequently as proof that the founders intended to establish the United States on biblical principles. Those who read Adams this way point to his support for a "mild establishment" of Congregationalism in Massachusetts and his use of religion against rival Thomas Jefferson in the presidential election of 1800. With regard to the first, Adams, like Washington, assumed that robust religion was essential to the cultivation of a national morality. As he remarked in a letter written during the Revolution, "It is religion and morality alone which can establish the principles upon which freedom can securely stand." Adams believed that the former lent important service to the encouragement of the latter.[15] Thus, after the Revolution he continued to push for qualified state support of a "publick religion" (in the form of the Congregational Church) in Massachusetts, while still insisting that citizens have the freedom to practice their own religions without interference.[16]

The election of 1800 put Adams's belief in the political necessity of religion in service to partisan politics. During his reelection campaign, the president's supporters took advantage of rival Jefferson's reputation for being, shall we say, religiously unorthodox. They reminded the public that Adams understood religion's importance to the young nation's public good, while they warned that a Jefferson presidency would be hostile to religion and a threat to the country's moral foundation. Seizing on Jefferson's well-known suspicion of organized religion and his intimacy with the atheistic French, an Adams sympathizer put the president's reelection to the public in these stark terms: "GOD—AND A RELIGIOUS PRESIDENT . . . [or] JEFFERSON—AND NO GOD." According to this writer, to vote for Jefferson was to vote to "destroy religion, introduce immorality, and loosen all the bonds of society."[17]

But despite the effort to distinguish himself from Jefferson at the height of their political rivalry, Adams actually subscribed to religious convictions that closely resembled Jefferson's more infamous ones. Like Jefferson, Adams was more fond of (and more indebted to) the Enlightenment than traditional Christian doctrine. He ignored the debates over the divinity of Christ and privately challenged the doctrine of the Trinity, and he preferred the Unitarians' emphasis on natural philosophy and reason to the biblical orthodoxies of traditional Protestant denominations (especially those nasty Presbyterians). He believed in the immortality of the soul, but he could not swallow the Calvinist doctrine of predestination. He professed to be a Christian, but he could not stand the clergy as a group, and he remained suspicious of popular religious enthusiasm and revivalist movements.[18] As church-and-state expert Derek Davis observes, in most matters of belief and principle, Adams and Jefferson "were almost totally agreed on religion."[19]

For Adams, as with the presidents immediately before and after him, good religion consisted simply of recognizing divine providence in the movements of history and honoring God through a dedication to good works. In fact, it was because Adams placed so much emphasis on morality in his understanding of religion that he could see the benefit of establishing a "publick religion" in service to the state of Massachusetts, but he rejected the idea that the federal government should be in the business of actively encouraging religion as an instrument to virtue.[20] In fact, he went further in his advocacy of separation between church and state than many of his contemporaries by arguing that ministers should not be permitted to hold political office.[21] Truth is, Adams had no interest in establishing a Christian orthodoxy with governmental support, at either the state or the federal level. His only interest was in tapping the moral resources of religion to provide a foundation of virtue for the new republic.

Surely the disparity between the religion of contemporary evangelicals and the religious commitments of the founders themselves is no more apparent than in the case of Thomas Jefferson. Jefferson was no evangelical, whether one means the eighteenth- or twenty-first-century variety. Even though Jefferson frequently expressed reluctance to share his religious beliefs in his private correspondence, we nonetheless know quite a bit about his religious commitments. The religion that emerges from his writings is not the traditional orthodoxy of evangelicalism, but rather the rational theism of the Enlightenment. Jefferson too explicitly denied the concept of the Trinity, arguing that it and other metaphysical doctrines were "superstitions" that got in the way of the genuine teachings of Jesus.[22] He rejected Calvin's idea of predestination and the priority of grace over works, arguing that it was a hideous teaching that discouraged moral effort.[23] He respected the Bible's authority only insofar as it served as a source for the moral pattern of Jesus. Jefferson famously edited his own version of the Bible, from which he deleted all reference to miracles, the virgin birth, Christ's resurrection, and the second coming. What remained was a volume he called "The Life and Morals of Jesus of Nazareth," the kernel of which was Jesus' modeling of reasonable morality. Jefferson assumed that genuine Christianity was that which conformed to the dictates of reason and commended good behavior; everything else was superstitious accretions on the original message of Christ. Reason, not revelation, was the most important source of religious insight for Jefferson, a perspective starkly different from evangelical insistence on biblical authority. To the degree that current calls for a return to a "Christian America" assume that the founders were working from a faith perspective similar to latter-day evangelicalism, Jefferson remains a striking counterexample.

Largely working from an interpretation of Christianity that was light on traditional doctrine, emphasizing instead only its moral teachings, some of the most prominent founders likely did not intend for the new government of the United States to be in service to traditional Christianity. To be sure, there were traditional Christians among the founders. Samuel Adams was by all accounts a loyal descendant of Massachusetts Calvinism; in fact, he is often called "the last American Puritan." John Witherspoon was a Presbyterian clergyman. My point here is not to claim, as many strict separationists in the church-state debate erroneously do, that none of the founders were working from classical Christian worldviews. Some of them may even have hoped for a "Christian America" roughly along the lines imagined by some evangelicals today. But undoubtedly other founders did not share this hope, including some of the most prominent men involved in the Revolution. Because the religious commitments of the founders were so diverse, it is impossible to derive a single interpretation of their "original intent" for religion's role in the new republic. Whose original intent do we mean? The Calvinist Sam Adams or the radical anti-Christian Tom Paine? The common-sense Presbyterian John Witherspoon or the Unitarian-leaning rationalist Thomas Jefferson? The religious backgrounds and motivations of the founders varied so much that historical study can yield nothing more than a general sense of their "original intent*s*"—plural.

But what about some of those decisions by the Continental Congress that themselves implied a vision of a "Christian America"? The Continental Congress periodically called for days of fasting and prayer in the lead-up to and prosecution of the Revolutionary War, as well as for days of thanksgiving to God when the war seemed to be going well.[24] As Derek Davis has observed, "Undoubtedly, Congress's regular proclamation of days of fast and thanksgiving served to reinforce the belief of Americans that God was acting for them," implying a theological interpretation of the war that encouraged the close cooperation of religion and politics.[25] On the second day of its assembly in 1774, Thomas Cushing of Massachusetts proposed that Congress's sessions be opened with prayer, a motion that eventually passed with the backing of prominent leaders like Samuel Adams (and over the objections of equally prominent patriots like John Jay and John Rutledge).[26] The practice of employing chaplains to lead the assembly in prayer continued after independence was won; all the while Congress was debating the wording of the First Amendment, and over the strong objections of James Madison.[27] In fact, on the same day that the Congress of the new nation adopted the religious freedom clauses of the First Amendment, it voted again to appoint chaplains for the House and the Senate, a practice that continues to this day.

Those who call for a return to our religious roots point to instances like these as signs that the founders imagined their new nation to be founded on Christian beliefs. The fact that Congress employed chaplains and that presidents issued religiously expressive proclamations of thanksgiving in the very same period in which the First Amendment was being crafted and ratified proves that they did not see these practices as a violation of the religious freedom protected by the Bill of Rights. Constitutional historian Derek Davis warns, however, about reading too much about the "original intent" of the framers from the acceptance of these religious practices. Rather than intentional, principled stands on the appropriate relationship between religion and government, the use of chaplains and proclamations of thanksgiving simply represented the continuation of traditions that, in eighteenth-century culture, were relatively uncontroversial. In a time in which the principles of separation of church and state were still being worked out, and in a moment of collective anxiety over a war of independence, Davis contends that it is unsurprising that the early American leaders continued these practices of appealing to divine guidance and sanction. But he insists that we see them in historical context and recognize that they normally were undertaken without much critical reflection. In other words, they were examples of long-standing tradition, not of "original intent"—that is, not an intentional interpretation of the right relationship between "church" and "state" being forged more deliberately in the First Amendment.[28]

Furthermore, any attempt to apply directly the designs of eighteenth-century patriots (however we understand them) to our very different twenty-first-century political culture requires considerable historical gymnastics. The truth is that the time of Washington, Jefferson, and Madison was very different from our own. Our understanding of religion and our awareness of (and appreciation for) diversity are broader than our revolutionary ancestors could imagine. Our understanding of American politics too is different from what it was in the days of the early republic, when the United States was more like the European Union than the centralized government it is today. To try to apply an interpretation of original intent directly to the religious and political cultures of contemporary America is historically dubious and an oversimplification of the complex relationship required between religion and the state in our day.

We cannot say with any certainty that the founders all intended for the United States to be a Christian nation, any more than we can say with confidence that they wanted it to be a completely secular republic. The legacy of the founders is messier and more complicated than either of these simplistic readings, and this muddled legacy is all that history gives us. What we can take from reflection on our history is the assurance that, from America's founding, religious voices, ideas, and perspectives have played an important role in shaping American identity, at the very same time that our constitutional structure ensured that religious freedom and pluralism would be written into our national character. Beginning with the founders, the overall trajectory of American history has been a dynamic tension between the so-called separation of church and state and a robust role for religion in the public life of the United States.

PUBLIC MORALITY AND RELIGION: LESSONS FROM VIRGINIA

One reason that Falwell and other members of the Christian Right have been concerned with Americans' departure from biblical authority is that they assume that morality *requires* religion. They take for granted that religion (specifically Judeo-Christian religion) is the essential source of Western notions of right and wrong, and they also suggest that to be moral—as individuals or a society—we *need* to be religious. Belief in God somehow makes a person (or a society) more open to moral behavior, while the lack of religion strips a person (or society) of the motivations and teachings necessary to maintain a moral life. From this perspective, America is in the grips of moral decay, precisely because we as a nation have departed from biblical principles. Righting the national ship, then, requires that "the authority of Bible morality must once again be recognized as the legitimate guiding principle of our nation."[29] Hence Falwell named his organization dedicated to the recovery of America's Christian roots the *Moral* Majority, for good religion and good morality are roughly the same thing: "We as American citizens must recommit ourselves to the faith of our fathers and to the premises and moral foundations upon which this country was established. Now is the time to begin calling America back to God, back to the Bible, back to morality!"[30]

As we have seen already, some of the founders also believed that religion was important (perhaps even necessary) to the moral foundation of civil society. In his Farewell Address of 1797, for instance, Washington linked religion and morality in a way that enamors current defenders of a biblical America:

> Of all the dispositions and habits which lead to political prosperity, religion and morality are indispensable supports. . . . Let it simply be asked where is the security for property, for reputation, for life, if the sense of religious obligation *desert* the oaths, which are the instruments of investigation in courts of justice? And let us with caution indulge the supposition that morality can be maintained without religion. Whatever may be conceded to the influence of refined education on minds of peculiar structure, reason and experience both forbid us to expect that national morality can prevail in exclusion of religious principle.[31]

With these parting words, Washington certainly expressed the view that a society that fails to maintain religion is doomed to moral decay. Though he did not link them so stridently as Washington, John Adams also assumed that religion contributed essentially to the maintenance of public morality. Indeed, as we have seen, his backing of a "mild establishment" of religion in Massachusetts was based in his assumption that support of religion would protect a moral basis for society. In their assumption that public morality required a publicly supported religion, Washington and Adams simply reflected the majority view in the eighteenth century. Most people back then had a hard time imagining a society that could maintain moral standards without explicit religious influence.

These days it is more apparent to most of us that people can be good moral citizens even if they subscribe to a different religion than we do—or to no religion at all. This fact was apparent to some important contributors to the early republic, too. Eventually their understanding of the relationship between religion and public morality—that religion can contribute to public morality, but public morality does not *require* religion to succeed—won out over the assumptions of Washington and Adams. No episode in colonial history illustrates that victory better than the contest over religious freedom in Virginia.

In 1783 in the newly independent Commonwealth of Virginia, Patrick Henry called for the General Assembly to adopt a "General Assessment" in support of religion. The Bill Establishing a Provision for Teachers of the Christian Religion would provide tax dollars to support clergy of all Christian denominations as they provided religious education throughout the state. Henry's motive for pushing the bill was not primarily to protect an "established" religion. Indeed, while the bulk of the funds would go to Anglican clergy (simply because that church was still the dominant religious presence in Virginia), Christians who belonged to another sect could earmark their taxes for clergy of their own communities, or alternatively toward the building of schools within their county. Thus, Henry believed that the state could protect the freedom of individual conscience while still doing its part to safeguard the health of Christian education within its borders.

Why did Henry believe religious education was an appropriate preoccupation for the state's General Assembly? He supported the bill because he believed that robust religion was vital to the encouragement of public morality. That assumption was captured in the first line of the bill: "WHEREAS the general diffusion of Christian knowledge hath a natural tendency to correct the morals of men, restrain their vices, and preserve the peace of society . . ." Concerned for the moral foundation of the commonwealth, Henry wanted to ensure the survival of the one institution he believed essential to cultivating ethical behavior and social cooperation. A man of his time, Henry assumed that a society that ignored religion was one that would struggle to maintain order, decency, and cohesion.

Among the opponents of Henry's bill was the young James Madison. In 1785 Madison anonymously but publicly attacked the proposed bill in his now-famous "Memorial and Remonstrance." In this tract, Madison argued that tax support of religion represented a "dangerous abuse of power" and an "encroachment" on the independent sphere of religion. He insisted that religion was an "unalienable right," a relationship with the Divine that "must be left to the conviction and conscience of every man [*sic*]," rather than an obligation that could be imposed by the state. He worried about the slippery slope; the bill clearly gave preference to Christianity over other religions, and he suspected that "the same authority which can establish Christianity, in exclusion of all other Religions, may establish with the same ease any particular sect of Christians, in exclusion of all other sects." In other words, a seemingly innocuous bill (to Christians, at least) that required support of Christian clergy, but allowed latitude for directing that support to the denomination of one's choosing, could just as easily be restricted, in a later moment, to require the support of a specific denomination's clergy over all others. To Madison, the Bill Establishing a Provision for Teachers of the Christian Religion represented the state's unjustified invasion of the jurisdiction of religion.

Most important for our purposes, though, is Madison's attack on Henry's main reason for supporting the bill. Madison argued that government support of religion was not necessary for either the good of religion or the stability of the state. Pointing to history, Madison reminded his readers that "it is known that this Religion [Christianity] both existed and flourished, not only without the support of human laws, but in spite of every opposition from them." Just as important, a good society does not need to control religion to ensure its own stability:

> Rulers who wished to subvert the public liberty, may have found an established Clergy convenient auxiliaries. A just Government instituted to secure & perpetuate it needs them not. Such a government will be best supported by protecting every Citizen in the enjoyment of his Religion with the same equal hand which protects his person and his property; by neither invading the equal rights of any Sect, nor suffering any Sect to invade those of another.

From Madison's perspective, government-mandated support for religion not only violates the natural rights of its citizens; it also fails to achieve its objective, namely, the stability of the state. It was unnecessary, and in fact such an invasion of personal liberties put society at risk. It signaled an early assault on the natural rights of citizens, therefore encouraging a hostile and disrespectful attitude toward government and social order. Far from ensuring public morality, government intrusion in the matters of religion *undermined* the moral foundations of society. According to Madison, this "first experiment on our liberties" was a good way to put them all in jeopardy.

Madison fought back Henry's bill and paved the way for Virginia to establish religious freedom instead.[32] Many of the points he made successfully in that debate proved persuasive in the federal consideration of "church and state" relations as well. Madison is largely credited as the principal author of the Constitution, a document that quite intentionally makes no reference to God or religious authority. In fact, the only reference to religion at all in the body of the Constitution is in Article Six, which states that "no religious Test shall ever be required as a Qualification to any Office or public Trust under the United States." The importance of this prohibition on religious tests for office cannot be overstated. It ran counter to that assumption, prevalent in the eighteenth century, that religious conviction was necessary for a person—and a civil officer more specifically—to be morally trustworthy. Rejecting Henry's notion that morality requires religion, Madison made sure that the U.S. Constitution explicitly prohibited a religious test for office. Instead, Article Six guaranteed that a citizen could qualify for the highest offices without subscribing to a particular religion—or any religion at all. According to the legacy of James Madison, neither promoting religion among the general population nor requiring it in our leaders is necessary for the cultivation of a moral society.

A careful reading of the "intent" of Madison, Jefferson, and others vital to the formation of the American Republic reveals that many of the founders were not enthusiastic about—were even deeply suspicious of—talk of the United States as a Christian nation. Most of the prominent statesmen of the Revolution believed in an institutional separation of religion and state. Many of them rejected the argument that public morality could be secured only through government sponsorship of religion, and even among those whose words suggested a necessary link between religion and morality, the religion they had in mind clearly was a generic and rational theism, not the doctrines and creeds of traditional

Christianity. To argue that the founders intended the United States to be a Christian nation similar to the aspirations of some (not all) modern evangelicals is to read today's political agendas back into the words of our eighteenth-century ancestors.

At the same time, in criticizing Christian calls for a biblical nation, secular liberals often overstate the "separation of church and state" in American history. Too often, separationists assume that the popularity of that phrase means that religion can have no public input at all. But to argue that the separation of church and state has ever been absolute in the American moral tradition, that religion was intended to be a "private" affair cordoned off from public life, betrays an equally tenuous hold on our history. To that misunderstanding we now must turn.

3

But What about the Separation of Church and State?

The "wall of separation" has been a popular catchphrase for interpreting the First Amendment's religion clauses. It is an enduring metaphor that seems to capture the strict separation the Constitution requires between the influences of religion and the powers of the state. To some secular liberals, a strict divide between religion and politics is one of the essential tenets on which the United States was founded. In fact, many Americans assume that the image comes straight from the First Amendment itself. In reality, however, the "wall of separation" occurs nowhere in the Constitution or the Bill of Rights. The First Amendment declares that "Congress shall make no law respecting an establishment of religion, or prohibiting the free exercise thereof." Nowhere does it describe the proper relationship between religion and state as a "wall." How this image came to symbolize the relationship between religion and government in the United States is an interesting story of Supreme Court jurisprudence laced with a splash of interreligious bigotry.

A POROUS WALL

When President Thomas Jefferson used the phrase "wall of separation" in a letter to some Connecticut Baptists, he did so to reassure them in their struggle against religious discrimination. In 1801, when the Danbury Baptists Association wrote to Jefferson, the idea of constitutionally supported religious freedom was new enough that religious minorities were still skeptical. Prohibited from public preaching in Virginia and driven out of some areas of New England, Baptists were just one religious minority used to being treated unfairly in colonial America. So they welcomed the protections of religious freedom that were incorporated in the First Amendment to the new nation's Constitution, and they worked hard to rally public support for the ratification of the Bill of Rights. But in the early years of the United States, the First Amendment was generally understood to restrict only the *federal* government from impinging on religious freedom. The states were free to keep their established churches and to support them with tax dollars, and several of them did so well into the nineteenth century.[1] Connecticut was one such state in the first decade of the nineteenth century that maintained official support of Congregationalism.

So when this group of Connecticut Baptists wrote to newly elected President Jefferson for reassurance of his commitment to religious freedom, they did so with the realities of religious discrimination all around them. They expressed their hope that his influence would prevail upon their own and other states to eliminate the practice of bestowing official favor to one religion over others. In response, Jefferson assured them of his commitment to religious freedom, and he employed his now-famous metaphor to do so. He agreed with his Baptist admirers that "religion is a matter which lies solely between man & his god, that he owes account to none other for his faith or his worship, [and] that the legitimate powers of government reach actions only, and not opinions." He pointed to the decision of the American people to ratify a Bill of Rights that prohibited the establishment of religion and interference with the free exercise of religion, and he concluded that by this action Americans had built "a wall of separation between church and state."

Widely credited with being the source of this enduring image, Jefferson actually was not the first prominent American to use it. The Puritan Roger Williams was banished from Massachusetts in the 1630s for, as he saw it, insisting on his right to religious freedom. In defending that right, Williams argued against the conventional Puritan practice of using civil punishments to enforce a particular religion. To confuse the jurisdictions of religion and state, he said, "opened a gap in the hedge or wall of separation between the Garden of the church and the wilderness of the world."[2] The government's priority should be to protect the "bodies and goods" of its citizens and to preserve civil peace, aims that were better served if it stayed out of the business of endorsing, promoting, and enforcing religion. Persecution on matters of religion caused more strife than it avoided, and too close association with the state usually caused the church to sacrifice its purity for political gain. The institutions of religion and state should mind their own business, argued Williams, for to honor that "hedge or wall" between them was the best path toward protecting both piety and civil peace.

Clearly both Williams and Jefferson thought there was something useful in describing the relationship between church and state as a "wall," for the image spoke vividly of the danger to be wrought by allowing the institutions of one to violate the jurisdiction of the other. But Williams certainly did not imagine a society in which religion made no civic contribution, if his own life and career are any indication. He spent a lifetime arguing in public *as a religious thinker* for both religious freedom and the need for some sense of civic duty, and in doing so he personified the appropriate contributions religion can make to public conversation. All the while he was pointing out the error in Massachusetts's policy of religious uniformity, he was using theological language to do so. Later in Rhode Island, he invoked religious values to inspire his fellow citizens to take seriously their shared civic responsibilities, like paying taxes and participating in civil defense. Despite advocating for that "hedge or wall" between religion and state coercion, Williams evidently considered it appropriate that religious people play a role in political discourse and decision making, and in fact he explicitly rejected the idea that religion is simply a "private" experience with no "public" consequences or contributions to make. To his mind, the "wall of separation" between church and state was not so impenetrable as to bar religion completely from the public square.

In his own use of the term "separation," Thomas Jefferson may have signaled more of a preference for a secular society than Williams, but his viewpoint was hardly characteristic of the founders or popular sentiment in the early nineteenth century. Jefferson's suspicion of public religion was rooted in his skepticism regarding "superstitious" beliefs (which he believed most traditional creeds to be) and was fueled in particular by the animosity between him and clergymen in New England, who publicly maligned him in support of John Adams during the presidential election of 1800. Legal historian Philip Hamburger has gone so far as to suggest that Jefferson's use of the phrase "separation of church and state" in his letter to the Danbury Baptists was a calculated attack on the public activism of Federalist clergy. Jefferson thought that his support for a separation between religion and state would be enthusiastically embraced (and publicized) by the marginalized Baptists, and that their support would help make his the authoritative interpretation of the First Amendment. As it turns out, the Danbury Baptists (good descendants of Williams that they were[3]) did not endorse Jefferson's desire for religion's complete separation from political matters. Like most people in the early republic, Baptists assumed that public religion was good for society, for it encouraged virtue and citizenship among people and moral influence on laws and government. They had little interest in a complete separation of religion from politics; they simply wanted the freedom to practice their own religion without civil penalty.

The idea of a separation of religion from politics never really picked up steam until the end of the nineteenth century, and then only because of religious bigotry prevalent in the United States at the time.[4] The nineteenth century brought waves of European immigrants to the shores of America, and many of these immigrants were Catholics. This growth in American Catholicism deeply concerned "nativist" Protestants, many of whom doubted the average Catholic's ability to distinguish between religious and civil allegiance. They feared that a Catholic majority would render the United States beholden to the pope; so over time a number of Protestant elites and public intellectuals pushed for the codification of a more explicit separation of church and state. They labored to pass a constitutional amendment spelling out such separation, but when this effort failed, they turned their efforts to the First Amendment and to the courts. If they could not manage to get the separation of church and state explicitly spelled out in the Constitution, they would make sure that the Supreme Court's authoritative interpretation of the First Amendment required just such an arrangement.

The U.S. Supreme Court finally gave them what they wanted (sort of) with *Everson v. Board of Education* in 1947. In *Everson*, the court considered a New Jersey law that provided state funding for busing students to private schools, including religious schools. The ruling in the case included a strident assertion of the "separation of church and state" that set the stage for decades of Supreme Court jurisprudence on the issue. Writing for the majority, Justice Hugo Black cited Jefferson and Madison as authorities to declare that

> the "establishment of religion" clause of the First Amendment means at least this: Neither a state nor the Federal Government can set up a church. Neither can pass laws which aid one religion, aid all religions, or prefer one religion over another. Neither can force nor

> influence a person to go to or to remain away from church against his will or force him to profess a belief or disbelief in any religion. No person can be punished for entertaining or professing religious beliefs or disbeliefs, for church attendance or non-attendance. No tax in any amount, large or small, can be levied to support any religious activities or institutions, whatever they may be called, or whatever form they may adopt to teach or practice religion. Neither a state nor the Federal Government can, openly or secretly, participate in the affairs of any religious organizations or groups and vice versa. In the words of Jefferson, the clause against establishment of religion by law was intended to erect a "wall of separation between church and state."[5]

In *Everson,* Black and his colleagues made clear that the First Amendment's establishment clause required strict separation between religion and civil government, separation that applied to the states as well as the federal government. Indeed, Black ends his opinion with this assertion: "The First Amendment has erected a wall between church and state. That wall must be kept high and impregnable. We could not approve the slightest breach."

The anti-Catholic strict separationists appeared to have won; the Supreme Court authoritatively declared that the First Amendment placed a "wall" between religion and the state. There are, however, a couple of reasons that we should not consider this wall as "impregnable" as the language suggests, despite—or because of—the Supreme Court's decision in *Everson.* Some legal scholars argue that the language in *Everson* reflects more of Justice Hugo Black's own anti-Catholicism than a legal interpretation deeply rooted in American history.[6] But another reason that the "wall" should not be taken to be as "impregnable" as the language in *Everson* suggests lies in the verdict itself: Ironically, the ruling that asserted this strident separation of church and state then ruled in *favor* of New Jersey's use of public funds to bus students to and from religious schools! The mixed message sent by the verdict has led to a complicated (and arguably contradictory) series of Supreme Court rulings on church-state issues over the last sixty years. School-sponsored Bible readings and prayers at public schools are unconstitutional, but the use of public funds to aid students of private religious schools may not be (under certain conditions). Religious holiday displays on government property are sometimes permissible, but sometimes they represent an unlawful state endorsement of religion. The Ten Commandments sometimes may appear appropriately on or in government buildings as a testament to our nation's legal heritage, but in other circumstances they resemble too closely an official endorsement of "Judeo-Christian" religious morality. The proper legal relationship between religion and the state has been so confusing since the middle of the twentieth century precisely because *the Supreme Court has never consistently insisted that the two be separated by a "wall . . . high and impregnable."*

What is true for the institutions of religion and state is true more broadly for religion in American public life. The appropriate role for religious perspectives in political conversation and decision making is more complex than the strict separationists allow. To some degree it may be useful to keep the *institutions* of religion and the *institutions* of the state as distinct as possible. At the same time, the First Amendment declares simply that government may not enforce laws that represent the "establishment of religion"; it does not rule out religious contributions to public discourse and to the debate over laws that possess a clear secular purpose. Furthermore, the First Amendment insists that government may not impede the "freedom of religion," and restrictions on religion in public debate may represent a violation of that constitutional protection, insofar as such restrictions serve as a litmus test by which citizens are disqualified from political participation.[7] Given that the image does not appear in the First Amendment and, at face value, proscribes more than the Constitution itself, it is unfortunate that so many Americans insist on reading the "wall of separation" as an axiomatic reflection of the framers' intentions for the role of religion in public life.

Dogmatic assertions of separation also defy the greater testimony of history. In reality, the "wall of separation" has always been more penetrable than Justice Black preferred, for religious voices and communities have played an important role in influencing American culture, especially American *moral* culture. The disestablishment of religion in the U.S. Constitution did not cause the demise of "enthusiastic religion," as Thomas Jefferson had hoped. Jefferson assumed that without state support religion would be forced to compete in the marketplace of ideas, a popularity contest he expected rationalistic Unitarianism to win over "superstitious" religions and their adherence to traditional creeds. In fact the opposite happened; Unitarianism failed to secure a strong following nationally, but evangelically oriented denominations like the Methodists, Baptists, and Presbyterians ballooned in numbers and energy in the early nineteenth century. The growth of these "superstitious" groups was fueled by what is often called the Second

Great Awakening, a period of revivalism in the early 1800s that led religious people and communities to become more involved in social issues. "Enthusiastic" evangelicals applied their religious energy to the public needs of the new republic, interpreting social activity as a religious duty. The result of their public involvement was that evangelical Christianity played a major role in the development of the American moral tradition through the nineteenth and twentieth centuries.

In fact, the story of public activism and the evolution of the American moral tradition in the nineteenth century *is* the story of American evangelicalism. When we think of evangelicals today, we imagine independent megachurches or the socially conservative segment of certain Protestant denominations—Southern Baptists and Presbyterians, to be sure. But in the early nineteenth century, most of our "mainline" denominations were evangelical, in the sense that they were traditions that emphasized the authority of Scripture, the importance of the cross to salvation, the need for conversion, and the obligation for Christians to evangelize the world.[8] Methodists, Baptists, Disciples of Christ, Presbyterians, and a host of other denominations shared the evangelical spirit, and evangelicalism inspired both socially conservative and socially progressive causes. Evangelicals were busy in the public sphere, pushing for better economic safety nets for the poor, legal address of widespread alcohol abuse, expanded political rights for women, improved educational standards for the nation's children, and justice for its African American underclass. Often pushed by a heightened expectation of Christ's imminent return, and thus the need to prepare the world for God's renewed kingdom, evangelicals regarded social reform as a necessary corollary to their religious beliefs.

But in the 1800s, it was not only doctrinally traditional evangelicals who felt compelled by their religious convictions to contribute to moral debate and social change. Liberal Christians implored their fellow Americans to invest in public school systems that would reflect progressive evangelical values of liberty and national optimism, and the popular *McGuffey Readers* institutionalized progressive Protestant values at the same time that they taught children to read. As industrial development and increased immigration led to higher concentrations of working poor in the nation's cities, progressive Christians agitated for a social network for the poor. Intellectuals like William Ellery Channing formed societies to advocate for a national policy of nonviolence, rooted in the moral optimism of liberal evangelicalism. And many of these religiously based reform societies not only took up women's concerns but also featured women in prominent leadership roles, in ways that were alarmingly countercultural. Frances Willard of the Woman's Christian Temperance Union was the most prominent example of the public presence afforded women by Christian social reform movements.

As historian Sidney Ahlstrom has written, "Nothing in America was safe from the reformer's burning gaze during the first half of the nineteenth century. Everything from diet and dress to the social structure itself—even the family and motherhood—were [*sic*] up for critical review."[9] In pushing for these social changes, religiously motivated reformers contributed to the foundation of an emerging moral tradition in America.

IN OUR DARKEST HOUR

Among religion's most important contributions to the American moral tradition was its leadership in the national crisis over slavery. To be sure, religion contributed to both sides of the debate over slavery. Defenders of the practice regularly rooted their arguments not only in the economic necessity of slavery and white fears of an emancipated black race, but also in the Bible's apparent permission for slavery. Proslavery advocates like Samuel How (1790–1868) pointed to passages like 1 Timothy 6:1–5, which counsels slaves not to "despise" their Christian masters but to "do them service." He read biblical examples of patriarchs like Abraham owning slaves as precedent for the southern slave industry, and he interpreted the Tenth Commandment in the Decalogue ("You shall not covet your neighbor's . . . male or female-slave") as proof that the Bible protected slaveholding with conventional property rights.[10] Presbyterian James Henley Thornwell (1812–1862) also implicated God in the institution, remarking that "the relation betwixt the slave and his master is not inconsistent with the word of God." He insisted that slavery was the "good and merciful" way to organize "labor which Providence has given us."[11] And South Carolina's first Catholic bishop, John England (1786–1842), went so far as to imply that slaveholding was an expression of Christian charity:

> The situation of a slave, under a Christian master, insures to him food, raiment, and dwelling, together with a variety of little comforts; it relieves him from the apprehensions of neglect in sickness,

> from all solicitude for the support of his family, and in return, all that is required is fidelity and moderate labour.[12]

Because of these clear advantages to the slave, England was unsurprised that he had "known many freedmen who regretted their manumission [i.e., freedom]." These appeals to Scripture and religion served as a powerful defense of slavery in a national culture so influenced by evangelicalism.

At the same time, many abolitionists rejected slavery on religious conviction. Moses Stuart of the Andover Seminary in Massachusetts responded in excruciating detail to the apologists' use of biblical passages to justify slavery; while he ultimately admitted that the Bible did not explicitly outlaw the institution, he insisted that the evils prevalent in the American version—namely, physical abuse and the common practice of slave rape—rendered it sinful. He also rejected as unbiblical the assumptions of white racial superiority at home on both sides of the debate.[13] On the eve of war, Protestant preacher Henry Ward Beecher insisted that slavery violated the core sentiments of Christianity. He called slavery "the most alarming and most fertile cause of national sin," and claimed that "where the Bible has been in the household," there would result "a government that would not have a slave or serf in the field."[14] Presbyterian minister and newspaper editor Elijah Lovejoy argued that Christian abolitionists "hold American Slavery to be a *wrong*, a legalized system of inconceivable injustice," in part because they consider slavery to be a social "sin" that would "speedily work the downfall of our free institutions, both civil and religious."[15] Fellow Presbyterian Albert Barnes found it "impossible to convince the world that slavery is right, or is in accordance with the will of God," for "no alleged authority of the Bible will satisfy men at large that the system is not always a violation of the laws that God has enstamped on the human soul." According to Barnes, slavery violated the natural laws of morality and justice that underwrote both American democracy and Christian religion, and he publicly feared that the claims of slavery's biblical legitimacy would undermine confidence in both.[16]

Certainly the abolitionist who had the biggest cultural impact was Harriet Beecher Stowe. Although *Uncle Tom's Cabin* is now routinely dismissed as an excessively sentimental novel filled with unflattering racial stereotypes, in the 1850s the novel was a powerful indictment of American slavery. It was, in a real sense, a political tract, a public appeal for abolition. Stowe used her novel to illustrate the brutality of slaveholding, the trauma it inflicted on families, and the inconsistency of slavery with the character of Christianity. Devoutly pious, Stowe emphasized how the terrors of slavery represented the antithesis of the redemptive love of Christ. Characters like little Eva St. Clare and Uncle Tom himself serve the novel as Christlike figures who highlight the contrast between Christian virtue and the vices of the institution. In the nineteenth century, Stowe's novel sold more copies than any book other than the Bible, and it inspired massive opposition to the Fugitive Slave Law (which made it illegal to aid escaped slaves) and to the institution of slavery in general. To the extent it had this public effect, much of the novel's success was a result of its appeal to popular American evangelicalism. *Uncle Tom's Cabin* spoke the language of the American people, which in the nineteenth century was the language of religion. In the South the book was panned and banned, but the energy with which Southerners attacked it testified as much as anything else to the effect it was having on the public debate over slavery.[17]

Of course, white Northerners were not the only voices of abolition in the years leading up to the Civil War. African American preachers also contributed religious perspectives to the public debate. David Walker (1796–1830), a free black man from Boston, in 1829 published an *Appeal, in Four Articles; Together with a Preamble, to the Coloured Citizens of the World, but in Particular, and Very Expressly, to Those of the United States of America.*[18] In what religious historian Mark Noll calls "the era's most widely noticed attack on the slave system by an African American,"[19] Walker offered a militant Christian appeal to fellow black Americans to throw off the yoke of slavery and rebel against their masters. Walker used his Christian belief in human beings as the *imago dei*—created in the image of God—to argue for the full humanity of African Americans, in direct contradiction to the assumptions of white superiority advocated by (among many others) Thomas Jefferson. He rejected the idea that the Bible permitted slavery by pointing out the incompatibility of slave abuse with the pacifist pattern of Jesus. He quoted the Declaration of Independence to insist that African Americans were entitled to the same God-ordained "unalienable" rights that white Americans were guaranteed. Explicitly appealing to religious values, Walker encouraged slaves to rise up violently against southern white power. One of the several covert means by which he distributed his *Appeal* to slaves and sympathizers in the South was to sew copies of the tract inside the suits of sympathetic sailors to smuggle them through southern ports!

White readers on both sides of the slavery debate were generally not all that interested in the perspectives of African Americans, but Walker was an exception. The militancy and popularity of his tract frightened southern slaveholders, and his *Appeal* was banned in much of the South. Taken just as seriously (and equally frightening to slavery's defenders) was the public witness of Frederick Douglass (1817–1895), an escaped slave from Maryland who became the most identifiable African American voice for emancipation. In his public lectures for the American Anti-Slavery Society and his other writings, Douglass rejected both slavery and the conventional Christianity that so easily endorsed it in the South. Yet he rejected neither religion nor religious reasoning. In his autobiography, *Narrative of the Life of an American Slave*, he famously wrote:

> I love the pure, peaceable, and impartial Christianity of Christ: I therefore hate the corrupt, slaveholding, women-whipping, cradle-plundering, partial and hypocritical Christianity of this land. Indeed, I can see no reason, but the most deceitful one, for calling the religion of this land Christianity. I look upon it as the climax of all misnomers, the boldest of all frauds, and the grossest of all libels.[20]

Douglass rejected an interpretation of Christianity that permitted ministers to own slaves, enabled slaveholders to teach Sunday school in clear conscience, and allowed human beings to be bartered for the purchase of—of all things!—Bibles. But Douglass was clear to distinguish between the "Christianity of America," which was the subject of his ire, and the essence of true Christianity, which he believed the southern slaveholders had perverted beyond recognition. In his indictment of white America's religious duplicity, he employed religious language and biblical allusion, going so far as to invoke verbatim Christ's diatribe against the Pharisees as a condemnation of the hypocritical religion of the southern slaveholder.

All of our examples so far involve regular Americans contributing to nineteenth-century debate from explicitly religious perspectives and in intentionally religious language. Political leaders too invoked religion in the fight against slavery, none more eloquently than President Abraham Lincoln. Lincoln increasingly understood emancipation and the Civil War itself as theologically significant events. In his Second Inaugural Address, Lincoln translated the tragedy of the war into ultimate religious terms. He acknowledged that both sides justified their cause theologically: "Both read the same Bible, and pray to the same

God; and each invokes his aid against the other." But he also sought to make theological sense of the senseless tragedy that had befallen the nation. Days away from military victory, Lincoln rejected triumphant rhetoric and instead called the nation to a period of theological introspection:

> The Almighty has His own purposes. "Woe unto the world because of offenses; for it must needs be that offenses come, but woe to that man by whom the offense cometh" [Matt. 18:7 KJV]. If we shall suppose that American slavery is one of those offenses which, in the providence of God, must needs come, but which, having continued through His appointed time, He now wills to remove, and that He gives to both North and South this terrible war as the woe due to those by whom the offense came, shall we discern therein any departure from those divine attributes which the believers in a living God always ascribe to Him? Fondly do we hope, fervently do we pray, that this mighty scourge of war may speedily pass away. Yet, if God wills that it continue until all the wealth piled by the bondsman's two hundred and fifty years of unrequited toil shall be sunk, and until every drop of blood drawn with the lash shall be paid by another drawn with the sword, as was said three thousand years ago, so still it must be said "the judgments of the Lord are true and righteous altogether." [Ps. 19:9 KJV]

Lincoln's religious interpretation of the Civil War arguably captured what no nontheological language could have expressed. With unsurpassed eloquence, he gave utterance to the apparent meaninglessness of the war, while also maintaining a sense of hope. He expressed profound humility while maintaining that abolition was on the side of the right. In doing so, he promised to lead a modest, repentant response to the war. Sadly, Lincoln did not live to ensure a sympathetic reconstruction of the South, but his religious assessment of the Civil War has gone down in history as one of the most profound public speeches by an American president.

As Lincoln, Douglass, Stowe, and many others demonstrate, religion and politics clearly were never "separate" in the public debates over slavery in the middle of the nineteenth century. Both defenders of slavery and its opponents appealed to religion in marshaling public support. On the proslavery side, biblical arguments were instrumental in clearing the collective conscience of a thoroughly evangelical culture, but religion motivated, energized, and gave expression to the abolitionist movement as well. In fact, historians agree that without the contributions of religious perspectives, the abolitionists never would have succeeded in affecting public opinion in the North and challenging political inertia in Washington.[21] It was religious leaders who grabbed the attention of the American people and helped turn the antislavery movement into what historian Sydney Ahlstrom called a "massive juggernaut."[22] Through their explicitly religious appeals to public sentiment and their tireless activity on behalf of emancipation, churches and other religious organizations pushed the country to commit to abolition.

THE SOCIAL GOSPEL

At the beginning of the twentieth century, the United States was in the midst of another kind of revolution, this time an economic one, and the changes this revolution wrought on American society brought new social problems that would cry out for a moral response. The American economy was becoming thoroughly industrialized, for this was the era of big coal and steel, the era of Andrew Carnegie and Henry Clay Frick. American industrialization required massive workforces, and the availability of jobs had attracted large numbers of people to the nation's cities, which became centers for this new economy.

But there was a dark underside to this intense economic development. Unbridled capitalism aggravated the disparity between the nation's economic classes. Industrialization made the steel and coal magnates rich while doing nothing to improve the hard circumstances of laborers and immigrants. In fact, the gulf between the rich and the poor widened exponentially as the American economy modernized. As the emergence of these new industries created the need for a growing workforce, it pushed the limits of what cities could support. Not just eastern cities like New York and Pittsburgh, but also midwestern towns like Chicago and Kansas City grew by leaps and bounds, as people flocked to them in search of work. As these cities grew, urban crises began to mount. Housing was often insufficient; there were not enough places for workers to live, and those that did exist were barely adequate for human beings. Wealthy property owners felt little pressure to ensure that the living conditions in their apartment buildings were more than squalor. The push for jobs and lack of oversight kept wages low and workweeks long; working conditions were often hard and dangerous; and frequently whole families—even young children—were forced by need to labor in these conditions. Labor unions were rarely successful and violently opposed by industrialists, so that no one—except a handful of radical socialists—seemed to speak for the struggles of the American working class.

Into this problem stepped a movement that raised the sensitivity of upper-class Americans to the plight of the working poor and profoundly influenced the way Americans responded to the issues of industrialism. The movement, called the social gospel, drew primarily liberal evangelical Protestants who insisted that Christian theology and morality had something to say about the economic crisis. Representatives of the social gospel charged American Christianity with being complicit in the injustices of the industrialized economy, because Christians had failed to apply the principles of Jesus to the need for social welfare and fairer labor relations. The churches had been content to preach an otherworldly Christian message that emphasized individual salvation to God's kingdom in heaven, instead of addressing the injustices of the here and now. Worse yet, their failure to address social problems implied that Christian morality had nothing to say about such problems. The social gospel movement insisted that social reform was the *heart* of the Christian gospel and was central to Jesus' own ministry. Motivated by Jesus' example and informed by his message, the social gospel argued that it was the responsibility of churches to engage the social crisis and to struggle to make American society reflect Christian justice and love.

Early advocates of this social gospel included a Congregationalist pastor named Washington Gladden, a Catholic cardinal named James Gibbons, an Episcopalian economist named Richard Ely, and an Anglo-Catholic socialist named Vida Scudder. But the most influential of all the defenders of the social gospel was a New York Baptist named Walter Rauschenbusch (1861–1918). For eleven years a pastor in a gang-infested district of New York City called Hell's Kitchen, Rauschenbusch saw firsthand the dark side of the industrialization and urbanization of America. Most of his congregants were immigrant factory workers, and he matured as a social thinker and activist through his relationships with them. Moving to Rochester to begin a career as a seminary professor, Rauschenbusch published in 1907 *Christianity and the Social Crisis,* a blockbuster account of Christianity's relevance to the social injustices of industrial capitalism. In this book, he criticized the economic disadvantage at which industrialism put the working class—not only the low wages, long hours, and unfortunate working and living conditions, but also the emotional and psychological stress the crisis put on labor families. He argued against land monopolies and capitalists' accumulation of financial power; he argued for profit sharing with laborers. He criticized capitalism's emphasis on self-interest that had pitted the social classes against one another, instead of encouraging solidarity, social cooperation, and the common good.

In response to the cutthroat ethos of unchecked capitalism, Rauschenbusch argued that what was needed was a "social Christianity." In the thoroughly evangelical culture of early twentieth-century America, Rauschenbusch believed that Christianity could make a difference in the prospects for America's working class, by calling for the moral reform of the economy. He insisted that such a public position would require the church to abandon its emphasis on otherworldly religion, and instead labor for the historical transformation of human society into the kingdom of God. As he put it in *Christianity and the Social Crisis*, for Jesus "The kingdom of God is still a collective conception, involving the whole social life of man. . . . It is not a matter of getting individuals to heaven, but of transforming the life on earth into the harmony of heaven."[23]

Rauschenbusch believed that the gospel was deeply political in that its core values served as a plumb line for measuring the righteousness of societies: "The kingdom of God is the true human society; the ethics of Jesus taught the true social conduct which would create the true society. [Therefore,] this would be Christ's test for any custom, law, or institution: does it draw men together or divide them?"[24] The social gospel also served as a call for Christians to be active in the moral transformation of their nation. According to Rauschenbusch, this social transformation would depend on a moral return to the "fundamental virtue" of "just love."[25] A "Christianized" America would temper the self-interest of capitalism with a concern for the common good, especially the welfare of the disadvantaged. It would require mechanisms to ensure that workers could share in the benefits of an industrialized society, and that all citizens were guaranteed sufficient food for their families, adequate health care, and suitable housing. In the spirit of Christian justice and love, then, Rauschenbusch actively advocated for a mandatory eight-hour workday, regulations to protect worker safety, closer governmental oversight of monopolies, public ownership of major utilities and transportation systems, and election reform.[26] To stand for this social gospel was the supreme religious obligation, as well as the first public responsibility, of the modern church.

Certainly the social gospel's vision of moral reform was significantly shortsighted in a number of ways. For one thing, its proponents were often better at criticizing capitalism than offering specific, realistic proposals for how to address its problems. The movement also largely ignored the issue of racial injustice (choosing instead to prioritize the plight of white workers) and sometimes explicitly reflected the racism of the larger culture.[27] Thanks to immigration from eastern Europe, the number of Jews in America tripled in the early twentieth century, but their presence (as well as the growing number of Catholics in the United States) was usually not accounted for in the staunchly Protestant vision of most social gospel advocates. Finally, the calls to "Christianize" America often ignored the growing pluralism in the United States during this time, which included an increasing number of Americans who had no interest at all in religion.

Rauschenbusch, though, was sensitive to concerns with the language of "Christianizing" American society. He assured his critics that the term did not represent a retreat from his commitment to the separation of church and state. He was not calling for a collusion of church with government. He was instead arguing for the moral transformation of American society, but from principles that were essentially and historically tied to his Christian belief. Rauschenbusch believed that these values of the social gospel were not exclusively Christian. Freedom, love, justice, and equality had their highest achievement in the teachings of Jesus, assumed Rauschenbusch, but they also found expression in the moral teachings of other religious and philosophical perspectives.

At the same time, despite the universal reach of these moral values, Rauschenbusch refused to heed suggestions that he drop his religious vocabulary. For Rauschenbusch, participating as a Christian in the public debate over social injustice required him to do so in theological language, to maintain his own integrity but also to maximize the positive appeal of his call for reform. He believed religious language was essential to making the public case for social justice in a culture heavily influenced by evangelical Christianity. "To say that we want to *moralize* the social order would be both vague and powerless to most men. To say that we want to *christianize* it is both concrete and compelling."[28] Theological arguments captured the ultimate significance of social responsibility and promised to be the most compelling strategy in the thoroughly Christian culture of early twentieth-century America.

Christianity and the Social Crisis outsold every other religious text for a three-year period, a sign that Rauschenbusch's instincts were right. It awarded Rauschenbusch rock-star status among socially minded liberals, and it gave him a platform from which to contribute to the public consideration of the ills of industrialism. Through activist newspapers, on the lecture front, and in his writings, Rauschenbusch became a major cultural voice for the needs of the American industrial worker. The movement he led prompted public conversations about economic justice and spurred mainline churches to set up denominational offices dedicated to influencing public policy on social questions.[29] In turn, the heightened social activity of these churches influenced elite members of American society who belonged to them. As a result, the religious message of the social gospel helped to raise the nation's collective consciousness about the dangers of unbridled capitalism, aided the empowerment of the American worker and the rise of labor unions, and inspired the era of governmental oversight that became the hallmark of the New Deal. Rauschenbusch and his theological understanding of justice and mutual responsibility had a profound effect on how America thought about social problems at the dawn of the twentieth century.

* * *

In this chapter we have traced the role of religion in some important public moral debates of the nineteenth and early twentieth centuries. If space would permit, we could strengthen the illustration by examining the well-known but essential role religion played in the civil rights movement of the 1950s and '60s, or the peace movement of the 1970s and '80s. The point of these quick historical vignettes is not to say that just because Americans in past generations used religious arguments in public, then it must be unambiguously fine to do so today. To argue that would be a simplistic misuse of history. Instead, I want to make a more limited claim. In response to those whose confidence in the "separation of church and state" prompts them to disqualify any expressions of religion in public discourse, I simply want to point out that public religion enjoys a rich history in the American moral tradition, one deeper than any separation between religion and public life would imply. The separation of religion and public life is an idea that never has been taken literally in American history, and those who argue that the United States was established on such a strict separation will have as difficult a time reconciling their reading with the facts as those who insist that the framers unanimously desired to make this a Christian nation. The actual story of our country is more complicated.

Because of the historical precedent for religion's involvement in the American moral tradition, we would seem to have license to imagine, at least, a role for it in our current moral debates. But making the case for its appropriateness is a harder sell in the highly diverse society we live in today. Many critics argue that the days of a dominant religious culture are gone, so that now religious arguments are inaccessible, if not incomprehensible, to those who do not share the beliefs they invoke. Given our increasingly pluralistic culture, then, religion in public serves only as a "conversation stopper." To this indictment we turn next.

4
Isn't Religion a Conversation Stopper?

The last chapter attempted to put to bed the assumption, popular among secular liberals, that the "separation of church and state" means that religion was not meant to play any role in American public life. Historically at least, nothing could be further from the truth. Religious voices and values have been instrumental in the evolution of the American moral tradition from the eighteenth century to today. Religion's public contributions certainly were not always positive. As we have noted, racist religious assumptions were common on both sides of the slavery debate in the nineteenth century and were vital to the cultural power that slavery's apologists enjoyed in the decades preceding the Civil War. But religion also has made some positive and profound contributions to our shared sense of right and wrong and has done so without necessarily violating the Constitution, which never requires that religion be completely separate from public and political life.

Even if we grant that religious arguments in public debate do not violate the First Amendment explicitly, we might say that such public religion violates the *spirit* of the Constitution and needlessly complicates political decision making in a pluralistic democracy. Religions contribute particular visions of "the good life," but in a society as diverse as ours, we cannot expect any one vision of "the good life" to appeal to all citizens. Because this is so, offering religious grounds for public policy simply manages to alienate anyone who does not subscribe to that religious vision. According to its critics, religion has shown a special capacity for alienating nonadherents and causing deeply felt division between segments of society. At the turn of the twentieth century, for example, the anti-Catholic bigotry of mainline Protestants aggravated class divisions in the United States, helped inspire oppressive restrictions on immigration that stood in place until the 1960s, and doomed the presidential aspirations of any non-Protestant until JFK.

A century later, evangelical leaders like Jerry Falwell and Franklin Graham offended and alienated many Americans by blaming 9/11 on America's support for the "homosexual agenda" and by insisting that the attacks on New York and Washington proved that Islam is a "wicked" and "evil" religion. Many believe that Roman Catholic bishops oppress women when they categorically oppose legal abortion on the basis of religious belief and papal instruction, Clearly, say the critics, religion is politically divisive. At its best, it commends visions of what is good and right that not everyone can accept. At its worst, it excludes and abuses those it defines as outside of what is right and good. In order to avoid this divisive intolerance, religion and its competing visions of "the good life" should stay out of the public sphere.

RELIGION'S CULTURED DESPISERS

These kinds of concerns about religion in public life are well represented among intellectuals. Many so-called political liberals insist that religious perspectives are too divisive and inaccessible to contribute to public discourse on the issues that most perplex us. For much of his career, the late philosopher Richard Rorty argued that religion in public discourse was a "conversation-stopper."[1] In what he called the "Jeffersonian compromise," Rorty argued that religion in the United States had given up its place in public life in exchange for the guarantee of its liberty. Religious people were assured their freedom to practice their faith in exchange for keeping their religion private.[2] In the spirit of this compromise, Rorty assumed that most Americans would agree that it was in "bad taste to bring religion into discussions of public policy," and that this was a good thing, since religious arguments were ill-suited for healthy public conversation. Religious arguments are built on premises of faith, not fact, and for those who do not share those religious premises, there is no way to respond with counterargument. How do you respond to an argument based on an interpretation of God's will if you do not believe in God? What do you do with scriptural references if you do not award Scripture any moral authority? According to Rorty, to offer a position in public moral debate that is rooted in a particular understanding of God's intentions for the world will elicit mainly silence as a response from those who do not share the tradition. As a result, religious arguments do not advance public conversation; they bring it to a grinding halt.[3]

Beyond their inaccessibility to people who do not share the convictions on which they are based, religious arguments are judged by some secular liberals as inappropriate in public conversation because they are categorically bad arguments—not just inaccessible but infantile. One public critic of religion who has gotten a lot of mileage out of this characterization of religion is Oxford scientist Richard Dawkins. In his book *The God Delusion*, Dawkins portrays religion as a pathology on par with insanity or brainwashing. It initially may have originated as an evolutionary strategy for the survival of the species, promoting the good of the whole over our instinct to prioritize self-preservation. But now religion is nothing more than an outdated enemy of rational reflection, a fanatical assertion of arbitrary and often destructive biblical laws that fly in the face of what reasonable people know to be right, good, and true. Occasionally Dawkins acknowledges a difference between fundamentalists (his true target) and more moderate believers, but he insists that the latter simply enable the former with their ill-fated attempts to make religion more palatable to the rational mind. In truth, he asserts, religious people are not reasonable; they cannot be, as long as they agree to the suspension of normal rules of reasoning in favor of blind adherence to dogma. Religious people are incapable of engaging in or being influenced by public persuasion: "dyed-in-the-wool faith-heads are immune to argument, their resistance built up over years of childhood indoctrination."[4] To Dawkins, such blind dogmatism impedes scientific discovery, threatens individual rights, increases global violence, and puts children at risk. Faith and reason are polar opposites, and as a result, "reasonable" citizens should insist that religion stay as far away as possible from public discourse.

The most influential advocate of what we might call this "exclusionist" perspective on religion in politics, though one less openly hostile to religion than Dawkins or Rorty, was the Harvard philosopher John Rawls. For Rawls, the fundamental problem with religion in political discourse was not that religion was infantile, but that our society was too diverse for us to hope that we would ever come to agreement on which religious or philosophical outlook was "right" or "true." So the basic question that Rawls wrestled with in his classic book, *Political Liberalism*, was this: Given that a certain amount of reasonable pluralism is an inevitable product of free democracy, how does a society like ours maintain its stability and a sense of justice? In other words, how do we protect a just order in the face of profound differences in the religious, philosophical, and moral worldviews that we citizens hold? Rawls responded that we do so by grounding our political system in a way that requires no adherence to any of those different worldviews. Liberal democracy must be defended and exercised on *political* grounds only, with no necessary attachment to a particular philosophy or religious outlook. Mutual commitment to a just society requires that citizens conduct their public debate and decision making on the basis of what he called "public reason."

What does "public reason" look like? First and foremost, it does not appeal to any particular religion, or any specific philosophy for that matter. Instead, it appeals to rational argumentation and reasons that ideally all citizens could recognize and understand: "The point of the ideal of public reason is that citizens are to conduct their fundamental discussions . . . based on values that the others can reasonably be expected to endorse."[5] What Rawls rules out is not only religious reasons but also appeals to any philosophical worldview (e.g., utilitarianism or Marxism). These are what Rawls called "comprehensive doctrines." A comprehensive doctrine is essentially a worldview, in that it "includes conceptions of what is of value in human life," commends certain standards for behavior, and posits an explanation of the ultimate "meaning of life."[6]

For instance, Christianity as a comprehensive doctrine orients all of life around the profession of Jesus Christ as Lord, lifting up Jesus' earthly life as the standard for human behavior and bestowing cosmic significance on the events of this world as they disclose something about humanity's relationship with the God of the Bible. Economic utilitarianism can be a comprehensive doctrine if it is used to interpret not just market relationships but also the fundamental nature of human beings. A utilitarian might argue that maximizing happiness is what it means to be human, and that a good society is one that achieves the most happiness for the most people, or one that gets out of the way to allow individual citizens to maximize their own happiness. Both Christianity and this kind of widely cast utilitarianism make claims for what constitutes "the good life" across the varied spheres of human activity—personal, political, social, and economic—and that is what makes them comprehensive doctrines.

In a pluralistic society like ours, argued Rawls, different citizens will subscribe to different comprehensive doctrines, so that it is not fair to institutionalize one at the expense of others, or to foist one on citizens who do not subscribe to it. Utilitarians may chafe under an institutionalized Christianity, just as Christians might resent the enforcement of a utilitarian politics. In response, Rawls argued that the most stable justification for the essential tenets of democratic society, the set of reasons most likely to gain acceptance by the widest group of citizens, is that which is independent of any comprehensive doctrine, independent of any particular conception of "the good life." Similarly, citizens' participation in democratic society should not rely on appeals to their comprehensive doctrines but should appeal to public reasons, arguments that anyone could reasonably be expected to accept, regardless of the worldview to which they subscribe.

One way Rawls described this commitment to public reason is with the image of a "veil of ignorance." He encouraged his readers to imagine that they are behind a veil that renders them unaware of their gender, race, ethnicity, religion, economic class, or any particularity that identifies them or their interests. They are, in other words, a generic citizen. Rawls argued that behind this veil, not knowing anything about the particulars of their lives, citizens would want to support social priorities and public arguments that had broad appeal, in order to avoid inadvertently excluding themselves by supporting policies that favor one social group over another or by offering arguments that appeal to a tradition to which they do not belong. This perspective behind the veil of ignorance is what Rawls had in mind when he insisted that public conversation ought to be confined to "public reason."

Rawls acknowledged and accepted that, in reality, citizens will deliberate privately on issues from within their particular worldview; Christians will think as Christians, Jews as Jews, Marxists as Marxists. But when it came to participating in *public* deliberation, Rawls expected citizens to appeal only to public reason. In fact, he insisted that citizens not only should debate social issues using public reason, they also should *vote* for particular public policies only if there are good public reasons (versus religious or philosophical reasons) to support their vote.[7] Not only should a traditional Catholic not offer religious arguments in public debate over stem-cell research, for instance; she also should not vote against funding for embryonic stem-cell research except on the basis of "public reasons" (that is, *not* Catholic reasoning) for her opposition.

A MATTER OF RESPECT

The exclusionist view of politics is very popular in law schools and the academy. Its popularity stems from the widespread assumption that public expressions of religion are necessarily divisive and disrespectful. We do not need to look far for examples of religious arguments that easily fit Rorty's description as "conversation-stoppers." Members of the Religious Right occasionally claim publicly that HIV/AIDS is God's punishment for the "sin" of homosexuality. Opponents of civil status for gay marriages sometime invoke simple declarations of God's will; the Bible says that marriage is to be between a man and a woman. Protesters outside abortion clinics insist that abortion is murder by citing Psalm 139. In each case, religious values or sources are simply asserted as valid and authoritative, with no attempt to argue the point or make a connection with other religious and philosophical perspectives. For someone who does not share the religious starting point, the assertion that abortion or homosexuality is wrong because the Bible says so elicits the response, "So what? The Bible holds no authority over me." With that rejection of the only semblance of argument offered, the conversation appears to be over. Let the shouting match begin!

The mistake that secular liberals often make, however, is assuming that this is the only form a religious argument can take. From their perspective, religious arguments are necessarily based only on assertions of convictions that are matters of faith, and so categorically are not open to rational evaluation. If they are not open to reason, they cannot contribute meaningfully to conversation among a religiously and philosophically diverse public for whom reason is the proper "universal" language. Insisting on making religious arguments in public sends the message that I consider it unimportant to persuade you, to take you seriously as a conversation partner, if you do not subscribe to my religion. It suggests that I would rather assert my position against yours than seek mutual understanding. Ultimately, religious arguments in public debate are divisive and disrespectful because they are "inaccessible" and "unreasonable."

This hard opposition between faith and reason underestimates the "reasonableness" and "accessibility" of religious arguments. Despite how Dawkins and others characterize millennia of religious tradition, religious thinkers historically have demonstrated a sophisticated facility with rational deliberation. Augustine of Hippo, Thomas Aquinas, Maimonides, John Milton, Hugo Grotius, Anne Hutchinson, Isaac

Newton, Lucretia Mott, Martin Buber, Dorothy Day, Dietrich Bonhoeffer, John Courtney Murray—inexhaustible is the list of deeply religious figures who made profound contributions to Western intellectual history. Likewise, for many believers today, faith and reason are not mutually exclusive; they are complementary sources for knowing the right and doing it. Seldom in the history of Western religions have faith and reason been seen as absolute foes.

Religious arguments are not categorically conversation-stoppers, for to assume so is to underestimate how comprehensible a religious argument might be, even to someone outside that religion. There is a profound difference between *understanding* an argument and *accepting* it. With a little bit of religious literacy and some effort to explain, even heavily theological arguments can be made comprehensible to someone outside the tradition from which the arguments draw language and ideas. When done well, religious arguments will have a logic, a line of reasoning, that can be understood even by those who ultimately reject the theological premises on which the arguments are based or the conclusions that they draw. Believers might make the case that their religiously based position resonates with values in the American moral tradition, or that it appeals to sources of moral insight (like common experience or reason) that religious believers share with others. Religious arguments, then, may not ultimately be *persuasive* to someone outside the tradition, but they often can be *understood* by them. If mutual respect simply requires that we work to make ourselves understood by others—and struggle to understand their points of view—then a religious argument can convey respect just as successfully as a nonreligious one.

Not only is it unnecessary for religious people to leave their faith convictions at the proverbial door of public discourse, it is generally impossible for them to do so. Rawls was right to understand voting as a public act, the culmination of public debate, and not simply a private decision. He was wrong to think that citizens can jump out of their religious or philosophical skins before casting their votes, or before participating in the public debate that precedes their votes. We all operate from worldviews that shape our understanding of the moral universe in which we live. These worldviews may have a number of sources and often are in constant evolution, but they are the perspectives from which we necessarily interpret and judge matters that confront us. For many religious people, faith tradition is (or is an important part of) their worldview, through which they understand, interpret, and pull together the different arenas of their lives. Religion is who we are, and as such, it is necessarily the lens by which we think about issues like abortion, war, economic fairness, and politics in general. To insist that religious people leave their theological coats at the door before entering public debate is to ask them to do the impossible. It is to require them to think and speak from no particular worldview at all. But to borrow a phrase from another prominent philosopher, there is no view from nowhere—it is impossible to think about moral and political issues from some generic position with no assumptions about what constitutes "the good life."[8] When individuals, communities, or governments take a position on a particular policy issue, they necessarily assert beliefs about what it means to be human, to live ethically, and to pursue the good life. To ask religious people to remove their faith from their understanding of what is right and good is unfair, unreasonable, and frankly impossible. The "myth of neutrality," as one theologian has put it, is just that, a myth.[9]

Ultimately, insisting that religious people mask their deepest convictions by removing them from public arguments asks people of faith to act disingenuously, an odd and dangerous way to demonstrate the mutual respect that political liberals demand. Do we really want to make dishonesty and deception a requirement for public involvement? By contrast, true mutual respect is better demonstrated when we are honest with one another about our opinions and motivations. We show mutual respect in public conversation when we value others enough to tell them the truth and why we think it is the truth, and when we patiently listen to others as they attempt to do the same. As Jeffrey Stout has argued,

> I would encourage religiously committed citizens to make use of their basic freedoms by expressing their premises in as much depth and detail as they see fit when trading reasons with the rest of us on issues of concern to the body politic. If they are discouraged from speaking up in this way, we will remain ignorant of the real reasons that many of our fellow citizens have for reaching some of the ethical and political conclusions they do. We will also deprive them of the central democratic good of expressing themselves to the rest of us on matters about which they care deeply. If they do not have this opportunity, we will lose the chance to learn from, and to critically examine, what they say. And they will have good reason to doubt that they are being shown the respect that all of us owe to our fellow citizens as the individuals they are.[10]

There is something truly sinister about a public forum that encourages religious participants to masquerade as something else in order to get a hearing, and something genuinely oppressive in being required to submit to this kind of deception.[11] On the other hand, public discourse that encourages citizens to argue truthfully, honestly, and forthrightly maximizes the potential for genuine conversation, while simultaneously reflecting some of the best virtues and freedoms of a democracy.

RELIGION'S POSITIVE CONTRIBUTIONS

However, why might it be a good thing for public discourse in America that we make clear the way for religious persons to participate in public debate without having to hide their religious reasons and motivations? In other words, what could possibly be the *advantage* to a political environment that is open to religious reasoning?

First, religious perspectives help return the language of morality to our political discourse. In our current political climate, too often we distinguish between the "political" and the "moral." With the first term we refer to public issues, and often we assume that the criteria by which we decide these public issues should themselves be strictly political. Thus, political disagreements should be settled pragmatically, through realistic attempts at compromise or democratic resort to majority rule. We might even settle these political disagreements by appealing to the feasibility or economic costs of the issues in question. But due to their public nature, what we may not do is invade our political discussions with the "private" language of morality. Moral concerns are private preferences, or at least a strong segment of our political culture assumes this is true.

Consistent with classical notions of politics, however, religious viewpoints remind us that the political issues that collectively perplex and divide us are usually about moral choices, and so require the language of morality and the discipline of practical reasoning to make some sense of them. Religious traditions remind us that the hard distinction between "private" and "public" is a relatively recent invention. Many of our public disagreements require conversation that includes the language, ideas, and preferences of morality in order for us to understand them, for us to understand each other, and for us to have any hope of progress in them.

Second, religious perspectives can contribute constructively to public discourse by bringing centuries of moral tradition to bear on current disagreements. Religious perspectives remind us that the problems that divide and perplex us are seldom new. Often they are contemporary versions of age-old questions, questions that theologians and philosophers, religious believers and public citizens have struggled with for generations. When they reflect their traditions learnedly and responsibly, religious people represent that history of considered moral reflection.

For instance, in the vigorous debate over the war in Iraq, most pundits acted as if the idea of "preventative war" was an unprecedented departure from Western notions of a just war. Opponents of the Bush administration's run-up to war insisted that declaring war on the basis of a pending threat, rather than waiting to respond to an actual act of aggression, violated the tradition of justified warfare.[12] For its part, the Bush administration seldom contested this reading of history, choosing rather endlessly to cite "national interest" rather than to offer a justification for the war based in any deep consideration of Western just-war thinking. Both sides of the debate over the Iraq war assumed that "preventative war" did not fit in the categories of just-war theory.

In reality, however, many classical thinkers wrestled with questions of preventative war. Augustine, one of the principal architects of just-war theory, focused his justification of state violence on the "parental" responsibility of rulers to protect the innocent.[13] This metaphor, with its emphasis on protection as well as punishment, appears at least to open the door to the use of violence to prevent an assault, as well as to respond to one. The seventeenth-century Dutch legal theorist Hugo Grotius interpreted just-war theory's principle of "last resort" to include the preemptive protection of innocent persons and their economic interests.[14] By contrast, the twentieth-century American theologian Reinhold Niebuhr explicitly rejected the idea of preventative war as a sign of the political hubris of a superpower. Niebuhr insisted that "a democracy can not of course, engage in an explicit preventative war." But he predicted that the United States could become so enamored with its global power and at the same time "driven to hysteria" by its frustrated attempts to win the world for democracy that it might be tempted to provoke war as a way to impose its political will once for all on the "tortuous course of history."[15] In other words, for Niebuhr the temptation of preventative war was a sure sign that the nation had succumbed to vain idealism. As we will discuss in a later chapter, Christian theology possesses a wealth of historical resources for thinking about the ethics of war, even in our age of technologically sophisticated weapons and blurred definitions of legitimate political authority. Informed religious perspectives can enrich our public debate over issues like war by helping us to tap these resources from the past.

Third, including these religious points of view promises to enlarge the context in which we think about moral issues. In contrast to the hyperindividualism that dominates American culture, religion often insists that we think beyond ourselves, to ask how our moral choices affect and are affected by other persons, communities, and creatures—and how our choices are affected by our knowledge of and relationship with the divine. The great monotheisms encourage this expansive perspective by putting human beings in our place, so to speak, by asserting that we are simply a part of a larger divine intention. Asian traditions like Buddhism and Hinduism make a similar point about interconnectedness in the belief in reincarnation and the idea of *karma*, the determination of one's future by one's present actions. Native American religions often stress the interdependence of human beings and other creatures in a way that enriches our understanding of the environmental implications of human activity. In various ways, religious perspectives can remind us that we and our moral decisions are parts of a greater whole. That greater whole may be defined in different ways—the community, the nation, humanity, the ecosystem—but religion encourages us to keep expanding our sense of context, reminding us of the effects of our decisions on other members of the cosmos.

Given American culture's preoccupation with the self, unattached and unencumbered by responsibilities to a greater good, religion's reminder to think about moral responsibility more broadly is an important contribution to our ethical discourse. Compare religion's emphasis on connectedness with the isolationism that consistently lurks in our foreign policy, preventing us from responding to genocide or assaults on human rights unless to do so would be in our "national interest." Or contrast religion's emphasis on interdependence with an economic climate that treats "welfare" as a dirty word, rewarding only those who "pull themselves up by their bootstraps," while ignoring the way that social policies help to create poverty and keep people poor. Compare religion's emphasis on the "bigger picture" with the shortsightedness that has led us to destroy so much of the world's ecosystem.[16] Religion's insistence that we understand ourselves as part of a larger whole, and its corresponding emphasis on the greater good in making our moral choices, provides a necessary counterforce to the extreme individualism encouraged by so many segments of the popular and economic culture in the United States.

Fourth, religious language sometimes can articulate moral priorities that are widely shared across the American public, both religious and nonreligious. The theological presuppositions normally will not be shared by everyone, but sometimes religious vocabulary provides a particularly imagistic way of expressing a basic moral idea that intuitively many Americans hold to be right and good. We will raise this possibility again in later chapters, and I will argue that the "sacredness of life" is one example of a religious idea capturing a widespread intuition better than most other kinds of moral language. To the degree that this is possible, then, religious language may contribute to the prospects for finding some limited consensus in our moral debates, for in the midst of heated disagreement it can give voice to the intuitions that many (if not all) of us share. Exploring these religious concepts can also clarify how it is we differ in our interpretation and application of moral values we share at a more theoretical level. If religious language can facilitate this kind of responsible conversation, it can provide some grounds for healthier public moral debate, as well as hope for at least tentative consensus on some of the issues that most divide us.

Fifth, religious language serves moral discourse when it *critiques* the moral conventions of our society. Even an exclusionist like John Rawls recognized religion's potential for offering "prophetic witness" against social injustice, which is why his preference for "public reason" had so much trouble dealing with two historical examples of blatantly religious public rhetoric: Abraham Lincoln's Second Inaugural Address and Martin Luther King's fight for civil rights. Neither Lincoln nor King restricted himself to "public reasons," but these unapologetically theological interpretations of social crises have become classic expressions of the American character. How do we justify our reverence for these apparent violations of the separation of church and state? In part we honor them because they represent the power of religious appeal as social critique, the prophetic function of religion as an important contributor to the evolution of an American moral tradition. In both cases, religious language arguably did what no other language could: it made sense of the great moral tragedies facing the nation, it laid bare the "sin" of long-standing social practices, and it gave expression to the ideals for which we must strive. Lincoln and King are two remarkable examples of an enduring national custom: using religious perspectives to offer moral critique of a society in need of reform.[17]

Sixth, welcoming religious perspectives into our public discussions helps to give voice to that "quiet middle" that is so key to rescuing

American politics from the divisive extremes. Poll after poll demonstrates that most Americans' opinions on issues like abortion, capital punishment, war, and the economy are more complicated and more uncertain than the extreme viewpoints that enjoy so much media airtime. Most Americans would locate themselves between the radical right and the radical left, and many of those same Americans caught in the ideological middle derive their moderate views from religious perspectives. To embrace their perspectives would helpfully complicate our public debate over these kinds of issues and would help wrest control of the conversation away from the extremes. Opening the doors of our public conversations unapologetically to religious perspectives would serve to empower many of those in the ideological middle who know no other way to articulate their complicated opinions than to make reference to their religious worldviews.

Finally, the better angels of religious traditions provide reminders and resources for rediscovering civility, a desperately needed virtue in our current political climate. Rabbinic dialogue in the Jewish tradition, for instance, offers a pattern for engaging one another on potentially divisive moral issues. Christian figures like Roger Williams (a Puritan, of all things!) consistently commended respectful dialogue in their own contentious times. At the end of this book, we will explore in detail religion's potential for infusing public conversation with civility. It is worth noting now, however, that many of the religious traditions active in American culture possess historical resources and contemporary models for cultivating and encouraging a public debate that is open and forthright, in which participants refrain from demonizing their opponents and instead focus on the shared task of creating a morally responsible political culture.

Of course it is not difficult at all to find examples of religion performing just the opposite role, promoting incivility and intolerance at the expense of fruitful discussion and the search for consensus. My argument here is not that religion *necessarily* brings virtue and clear thinking to public debate. I admit that religious persons and communities can be a major part of the problem of incivility, especially when they buy into the divisive ethos that now dominates American politics. But I do believe that by expanding the invitation and empowering religious persons between the extremes to join the public conversation, we (and they) will discover that religious perspectives often represent rich traditions of deep reflection, subtlety, diversity, moderation, and tolerance.

RELIGION AND THE VIRTUES OF CIVIL CONVERSATION

Far from a disruptive and divisive force, then, religion can contribute healthy leadership to our moral conversations. If this is true, what should a public debate that welcomes religious perspectives look like? Harvard theologian Ronald Thiemann offers what I think is a refreshing vision of public conversation, one that intelligently rejects the disqualification of religion favored by many liberal thinkers, while insisting on standards of public virtue for all who would participate in the debate.

By Thiemann's reading of the founders' "original intent," the Constitution was meant to establish a framework for democratic society founded on the virtues of equality, liberty, and toleration.[18] Especially with a charter that so fundamentally protects freedom of speech, the United States cannot maintain its commitment to these public virtues if it sets "threshold requirements" by which participants in public discourse are excluded. Instead of doing what political liberals love to do, establishing a litmus test for judging which kinds of arguments may or may not be permitted, Thiemann argues that the principles of equality and liberty and the free-speech protections of the First Amendment require that we throw open the gates of public discourse so that everyone is welcome to participate.

Once we have established this inclusive public conversation, it is then the responsibility of citizens to distinguish good arguments in the conversation from bad ones. What makes an argument "good"? According to Thiemann, it is the argument's compatibility with the virtues of democracy, namely, equality, liberty, and toleration. He suggests several criteria by which citizens can evaluate consistency with these virtues, criteria he calls "norms of plausibility." Thiemann emphasizes that he does not mean these "norms of plausibility" to act as new threshold requirements; they are not restrictions on the kinds of contributions citizens are *allowed* to make to public conversation. Instead, given that anyone can offer virtually any argument in the public domain, these norms serve as a basis for measuring which arguments are *worth taking seriously*, and which fail to convey the virtues of healthy democracy.[19]

What are these "norms of plausibility" according to which we judge which are good (and potentially persuasive) arguments and which are bad? First, Thiemann suggests we should recognize a particular perspective worthy of conversation if it strives to be *publicly accessible*. By this Thiemann does not mean the same thing that exclusionists mean when they talk of accessibility. For exclusionists, an accessible public argument requires the deletion of all references to religion. By contrast, Thiemann means that arguments simply ought to be open to "public examination and scrutiny."[20] Arguments that strive for public accessibility are committed to the conversation enough that they want to be understood, and they want to be as open as possible so that they might be understood. The standard of accessibility recognizes that the ultimate objective of democratic conversation is to persuade others of your position, but persuasion cannot take place without understanding, and understanding requires an argument be open to questioning and critique.

This means that a religious argument may be a good public argument if it is open to having its theological claims tested and evaluated. Citizens who make religious assertions without argument, or who consider the interrogation of their claims off limits, are guilty of inaccessibility. As Thiemann notes, "Public accessibility should be *encouraged* in all arguments that seek to contribute to the democratic process of building an overlapping consensus. Such accessibility cannot, however, be *demanded* in a society that protects free speech as a fundamental right."[21] So persons certainly are free to offer arguments that are not accessible. The First Amendment protects the right to offer even arguments that are founded in nothing more than appeals to base instincts, irrational emotion, or private sources of "revelation" that offer no entry point for others in the public conversation. However, Thiemann encourages citizens to reject these arguments that do not strive for accessibility, as incompatible with the fundamental democratic ideals of liberty, equality, and tolerance.

Also among the "norms of plausibility" by which Thiemann thinks prepared citizens ought to distinguish proper public arguments from improper ones is the virtue of *mutual respect.* In order to be consistent with the virtues of democratic discourse, citizens ought to demonstrate a respect for their conversation partners, even those with whom they disagree. Religious citizens do not need to assume the dogma of relativism; mutual respect does not require a commitment to the belief that all perspectives are equally valid claims of truth. But respect does require me to listen to the arguments of others and to respect the moral conviction from which they are genuinely offered, even if I judge that moral perspective to be tragically wrong.

Mutual respect also implies a certain intellectual humility, an openness to having my mind changed. Cultivating the virtue of respect encourages me to enter public conversation open to the possibility that my best understanding of what I believe to be "true" may be improved, completed, or corrected by my engagement in conversation with others who disagree with me. Again, this is not to require relativism as a condition for proper public discourse, just a good dose of modesty and an appreciation for the improvements that others' perspectives may make to our own. Citizens who enter public "dialogue" certain that they have nothing to gain from their conversation partners show very little respect for others involved in the debate.

Finally, Thiemann's "norms of plausibility" include a commitment to *integrity*. By this norm he means that we should recognize as legitimate (and potentially persuasive) only arguments that exhibit a moral consistency within themselves. Integrity is thus measured by the consistency between a public position and its actual motivation. A position that is publicly offered on moral or religious grounds but is really motivated by political advantage or expediency lacks integrity. On this front, the recent tradition of presidential candidates staking out "heartfelt" but carefully strategic positions on abortion might be considered wanting on the measure of integrity.

Integrity is also measured by consistency between political positions. The late Joseph Cardinal Bernardin, the Roman Catholic archbishop of Chicago, was famous for insisting on a "consistent ethic of life" in public debates over abortion, euthanasia, and the death penalty. Many religious citizens who reject the practices of abortion and euthanasia in the name of the sacredness of life do not apply the same principle to the death penalty. But Bernardin insisted that a commitment to opposing abortion and euthanasia (which, as a traditional Catholic, he shared) lacked integrity without an equally zealous rejection of the death penalty. He argued that all three practices were a violation of the sacredness of life, and to oppose abortion and euthanasia but not capital punishment betrayed a moral contradiction. Bernardin's commendation of a "consistent ethic of life" is a perfect example of Thiemann's insistence on the virtue of integrity in public arguments.

All of these "norms of plausibility" are rooted in an understanding of the importance of open public conversation to democracy:

> Politics ought to provide the realm within which contending parties seek to *persuade* one another that a particular course of action best serves the common good of the citizenry, that is, helps forge an "overlapping consensus" concerning the issues of public importance. . . . If we despair of our ability to persuade one another, even in the most pluralistic of cultures, then we abandon a fundamental

> principle of democratic government—the commitment always to prefer noncoercive, nonviolent means of conflict resolution.[22]

By this measure, Thiemann judges that the attitudes of both secular exclusionists and many religious fundamentalists betray the ideals of democracy. In their effort to protect democratic discourse from the alleged divisiveness of religion, the first group shows little faith in democracy, so they preemptively rule out of order any participants—especially religious ones—whose particularity seems to intensify public disagreement. For their part, some fundamentalists attempt to circumvent the objectives of public discourse by asserting, manipulating, or coercing the public to think and act their way, with little genuine attempt to persuade a pluralistic culture of the superiority of their point of view. To the former, Thiemann insists that religious persons can and ought to be welcomed to make a sustained contribution to our deepest public debates. To the latter, Thiemann insists that they satisfy their responsibilities as citizens only when they represent their religious perspectives in ways that also respect the virtues of democratic citizenship. To both, Thiemann argues that

> if moral arguments are to be welcomed into the public debate, then religious arguments must also be allowed. But all these arguments—political, moral, and religious—should be governed by the criteria of public accessibility, mutual respect, and moral integrity. Arguments that do not meet those criteria cannot be banned from public debate, but citizens need to be encouraged to ignore or resist arguments that appeal to inaccessible warrants, that belittle one's opponents, that appeal to prejudice or base instincts, or that seek to coerce or manipulate the public discussion.[23]

Though it is a bit idealistic, I think Thiemann's vision is among the best for American public discourse, because he imagines a conversation that is open to wide participation, that protects the integrity of citizens by not asking them to be something other than what they are, and that encourages honest and forthright dialogue between citizens. At the same time, his ideal for public discourse also demands that citizens constantly evaluate their own arguments and those of others to measure their commitment to the democratic project: Does my argument (or that of my opponent) exhibit moral integrity, strive for wide accessibility, and demonstrate mutual respect toward those who disagree? Does it in this way affirm the basic democratic principles of equality, liberty, and tolerance? These are the kinds of questions all of us should learn to ask as we encounter contributions in public debate, and as we are contributing ourselves.

Insofar as Thiemann puts the onus on citizens (rather than ivory-tower philosophers) to evaluate good arguments from bad, arguments that are consistent with the basic American ideals from those that are not, he may be guilty of a bit of idealism. If what passes for political debate on Fox News, CNN, and MSNBC is any indication, we Americans are not as equipped as we need to be to fulfill Thiemann's vision of public moral discourse, for the virtues on which his vision depends are neither consistently exhibited nor widely cultivated. Then again, what Thiemann's proposal amounts to is a call for civic education. We need collectively to learn how better to protect these values of the American experiment. We need to reclaim the democratic norms of equality, liberty, and toleration that underwrite the virtues of public moral discourse, and we need to teach them to our children. Rather than rewarding incivility with media points and political advantage, we need to insist that our public moral debates be conducted with respect, integrity, and a spirit of genuine accessibility. I will have more to say about civility in public discourse at the end of this book, but for now it is enough to affirm that Thiemann's call for education in the area of "civic virtues" is perhaps as valuable as the vision of public discourse from which it stems.

PART TWO

Rethinking the Big Four

5
Abortion and Stem Cells

So far in this book, I have tried to complicate our understanding of the "moral values" debate in the United States by taking on the prevailing myths of the Religious Right and secular left. The Right's myth is that you do not stand for moral values unless you defend conservative positions on conservative hot-button issues, with the ultimate goal of returning America to its Christian roots. In response, I have suggested that liberal or progressive positions in the debates over issues ranging from gay marriage to the environment are themselves rooted in moral values, just different ones than those held up by the Right. Furthermore, I have suggested that the Right's assumption that America is rightly understood as a "Christian nation" is a distortion of our history that complicates our attempt to negotiate moral discourse in a religiously and philosophically diverse society.

The left's myth is that talk of moral values is out of place in politics altogether, because that language is simply cover for the imposition of religious norms on the public square, a clear violation of the "separation of church and state." In response to this perspective, I have suggested that the sharp distinction between "private" morality and the public sphere is equally misleading, ignoring the fact that most of the issues that preoccupy us collectively are not only political but also at their core moral. I have offered historical evidence that religion and politics have never been walled off from one another in the United States, and in fact religion has made vital contributions to the evolution of the American moral tradition. In line with that tradition, religious perspectives continue to offer something of great value to our public conversations over the issues that most divide us.

This chapter and the next two demonstrate some of the improvement that might result from careful consideration of religious perspectives on the "big four" of American moral debates—abortion, stem-cell research, euthanasia, and gay marriage. We will look at what concerns thoughtful conservatives about these issues, discovering in the process that the moral values they defend may be compelling priorities for many progressives and liberals too. We also will look at what drives many religious liberals to support embryonic stem-cell research and access to abortion, euthanasia, and gay marriage. In the process, we will discover that they too are motivated by moral priorities and that these moral values are ones that, in other contexts, conservatives might agree are important to defend. Ultimately, I hope to portray a debate over abortion, stem cells, euthanasia, and gay marriage that is more complicated than the "theocrat" and "hedonist" caricatures so beloved by the media. I also hope to suggest that in their surprising common ground and their more-expected differences, thoughtful conservative and liberal religious perspectives add something useful to these seemingly intractable public debates. We begin with what is the quintessential moral-values debate, the fight over abortion and embryos.

WHO COUNTS AS A PERSON?

In my home state of Vermont, known for its moral libertarianism, I have more than once followed a car sporting a bumper sticker that read, "If you don't believe in abortions, don't have one." Never a fan of bumper-sticker rhetoric anyway, I find this one to be monumentally foolish. While it may seem clever enough, it completely trivializes principled opposition to abortion and, by extension, embryonic stem-cell research (or ESCR, as I shall abbreviate it). Rather than responding to the philosophical or theological assumptions conservatives make about the moral worth of a fetus, the slogan dismisses those convictions out of hand. Now you may think this an unfair expectation to have of a decal, except that the bumper sticker represents fairly well the typical thinness of the debate over abortion and ESCR in this country, at least as the media portray it. Liberal spokespersons regularly characterize conservatives as misogynist, heartless, and hostile to women, personal freedom, and medical progress. Conservatives routinely characterize liberals on these issues as amoral at best, bloodthirsty at worst, willing to murder thousands of innocent babies to serve the gods of autonomous choice or endless scientific achievement. Comparisons to Nazism and genocide (employed at times by both sides of the debate) do not exactly nurture deep conversation between the two camps.

How do we resuscitate the public debate over abortion and ESCR? A healthier conversation begins with a move beyond the bumper stickers and sound bites to a deep consideration of the moral values at stake for each side, in particular their convictions about the moral status of the fetus. For traditional Catholics, many evangelicals, and other persons of faith, abortion is not simply a matter of personal choice. It is instead a tragic contest between the rights and interests of human beings of equal worth and dignity, the fetus and the pregnant woman. Catholics who adhere to Vatican teaching on abortion believe that the point at which an embryo should be considered a human being, on moral par with you and me, begins at the moment of conception. Most evangelicals and many other Christians share this assumption, and many Hindus and Buddhists hold similar views.[1] For those who think this way, abortion and ESCR represent threats to human beings who have done nothing to justify punishment, but who are being killed in the name of someone else's well-being.

Contrary to the implication of that bumper sticker, then, from a conservative's point of view, abortion is no more a private matter than is murder. In fact, abortion *is* murder from their point of view, since they assume that the fetus is a person like you and me. From this perspective, the bumper sticker might as well read, "If you don't believe in murder, don't commit one." Harming another member of society normally cannot be justified as a matter of personal choice, and liberal assertions of privacy do not apply. From this perspective, what is at issue in abortion is the government's responsibility to protect its citizens from harm, so that legislating against abortion is not the infringement of choice but the protection of civil order and the well-being of society's most innocent members.

Similarly, conservatives who oppose embryonic stem-cell research normally are not heartless enemies of medicine and scientific progress. In fact, many conservatives oppose ESCR out of a spirit of compassion for those they regard as most vulnerable, the unborn. Stem cells are, in a sense, the building blocks for all other cells in the body. Scientists label them undifferentiated, meaning they are generic cells, not specialized for any particular use in the body. They are also pluripotent, meaning they have the ability to develop into nearly any kind of specialized body cell. In other words, stem cells could be manipulated to become heart, nerve, liver, or skin cells. What makes them even more attractive to researchers is that they are "immortal," an unfortunate quasi-religious term scientists use to refer to stem cells' ability to divide indefinitely, providing (theoretically) an endless supply of stem cells. Stem cells can be found in different places in the body, including umbilical cord blood and perhaps amniotic fluid, but the most pluripotent stem cells (and thus the most promising to researchers) are those that exist in the inner cell mass of a human blastocyst, a week-old embryo. Scientists envision a number of uses for these stem cells. Studying their differentiation into more specialized cells promises to help us understand human reproduction and developmental biology, which could yield helpful information for dealing with the causes of infertility, prematurity, and birth defects. But most of the public celebration of stem-cell research has been in response to its potential for treating diseases like diabetes, Parkinson's, and Alzheimer's. Stem-cell research also has been expected to usher in an unprecedented age of reparative medicine, the ability to regenerate organs or tissues that have been destroyed through disease or accident.

Embryonic stem-cell research harvests stem cells from embryos in order to study them and develop these different applications, but at this point harvesting requires the destruction of the embryos.[2] Because of their assumptions about the moral status of the embryo, conservatives argue that ESCR amounts to the sacrifice of innocent human beings in the name of research, something that our society has considered cruel and immoral since at least the Nuremberg trials. Opponents of ESCR generally do not ignore the suffering that such research could theoretically address, though they rightly point out the scientific community's penchant for exaggerating how quickly we might see benefits from this research.[3] More importantly, they argue that the good end of medical research cannot justify using an immoral means to pursue it. Instead, they demonstrate their own commitment to alleviating suffering by vigorously supporting alternative means of researching devastating diseases. *Adult* stem-cell research is enthusiastically endorsed by many opponents of ESCR precisely because it represents the possibility of attending compassionately to the needs of people stricken with conditions like Parkinson's and Alzheimer's without the abuse of human embryos.[4]

There is a reasonableness to many conservatives' unease with abortion and ESCR. In fact, given the moral claim at work here—that an embryo or fetus is a moral person with the same right to live and the same interests as you and me—no conservative position is more logically consistent than the traditional Catholic perspective. Most conservatives will argue that, while abortion is normally wrong, we must grant a woman permission to terminate her pregnancy in cases of rape or incest, or when the pregnancy threatens the health of the woman. But starting from the assumption that the fetus is an innocent human being, it is difficult to see how the tragedy of circumstances that led to the pregnancy can justify the murder of an innocent person in these "exceptional cases." If the fetus is the same as a baby, then it remains innocent, even if it came into being as a result of a man assaulting a woman, and even if its existence threatens the well-being of the girl or woman carrying it.

The Vatican's judgment is that there are *no* exceptions to the illicitness of intentional abortion. Abortion is always the killing of an innocent human being, and no circumstances, however tragic, can justify that murder. Even in the so-called exceptional cases, the fetus is still not at fault; in the case of a rape, the fetus did not commit the violent act, and in the case of a medically problematic pregnancy, the fetus is not intentionally and maliciously threatening the woman's life. The fetus is an innocent bystander, and thus to have an abortion would be to kill a guiltless person for one's own good, something that in other circumstances a decent society would not allow.[5] Conservatives who allow for exceptions to the rule against abortion—including most evangelicals—are burdened with the task of explaining how the deliberate killing of an innocent human being in the exceptional cases is no longer bad. To my mind, few conservative thinkers have offered compelling arguments for how these compassionate exceptions to the prohibition on abortion are compatible with their starting assumption that a fetus is an innocent human being. The Vatican's position, however, takes the implication of that starting assumption to its logical conclusion.

To admire the logic of the Catholic position, however, is not to say that opposition to abortion and ESCR is irrefutable. The primary assumption, that an embryo or fetus is a person with rights and interests on par with my own, is a debatable claim. When do we become not just genetically human but *persons*, morally significant beings with interests to be protected and a right to existence? When and why should an embryo or fetus enjoy moral worth akin to my own? One of the contributions that thoughtful religious perspectives make to our public debate over abortion is the reminder that determining the "personhood" of a fetus is a *moral* question, not a *biological* matter. There is nothing in the developmental biology itself that tells us whether or when an embryo or fetus should be treated with the same respect as an infant. The common ploy of displaying models of midterm fetuses is not scientific verification that fetuses deserve protection; it is emotional extortion. Equally unpersuasive is the quick dismissal of conservative concerns in the name of scientific "objectivity." Conception, viability, birth, or any of the other biological markers that are identified as "the moment" when an embryo/fetus becomes a person worthy of protection are significant only when they are *morally interpreted* as important.

For instance, no biblical passage offers an explicit answer to the question of the moral worth of an embryo/fetus, but some conservative Christians draw on texts like Psalm 139 or Jeremiah 1 to argue that from the moment of conception an embryo ought to be respected as a person with a right to live. They argue that God's assertion in these passages, that "before I formed you in the womb I knew you" (Jer. 1:5), indicates that from the moment the cells who will be us come into being, we are known by God, and this relationship imputes to us importance and dignity. Building on this conviction, the late Pope John Paul II suggested that what makes someone a person in a moral and religious sense is precisely his or her individuality; a human being possesses a unique genetic identity and a personal relationship with God the Creator.[6] This moral designation is not something the pope could read off scientific data, nor is it something he simply lifted from a biblical verse. It is instead a theologically derived moral interpretation of personhood.

Importantly, when liberals reject conservatives' assignment of moral status to an embryo, they too are making *moral* judgments, not strictly scientific ones. Some think that what distinguishes human beings from other creatures is our rationality, so that rational capacity is the distinguishing characteristic of personhood. As a result, they argue that it does not make sense to regard an embryo or fetus as anything more than a collection of cells and tissues until significant development of the fetal brain—and thus the potential for rationality—has occurred.[7] Others identify our social nature as the defining characteristic of human beings; what gives us moral worth is our connection with other persons and communities. Extending this theme of sociality, they argue that an embryo or fetus is not a person with moral worth until it is connected in a web of relationships with other persons, most notably with the woman carrying it. In this way, a fetus does not have moral status from conception; instead status is conferred on it when the pregnant woman wants it and relates to it as a "child." Still others identify viability (roughly the end of the second trimester), or perhaps even birth, as the time when a fetus becomes a person, for it is our ability to survive without dependence on the organs of another person that makes us individuals in our own right. Each of these theories for when personhood begins is a *moral* argument for the significance of some moment in the developmental process. Each of them finds some support among liberal thinkers, allowing them to justify early abortion as something less problematic than the killing of an innocent human being.

Moral arguments for the beginning of personhood cannot be "proved" scientifically; they are *interpretations* of the ethical significance of what we know about human biology. Still, we can ask whether an interpretation is consistent with what science tells us about fetal development. For instance, most scientists now insist that fertilization is a nebulous process and not a precise event that can be pinpointed and isolated, as conservatives seem to require by insisting that personhood begins at the "moment" of conception. Furthermore, the majority of fertilized eggs do not survive very long in this process, a fact that suggests that millions of "persons" (as defined by conservatives) die every day before they are a week old. Further still, scientists tell us that an embryo is susceptible to division into two or more embryos through the first two weeks after fertilization. How can an embryo be a distinct individual in the eyes of God at conception, and then become two or three or more individuals?[8]

Liberal arguments for the beginning of personhood also come with problems. If we say that rational capacity is what makes someone a human being, what does that mean for those on the other end of life—advanced Alzheimer's patients, for instance—who no longer exhibit that capability? Are they no longer "persons," with rights and dignity? If we insist that personhood depends on social relationships, are we comfortable with the implications of saying that the moral worth of persons is something conferred on them by others, rather than something innate and inalienable? Is the argument that personhood begins late in pregnancy or only at birth consistent with the testimony of millions of pregnant women (and their partners) who have experienced the fetuses they carried as "persons" well before they emerged from the womb?

These kinds of questions suggest that liberal definitions of personhood are as fraught with challenges as the conservative assumption that personhood begins at conception. But in just this debate, religious perspectives remind us that we will never be able to determine the respect and protections embryos and fetuses deserve on the basis of science alone. Our attitudes toward them are products of our assumptions about what constitutes personhood. What gives you and me dignity, worth, and rights? Do embryos and fetuses share those defining characteristics? Answering these questions requires careful conversation between conflicting worldviews; it requires moral discourse. Sophisticated religious perspectives can help us navigate that complicated philosophical terrain of discerning what we regard as fundamental about being human beings.

IT'S NOT *ALL* ABOUT THE FETUS

Some religious perspectives also remind us that there is more to the morality of abortion and ESCR than just a debate over moral status. Because liberals generally do not believe that abortion or ESCR involves the violation of a person like you and me, they do not find persuasive the argument that abortion or embryonic research is equivalent to murder. But this does not mean that they regard abortion and ESCR as morally unproblematic. For many liberal thinkers, the primary moral obligation surrounding abortion is to protect women's health and well-being. Abortion should be a legal option in order to keep it safe, legitimate, and out in the open, rather than retreating to the days when abortions were performed in secret, often in medically dangerous conditions. Sometimes stopping a pregnancy is the best way to care for a woman's physical, psychological, or emotional health, and in those cases it is best to have unfettered access. Despite the way that some religious conservatives try to pit the "women's agenda" against "moral values," quite clearly this commitment to women's health is morally motivated and justified. Feminist theologians from Protestantism, Catholicism, Judaism, and a host of other religions argue that protecting women's well-being is a subset of social justice, to which these traditions have deep historical commitments.

Many religious liberals remind us that God created us not as spirits, but as fully embodied persons, thus giving theological importance to the defense of women's control over their own bodies. An essential aspect of the Christian doctrine of resurrection, for instance, is that Jesus promised a *bodily* resurrection, which is an implicit commentary on the importance of our bodies for determining who we are. Other religious traditions also emphasize the embodied nature of human being; Judaism in particular comes to mind.[9] We are our bodies, and minds, and spirits—we are integrated, whole beings, so that what happens to our bodies in this life is important, because it happens to us. Given the importance of bodily integrity to many religious liberals, then, it is important that women have the freedom to control what happens to their bodies, including whether or not to continue a pregnancy. Women should have the right to make choices about their bodies that conform to their convictions of conscience. Like the value of the body, freedom of conscience enjoys deep support in many religious traditions, including Christianity. (The list of theologians in Christian history who supported freedom of conscience includes somewhat surprising names, like John Calvin and more than a couple of Puritans!) If religious liberals agreed that a fetus is a person with rights on par with the woman carrying it, then the fetus's right to live would trump their appeals to freedom of conscience and bodily integrity. But since they do not believe that the fetus's interests are on the same moral level as the woman's, the religious and moral commitments to freedom of conscience and women's well-being determine what they believe is right—that women should have legal access to safe abortions.

When it comes to embryonic stem-cell research, liberals likewise emphasize different moral concerns than their conservative counterparts. To religious liberals, the chief moral issue in ESCR is fundamentally the need for compassion and the opportunity to improve the health of people debilitated by sickness. Judaism puts a great deal of emphasis on healing; in fact ethicist Laurie Zoloth argues that "the task of healing in Judaism is not only permitted, it is mandated; if stem cells can save a life, then not only can they be used, they must be used."[10] Rabbi Elliot Dorff insists that God the healer commissions human beings to participate in the project of healing, so that "the duty of saving a life (*pikkuah nefesh*) takes precedence over all but three of the commandments in the Torah."[11] Similarly, healing was a central part of Jesus' ministry; the Gospels abound with stories of Jesus performing miracles of healing, even when doing so violated long-standing religious conventions. With this biblical precedent in mind, many liberals argue that the divine mandate to do what we can to help people escape injury or disease justifies our pursuit of ESCR. Christian ethicists like Ted Peters go so far as to suggest that we have an *obligation*, as creatures created in the image of God, to exercise our God-given creativity and intelligence this way, for the betterment of humankind.[12] To Peters,

ESCR is an example of ethically responsible use of technological ability—it is, as Judaism teaches, the fulfillment of our obligation to "fix the world" in God's name. Rather than being preoccupied with the well-being of an embryo, liberal supporters of ESCR are concerned that we fulfill the responsibilities of stewardship, to do the most good with the gifts of intelligence and creativity that we have been given.

ESCR raises other moral issues for liberals, to which religion gives powerful language to respond. Thinkers like Zoloth point to "problems of process" and are concerned that we monitor the details of ESCR as zealously as we debate the moral status of the embryo. She warns that enthusiastic pursuit of ESCR will require a lot of embryos, which will in turn require a lot of eggs. She worries that this might place undue pressure on women to donate their eggs to research, a process that involves more medical risk than sperm donation.[13] Suzanne Holland, a self-identifying Roman Catholic bioethicist, worries about the nefarious effect of commercialization, where the demand for embryos creates a "market" for eggs—with unconsidered consequences. Such a market could place the obligation to provide eggs disproportionately on women from lower socioeconomic tiers, or it might have the opposite (and equally undesirable) effect, making eggs from wealthy and educated women more valuable than those of other segments of society. Either way, writes Holland, this would be an unfortunate development, because "if some eggs are worth more than others, . . . it pits two groups of women against each other in terms of market desirability on the basis of market-supported eugenics."[14] Holland is also concerned that the therapies that might come from ESCR "are likely to be cost-prohibitive for all but the wealthy and the well-insured . . . The poor, who are largely female, and most persons of color will simply be marginalized from these therapies, even as it is possible that their eggs are commercialized downstream for profit."[15] Holland raises serious questions about ESCR, but none has to do with the status of the embryo. In fact, she calls us to move "beyond the embryo," to understand the moral implications of ESCR as they relate to the concerns of women, to the needs of the poor, and to the already pressing demands on a dysfunctional healthcare system.[16] Both Holland and Zoloth invoke the deep commitment to social justice in their religions to make their arguments.

Clearly, embryonic stem-cell research is a moral issue for religious liberals. Where they differ with conservatives is the specific concerns they think ESCR raises. For many liberals, the chief ethical problem surrounding ESCR is *not* the status of the fetus. Instead, it is the specter of injustice that haunts the processes of medical research, as well as any advances that might come of this research. At the same time, many liberals see a moral obligation to pursue ESCR in order to address the health-care needs of millions of global citizens. ESCR is a "moral values" issue for liberals, but the values they see at stake are those of personal freedom, bodily integrity, compassion for the sick, and social equality.

SHARED COMMITMENT TO THE SACREDNESS OF LIFE

Certainly the public debates over abortion and ESCR have been dominated by assertions and accusations that do very little to help the discussion along. Simple declarations that abortion runs contrary to God's will (based on implicit biblical evidence at best) are routinely met with equally simplistic dismissals of religious convictions. Conservatives label liberals baby killers, while liberals accuse conservatives of being women haters. But commitment to healthier public conversation requires that we move beyond the superficial and divisive rhetoric to try to achieve some mutual understanding of perspectives different from our own. In this chapter, I have tried to represent some of the deeper thinking that goes on within both conservative and liberal camps on abortion and ESCR, in order to facilitate that understanding. Regardless of which arguments we ultimately find persuasive, spending some time trying to understand what others are thinking may help us capture what is most at stake for us in the debates surrounding abortion and ESCR.

But why take the time? Why tolerate religious perspectives, when their track record on these issues seems so dubious? One reason to do so is pragmatic: many Americans already think about these issues from a religious point of view. Both conservatives and liberals make claims about the moral value of an embryo or fetus, and many in both camps do so from theological grounds. Any hope of public consensus over abortion or ESCR, however limited, disappears if arguments cannot be couched in the terms most amenable to Americans' moral worldviews, the lens through which many Americans are so accustomed to thinking about these concerns. Because abortion and ESCR already are religious issues for a majority of citizens, on both sides of the debate, to proscribe that language marginalizes many Americans and virtually eliminates the chance that we will ever progress in our collective deliberations.

Beyond practical resignation to religion's current dominance of our debates, I think that religious arguments contribute positively to our public conversations. For instance, liberal religious emphases on respect for women and the integrity of free choice can encourage the promotion of social justice and equality. When these concerns are given theological grounding, they take on ultimate significance in a way non-theological language struggles to achieve. Similarly, conservative religious appeals to the basic value of every individual person as a child of God give vivid expression to the inherent worth of all human beings. The theological language of life's sacredness, while not unproblematic, serves as an antidote to a materialist culture that assigns worth to things and people only according to what they can do for us; it declares that we are valuable beyond the ways in which we are useful, attractive, or entertaining to other people. In a culture that sometimes seems to worship at the altars of unfettered autonomy and unchecked technological progress, conservatives insist that the value of human life is inherent and inalienable, and that the dignity of the individual cannot be sacrificed for the greater good if we want to remain a moral society. This declaration does not eliminate our need to debate whether or not it is right to consider a five-day-old embryo a person, but it reminds us not to sidestep the question of personhood just because we are enamored with the medical promise of ESCR. Can this point be made without theology? Perhaps, but it can hardly be made more eloquently than by the religious conservative's invocation of the *imago dei* (the "image of God") in each of us.

Philosopher Ronald Dworkin thinks that the language of life's sacredness or "sanctity" holds great promise in promoting dialogue over abortion, despite (or perhaps because of) its religious connotations. He believes it captures something important to both conservatives and liberals.[17] Dworkin notes that almost no one associated with a pro-choice position believes that abortions should be undertaken in a cavalier fashion, as an acceptable form of birth control. On the contrary, pro-choice politicians frequently speak of the "tragic" reality of abortion, even as they argue that it should be legal. To talk of abortion as tragic implies a sense of loss that accompanies abortion even in the minds of those unwilling to award full personhood to a fetus. This sense of loss, says Dworkin, betrays a regard for the sacredness of fetal life even among pro-choice thinkers. We can believe fetal life is sacred without committing to its full personhood and without retreating from the conviction that in tragic contests between fetal development and the best interests of the woman, the woman's best interests should win out. Nonetheless, it is an important discovery to recognize that, on some level, most liberals agree with conservatives that embryos and fetuses have significant moral worth. They may disagree about just how much worth they have and about what the implications of that worth are for abortion policy and ESCR. But in a debate this intractable, it is no small victory to get parties to recognize a little bit of common ground—and the religious language of sacredness helps to light the way.

From the other side, Dworkin also points out how the language of life's sanctity might better capture pro-life commitments than does the description of embryos and fetuses as persons. As we have noted, with the exception of traditional Catholics, most conservatives allow for justification of abortions in cases of rape, incest, and a threat to the woman's health. Those exceptions do not make much sense if you literally believe that fetuses are persons with rights, like you and me. In fact, Dworkin claims that the popularity of these exceptions proves that pro-lifers do not *really* think that a fetus is a person. Instead, what conservatives are trying to protect is something important but vaguer, something we might call the sacredness of life. Embryos and fetuses are worthy of great respect, even if they are not exactly babies, even if we cannot regard them as people with rights to protect without exception. Drawing this subtle distinction between the language of personhood and this admittedly fuzzier notion of life's sacredness allows the conservative to hold to his exceptions to the prohibition on abortion with logical consistency. It also suggests the potential for common ground with liberals, who themselves at a certain level acknowledge an inherent value to these beginning stages in the development of human life.

According to Dworkin, then, the language of life's sanctity or sacredness captures a certain level of shared moral conviction between conservatives and liberals in the matter of abortion, despite their pronounced disagreement over how to interpret and respond to that sacred value. In fact, despite its religious overtones, Dworkin believes that the language of "sacredness" captures a nearly universal regard citizens have for the inherent value of human life:

> If we can understand the abortion controversy as related to other differences of religious and philosophical opinion in that way, then we shall understand much better how and why we disagree. We shall also be in a better position to emphasize how we agree, to see how our divisions, deep and painful though they are, are nevertheless rooted in a fundamental unity of humane conviction. What we share is more fundamental than our quarrels over its best interpretation.[18]

While the pro-life and pro-choice caucuses differ substantially on whether abortion should be legally restricted, the recognition of their common moral commitment to the sanctity of life may provide some occasion for discussion and—dare we dream?—movement. When we see past the misleading debates over personhood to discussing competing definitions of our common commitment to life's sacredness, then the questions become: How do we as a society best reflect our value for the sacredness—the inherent worth—of all human life? How do we balance the value we place in existing persons (women, the sick), whom we may feel an obligation to assist, and the value we see in the earliest stages of human existence? Agreeing on the shared commitment to life's sacredness does not mean we have dispensed with the abortion dilemma by any means, but this religious language does give us a common vocabulary with which to talk about our disagreements. In a debate that has seemed to go nowhere in the last thirty years, the discovery of a common language and some shared moral commitments—however general—would be welcome indeed.

6

The End of Marriage as We Know It?

In 1996 the U.S. Congress (with President Clinton's signature) enacted the Defense of Marriage Act, which defined marriage for the purposes of federal policy as between a man and a woman. The majority of states followed suit, enacting heterosexual restrictions on marriage that remain in effect in most states. But in 2000 Vermont became the first state in the United States to permit "civil unions" between gay or lesbian partners. Four years later, the state Supreme Judicial Court declared gay marriage legal in Massachusetts, a provision that has been unsuccessfully challenged there ever since. In May 2008 the California Supreme Court ruled that state's eight-year-old ban on same-sex marriage unconstitutional, making California the second state in the United States to offer legal marriage to gay and lesbian couples, and the first where the privilege was open to couples coming from any other state.[1] The victory for gay-marriage advocates was short lived, for in November of that year voters approved Proposition 8, a constitutional amendment outlawing gay marriage in California. But in April 2009 Vermont made history again, becoming the first state to legalize gay marriage through legislative action instead of a court ruling, a pattern that Maine and New Hampshire (two states that previously had approved defense-of-marriage laws) soon followed.[2] Despite some reversals (such as Maine's fall 2009 vote to overturn same-sex marriage), the push to add more states to those that legally recognize civil unions or gay marriage grows stronger with each election year, a development that has only intensified the political and religious debate over homosexuality. In many ways, same-sex marriage has become the new abortion, a seemingly intractable debate that is regarded by many as a gauge for the moral direction of the culture.

Of course, much of the intractability resides with religious communities themselves, and religious conservatives are the most publicly outspoken opponents of same-sex marriages. But I think that a more careful consideration of thoughtful religious perspectives on this issue, from conservative to liberal, may provide the chance to move our civil conversation in a healthy direction. That progress is not likely to happen as long as the religious arguments do not evolve beyond contests of biblical proof-texting. Conservative invocations of Leviticus and Romans, and liberal dismissals of these passages as outdated, are not apt to convince, on either the religious or the political front. The fact is that the Bible has nothing explicitly positive to say about homosexuality, but it also provides no outright condemnation of gay and lesbian marriage, since the modern concept of committed homosexual relationships was completely foreign to the biblical world. A productive conversation about homosexuality, then, requires that we move beyond assaulting one another with biblical one-liners to a deeper discourse—theologically, historically, and philosophically informed—on the meaning of sex and love, the importance of social order, and the definition of moral good. As was the case with abortion and ESCR, we do not have the space here to do justice to the complexity of this important public controversy. But I do want to suggest a little of the deeper thinking happening among religious people on both sides of the debate, and ways that religious reasoning might serve the larger public discourse.

NATURAL SEX

Despite how it is depicted in popular culture, there is often more to conservative religious opposition to same-sex marriage than an irrational fear of homosexuality. Thoughtful conservatives argue against same-sex marriage on the basis of certain assumptions about what is "naturally" right and good about sex. David Novak, for instance, has argued that homosexuality runs counter to Judaism's understanding of the meaning and true purpose of sexuality. For Novak, "Sexual love in the sacred covenant of marriage is a participation in a higher relationship, that of God's everlasting love for his people."[3] It also reflects our nature, that we were created to be social beings, to exist in relationship and in community as God desires relationship with us. Our sexuality reflects our need for an "other," but like any other natural impulse, our sexuality may be abused or misdirected from its proper intentions. As a result, marriage serves as an institution through which that relational impulse with which we were created may be channeled in ways that further God's intentions for individuals and human society.

According to Novak, homosexuality is "inconsistent with human nature" and divine intention, because homosexuality is "counterprocreative" (that is, a homosexual act cannot produce a child) and therefore frustrates the institutions of marriage and family, the building blocks of stable moral society.[4] More fundamentally, however, Novak argues that Jewish tradition prohibits homosexuality because it runs counter to the "essentially bisexual nature of human beings."[5] In its desire for an "other" who is fundamentally different—namely, one of the opposite sex—heterosexuality corrects the human tendency toward self-absorption. Instead of leading us to seek someone who simply reinforces our own characteristics (good and bad), the "norm" of heterosexual human nature suggests that we properly find our completion in the complementarity of someone different from us. By contrast, homosexuality represents a denial of that need for complementarity, for difference. Moreover, Novak argues that "homosexuality is based on a fundamental lie," because it requires that one partner assume a false gender role.[6] The absence of gender diversity "belies the very biological truth of the essentially intersexual relatedness attested by the fact that the sexual organs and the organs of procreation are the same."[7] In Novak's reading of the Jewish tradition, homosexual unions are both unnatural and antisocial, and thus "elevating a homosexual relationship to the level of a 'marriage' was considered [to the rabbis] shocking and a sign of extreme social decadence."[8]

Novak's reliance on gender complementarity as a "natural" sign of how human beings were created to relate sexually to one another shows up in Christian arguments too. In a book called *Welcoming but Not Affirming*, theologian Stanley Grenz argues for a traditional evangelical stance on homosexuality and gay marriage. After carefully analyzing several standard biblical passages (for example, the Sodom and Gomorrah story and the Levitical code) and important periods in Christian tradition in a way that confirms the standard interpretation that homosexuality is wrong, Grenz steps back to ask what the theological meaning of sexual difference is to Christianity. His answer is that "we discover—or construct—who we are in our embodied maleness or femaleness in part through our interaction with the other sex."[9] Sexual difference is part of the *imago dei* (the "image of God") in which Genesis claims we all were created. Grenz argues that the "exclusive love shared by husband and wife reflects the holiness of the divine love present within the triune God" and extended to us, in a way that same-sex relationships cannot.[10] Beyond the admittedly important potential for bearing children, heterosexual marriage ritualizes the intimate and exclusive coming together of two into one that symbolizes the love that binds the Trinity together, as well as our own union with the Divine. But Grenz insists that without the physical complementarity of male and female, homosexual relationships cannot mimic this intimacy or exclusivity. As he puts it, "The specific body part each contributes to the act does not represent what distinguishes each from the other," so that "same-sex intercourse loses the symbolic dimension of two-becoming-one present in male-female sex."[11] It fails to ensure exclusivity, in that "there is nothing inherent in this physical act that would limit involvement to two persons."[12] Like Novak, Grenz believes the physical complementarity of male and female is important because it holds deeper theological meaning, as a reflection of God's intentions for human sexuality and as a symbol of the ideal love between human beings and God.

Most famously, the Catholic Church also has argued that the proper norms for marriage can be interpreted from the natural sexual compatibility of men and women. According to Catholic tradition, sex is rightly ordered when it is experienced and enjoyed in ways that are consistent with its *ends*, the reasons we were created sexual beings. The proper ends of sex, which we know from both the testimony of religious tradition and inferences from nature, are its "unitive" and "procreative" functions. Sex is good because it promotes a deep love and companionship between two people, a partnership that allows them to flourish as individuals but also to pursue their calling as a couple. Sex is also good because it makes it possible for a couple to receive the gift of children and to contribute to the future of humankind by raising a family. According to church teaching, "good sex" is sex that is consistent with *both* of these ends; each sex act must be open to satisfying the unitive and procreative functions. The Vatican regards extramarital sex to be categorically opposed to the unitive function of sex because it frustrates the project of developing committed, monogamous, marital partnerships. Similarly, contraception and assisted reproductive technologies separate the act of sex from its procreative end, the first by ensuring sex without pregnancy and the second by facilitating pregnancy without the experience of sex.

Homosexuality too is wrong in the eyes of the church because it is naturally incompatible with one of the fundamental purposes of sex, to create children. Thus, while sounding a sympathetic note toward gay and lesbian persons and their struggles, the Vatican nonetheless rejects homosexuality as behavior that cannot be solemnized or endorsed with the sacrament of marriage. The Catechism of the Catholic Church calls homosexual acts "intrinsically disordered." Homosexual acts and relationships "are contrary to the natural law. They close the sexual act to the gift of life. They do not proceed from a genuine affective and sexual complementarity. Under no circumstances can they be approved."[13]

The Vatican urges members of the church to regard gay and lesbian persons as fellow children of God worthy of respect and compassion. But the church cautions homosexual persons that its sensitivity to their situation should not be confused with endorsement; gay and lesbian persons should not act on their "unnatural" tendencies, but instead should embrace the calling to be chaste:

> To choose someone of the same sex for one's sexual activity is to annul the rich symbolism and meaning, not to mention the goals, of the Creator's sexual design. Homosexual activity is not a complementary union, able to transmit life; and so it thwarts the call to a life of that form of self-giving which the Gospel says is the essence of Christian living. This does not mean that homosexual persons are not often generous and giving of themselves; but when they engage in homosexual activity they confirm within themselves a disordered sexual inclination which is essentially self-indulgent.[14]

Official Catholic teaching rejects homosexuality—and thus the prospect of gay marriage—as both contrary to religious teaching and unnatural. It does so, not through an assault with biblical verses, but by proposing a biblically and theologically informed theory of sex.

In each of these religious arguments against gay marriage, we see a couple of moral claims that, however we might disagree with them, amount to more than just fear of gays and lesbians. Conservative rejection of homosexuality relies at least partially on assumptions about what makes for "natural" sexuality. They argue that the physical compatibility of the sexual organs and the need for male and female in order to produce offspring are themselves natural signs of "good sex," and thus that heterosexuality is the proper norm for human sexuality. They assume that the procreative function of sex is either a necessary justification for every sexual act (Catholicism) or the reflection of a divine intention that defines more generally what is proper sex and what is not (Novak). An openness to procreation, or at least the practice of sex in a way that is compatible with its procreative function, gives moral legitimacy to the other uses of sex, namely the "unitive" function, or the relational aspect of sex. But sex cannot be justified on its unitive function if it is practiced in a way incompatible with its procreative function. In other words, it is not enough to cite love and commitment to define sex as "good." As we will see, liberal critics reject this inextricable tie between the procreative and the "unitive" function in their readings of the traditions.

It is worth noting what is *not* included in these arguments. Absent in these rejections of gay marriage are biblical proof texts or assertions of the categorical promiscuity or moral laxity of gay and lesbian persons. Thinkers like Novak and Grenz demonstrate that concerns about gay marriage do not have to peddle in fearmongering or disparagement of the moral potential of gay individuals (or their heterosexual allies). The arguments of thoughtful opponents of same-sex marriage like Novak, Grenz, and even the Vatican are careful theological and philosophical perspectives that demand equally thoughtful response, rather than being easily dismissed as ignorant bigotry.

Whether these arguments still amount to homophobia depends on your definition of the term. If we take it literally, homophobia means irrational fear of gay persons and homosexuality, and I for one do not assume that everyone who argues against same-sex marriages is subconsciously afraid of being assaulted by a gay man, or having their children seduced by "the gay lifestyle." It is worth asking, however, if assumptions about the "unnaturalness" of homosexuality make one susceptible to dis-ease around the "abnormality" of gays and lesbians. Is this homophobia? Perhaps, perhaps not. At the very least, though, a commitment to civil conversation requires that arguments like these be met and assessed on their stated terms. These rejections of same-sex marriage are based on philosophical and theological claims about the proper uses, symbolic power, and social implications of sexuality, not just hatred of the different.

JUST SEX

On the other side of the debate, and despite the rhetoric to the contrary emanating from some conservative religious leaders, liberals who support gay marriage are not enemies of morality. Many liberals support same-sex marriage out of deep religious conviction. Like the other issues identified as the "big four," the issue of same-sex marriage raises for liberals moral concerns for personal freedom. In this case, liberals see the right to marry as a freedom that is impinged by restrictive civil definitions. As is the case with the other issues for liberals, same-sex marriage is not only about personal freedom but also about their moral claims regarding the true meaning of sex, marriage, and family, as well as the importance of social justice.

Most liberals reject the idea, represented by Novak and the Catholic magisterium, that the primary purpose of sexuality—and that which defines what is normal—is procreation. In particular, liberals normally reject the traditional Catholic notion that the unitive and procreative functions of sex must coexist (in each sexual act no less!) for a sexual union to be proper and licit. Instead, many liberals insist that a proper sexual relationship is defined by love, mutuality, and companionship and that marriage as an institution represents the long-term commitment to another person and those ideals. On this definition, many sexual relationships that maximize the virtues of domestic partnership, whether heterosexual or homosexual, are consistent with the moral ends of sexuality and the purposes of marriage, while those that harbor abuse, injustice, or inequality are illicit, regardless of the sexual orientation of those in the relationship. Many liberals might agree with Novak that our sexual lives are an important feature of our inherent sociality as human creatures, but they disagree with the assumption that the only proper way to understand the relational purposes of sex (and marriage) is through its compatibility with producing children.

Jewish ethicist Arthur Waskow, for instance, declares his tradition's historical emphasis on procreation to be outdated in our modern age of overpopulation. He instead describes a proper Jewish sexual ethic as one that emphasizes commitment, pleasure, companionship, justice, and family (however broadly construed). For Waskow, a proper sexual ethic emerges "from the need to make worthy, honest, decent, and stable loving connections among ourselves."[15] Similarly, Catholic ethicist Daniel Maguire breaks from the official teachings of his church to insist that gay and lesbian partnerships may be appropriate expressions of the aims and ends of marriage, apart from their inability to directly produce children. Against the naturalistic arguments for heterosexuality, Maguire points to historical record and scientific studies that confirm how common homosexual orientation is not only among human beings, but among numerous species in the animal kingdom. In response to the Vatican's focus on procreation in its definition of licit sex and true marriage, Maguire argues that marriage ought to be defined as "the unique and special form of committed friendship between sexually attracted persons," gay or straight.[16] Clearly for Maguire, Waskow, and other liberal religious thinkers, the unitive function—the presence of love and commitment—gives primary meaning to our sexual lives, and procreative possibilities are of secondary importance.

Rather than completely rejecting the importance of family to the ends of marriage, however, some liberals base their support for same-sex marriage on a reconsideration of what it means to be a family. They point to assisted reproductive technology as a way that gays and lesbians may have children. Noting the number of heterosexual couples who create their families through these technologies or through adoption, supporters of same-sex marriage point out the obvious fact that "natural" procreation is not the only way to become a family. Resisting the pressure to define families in strictly nuclear terms, some liberals argue for a more open reimagining of the family that recognizes not only gay parents but also the increasing frequency with which children are raised by single parents, grandparents, or other guardians. Jewish ethicist Martha Ackelsberg argues that "many of the values we associate with families can be, and have been, met in contexts other than the traditional nuclear family."[17] Agreeing with conservatives that families are the institutional context in which a society cares for the physical, emotional, and psychological needs of its children while training them to be responsible citizens, she nonetheless insists that these objectives can be met outside heterosexual nuclear units, and sometimes *better* in nontraditional families than in traditional ones. Giving nuclear families social priority relegates all other families to second-class status, while ignoring the fact that these "second-rate" family forms can provide for children and nurture them in the moral ideals of citizenship at least as well as the traditional formula.

Ultimately, from a liberal point of view, the debate over same-sex marriages is a fight for social justice. Those who support same-sex marriage argue that the civil privileges that accompany marriage should not be denied to gay and lesbian persons simply on the basis of sexual orientation. To many critics of traditional restrictions on marriage, the solution of civil unions is an unsatisfying compromise, because civil unions fail to secure the same rights and privileges for gay couples that heterosexual couples enjoy through marriage. Marriage comes with federal tax benefits unavailable to partners in a civil union. Marriage partners have normally uncontested next-of-kin authority in immigration and health-care issues. Unlike partners in a civil union, married spouses have the right to (and rights in) divorce, and both a marriage and its dissolution are recognized in all fifty states, regardless of where the couple was married.

As a result of these discrepancies, say same-sex marriage supporters, civil unions amount to a "separate but equal" segregation between heterosexual and homosexual domestic partnerships that relegates gay and lesbian couples to second-class status. This segregation is incompatible with American ideals, and many liberals argue for the extension of marriage to gays and lesbians as a matter of the equality imagined by the Declaration of Independence and the Bill of Rights. Beyond the appeal to political values, many religious advocates for gay marriage cite themes of social justice and mutual respect within their theological traditions to argue that ending the social discrimination against gays and lesbians is a matter of human rights.

For other liberals, however, the institution of marriage is so wrought with injustice that they argue gays and lesbians should want nothing to do with it. These critics point to the history of domestic violence and the abuse of children within marriages and ask why gays and lesbians would want to associate themselves with such a vehicle of injustice. Instead, they argue that there is a prophetic stance to be taken in completely rejecting marriage as a religious and legal institution. Protestant ethicist Marvin Ellison calls this the "de-centering" of marriage and its importance to our society. Taking his cue from the radical pattern of Jesus, whose attitude toward Sabbath laws was a challenge to the most important religious institution of his tradition, Ellison suggests that GLBT advocates should not argue for "equal protection" from marriage laws, but instead should call into question the deference our society shows toward marriage. He suggests that gays and lesbians should not seek but should reject the designation of their partnerships as "marriages," and should lead American culture in a reconsideration of family patterns.

To do so, says Ellison, would dethrone marriage from its social pedestal, expose its dangers to social critique, and invite us to imagine healthier family dynamics that potentially could achieve some of the objectives of marriage and the nuclear family more successfully that the traditional institution has accomplished.[18] His radical proposal is inspired by his commitment to Christianity, and its emphasis on social justice as a radical, countercultural moral value. To this Christian thinker the ideals of love and justice that his religious tradition emphasizes urge him to call into question the fundamental ways in which our society thinks about sexual commitment.

LET'S TALK ABOUT SEX (AND MARRIAGE)

These days the debate over gay marriage gives abortion a run for its money as the most polarizing issue in American culture. Conservative spokespersons characterize liberals as enemies of morality for their attack on the traditional family. Liberals treat conservatives as if they are ignorant bigots for their endorsement of discrimination against gay and lesbian couples. Hopefully, this chapter so far has shown how both stereotypes fail to capture accurately the more careful convictions of religious conservatives and liberals in this debate. Religious conservatives do not base their opposition to gay marriage in a hatred or fear of homosexuality, but rather in a principled understanding of the true purposes for sex and marriage as indicated by divine intention and the natural law. Religious liberals think about gay marriage as a referendum on moral values just as much as conservatives do, but they argue that the ideals of their traditions require a moral commitment to equal regard for all citizens who wish to celebrate their entry into committed and loving relationships. For conservatives *and* liberals, the gay marriage debate is a debate over moral values. They just do not agree on *which* moral values are most relevant and how to interpret them in light of this controversy.

In their disagreement, however, religious conservatives and liberals bring important contributions to our consideration of gay marriage. Most obviously, liberals remind us that one of the most essential "moral values"—especially to the Jewish and Christian religious worldviews that have been so important to the American moral tradition—is social justice. Contrary to the way conservatives sometimes talk, social justice is not a pollution of the Christian message born in nineteenth-century liberalism or the 1960s. Rather, social justice was arguably the core of Jesus' teachings; any reader of the Gospel of Luke picks up on the radical critique of social and economic inequality in Jesus' message. Before that, social justice was the axis on which the Torah revolved, as is clear from the way that the law in Leviticus and Deuteronomy takes great pains to provide for the poor, the "sojourner" (sometimes "alien" in NRSV), and the powerless in Israelite society. In all their talk of gay marriage as a matter of social justice, religious liberals are not opposed to moral values. Instead, they offer a corrective to truncated notions of morality by reminding us of the Jewish and Christian commitment to justice, equality, and mutual respect as moral values in themselves.

Another contribution religious liberals make to the debate over gay marriage is their reminder that definitions of marriage have always been historically contingent. In response to declarations that marriage has "always" been this or that, liberals remind us that marriage is at least in part a human institution that has been shaped by the historical context that surrounded it. As a result, marriage and the moral values that governed it looked different in pre-Christian Greek and Roman society than they did in Constantine's Christian empire. They took different shape again in medieval Europe, when the Catholic Church began to assert greater authority in the marriage arena, in part to correct the abuse of marriage as political and economic barter. Marriage evolved further still in early modern Europe and America, influenced by Protestant principles that differed substantially from Catholic teachings on sex and marriage.[19] Conservatives are fond of arguing that marriage has "always" been between a man and a woman, and strictly speaking, that is true in Western history. A lot of the other details surrounding marriage and family have changed significantly throughout history, however, and the broader implication that they have always taken some essential, unchangeable form underestimates the effect of historical context on how societies have defined the family. In calling for our assumptions about marriage to adjust to the times in which we live, liberals are helpfully reminding us that the institution has constantly changed to reflect the moral values of the societies in which it operated.

But conservatives also bring helpful reminders to the table of debate over gay marriage. Many supporters of gay marriage bristle at religious conservatives imposing their theological values on a political institution. Why should religious understandings of marriage be at all relevant to whether or not the state recognizes a gay partnership as a marriage? In response, conservatives properly remind us that marriage in Western history has always been and remains a religious and a political institution. Marriage has simultaneously been a celebration of a religious covenant between two people in the presence of God and a social contract with associated rights and relationships in the eyes of the state. Both religion and the state are invested in the meanings of marriage, so that no simple appeals to the mythical separation of church and state will do to help us navigate our disagreements. For better or worse (and I suspect it is some of both), we are stuck with negotiating the meaning of marriage as a phenomenon with both theological and social implications. In fact, marriage perfectly symbolizes the unavoidable intersection of religion and politics in this country. That is part of what makes the debate over gay marriage so difficult, but progress in the debate cannot be purchased by *denying* the intersection. Progress in the debate will be achieved only by negotiating our way *through* the intersection.

So conservatives do us a favor when they force us to acknowledge the essential relevance of religion to our collective consideration of marriage and family. They also serve our debates over gay marriage when they remind us that sex and marriage are not, contrary to some liberal rhetoric, private matters. Conservatives understand that marriage is a private relationship and a religious institution but also a pillar of Western societies. Marriage historically has been essential to nurturing society's future generations, to assuring productivity in various economic systems, and to channeling political power. As such, marriage has always served functions that were at least as important to political society as they were to the people involved in the marriage. When liberals characterize the controversy surrounding gay marriage as conservatives' intrusion into the private choices of other people, they demonstrate a profound misunderstanding of the history of marriage in Western culture. Marriage has never been only, or even principally, a private choice. Since it is also a public institution, it is fair game for political debate and competing proposals for how its parameters should be defined. Given the importance of marriage as a social institution, conservatives are right when they argue that changes in this institution will have a significant effect on American moral and political culture.

At the same time, to admit that change in the definition of marriage will have social consequences does not tell us whether these consequences will be good or bad. The claim that raising children within gay marriages is detrimental to the children's emotional and social development, for instance, has little data to support it.[20] At the same time, enough studies have confirmed the benefit that children receive from stable two-parent homes—and role models of both genders—that liberals need to take more seriously this component of the conservative defense of marriage. Progress on a shared interpretation of the empirical debate will not alone eliminate the disagreement over gay marriage, because there is more at stake on both sides than just the question of its effect on children. But in the current environment any productive conversation is a significant accomplishment.

The debate over gay marriage is so important and difficult because marriage is a part of the structural foundation of American society. Thus conservatives are right when they insist that choices about "acceptable" sex and forms of marriage cannot be simply private matters, and when they demand that religion has a real stake in the debate. But liberals are right to remind us that the forms marriage takes are not static ideas dropped down from heaven, but contingent (at least in part) on the moment in history in which we find ourselves. How to figure out what this moment demands is the task before us all.

7
Living and Dying Well

On February 25, 1990, a young Florida woman named Terri Schiavo suffered cardiac arrest in her home, and the prolonged lack of oxygen resulted in massive damage to her brain. Connected almost immediately to artificial nutrition and hydration (that is, a "feeding tube") at the hospital, Schiavo lingered in rehabilitation centers and care facilities for the next eight years while her husband Michael and her parents tried every course of treatment they could find—conventional and experimental—to stimulate her brain function. Finally, after already falling out with Terri's parents over treatment decisions, Michael decided that it was time to remove the feeding tube and allow Terri to die peacefully. But her parents strongly objected, and for the next five years Michael and Terri's parents fought in Florida court over the right to make decisions for Terri. The struggle dragged through state and federal appeals courts, and at different times the governor and legislature of Florida, the U.S. Congress, the Florida and U.S. Supreme Courts, and the White House got involved. Several times throughout the fight, Terri's feeding tube was removed and then reinserted after the parents petitioned the court for a stay. When all avenues of objection finally were exhausted, the court ruled that Terri's artificial nutrition and hydration could be stopped according to Michael's wishes. The feeding tube was finally removed on March 18, 2005, and about two weeks later, Terri died.

The public attention Terri Schiavo's story received illustrated the sharp disagreement that exists among Americans over end-of-life issues, while also demonstrating how complicated these issues can be. Some Americans believed that the removal of her feeding tube amounted to the doctors ending Terri's life, while others believed that her doctors and Michael were simply ending treatment that was clearly futile (akin to suspending a useless chemotherapy regimen), and that there should not be anything particularly controversial about that. Others believed that the removal of artificial nutrition and hydration amounted to "starving" her, an act more heinous than euthanasia, because it violates a patient's basic human right to sustenance.

The sharp disagreements surrounding the Schiavo story were partially a result of different interpretations of what was really going on in the case, but they also reflected the very different understandings Americans have about what makes for a "good death." Euthanasia, physician-assisted suicide (PAS), and similar end-of-life circumstances remain hotly contested "moral values" issues in our society.[1] Improving our public conversation over them will require that we thoughtfully explore the moral values at work on both sides of the debate—the competing ways that Americans define a "good death." This is a conversation that religious perspectives, both conservative and liberal, can help lead.

THOU SHALT NOT KILL

The Terri Schiavo case generally encouraged more political posturing than sustained public conversation. In particular it was not American conservatism's finest moment, as politicians accustomed to railing against intrusive government seemed all too willing to prod officials at the state and federal levels to intercede in this family's crisis. Governor Jeb Bush of Florida led fellow Republicans in crafting legislation that would give the state onetime permission to exert itself in this case. An advisor to Senator Mel Martinez (R-FL) created a memo that trumpeted the political advantages that Republicans would get from taking a public stand on Terri's situation.[2] President George W. Bush, in a blatantly choreographed photo op, interrupted his Easter vacation to return to the White House on Marine One to sign congressional legislation that might give Terri a hearing on the federal level. And then there was Senator Bill Frist (R-TN), surgeon and Senate majority leader, offering expert diagnoses of her condition from a couple of photos he had seen, causing many to question his competence in both the medical and political arenas. A family's tragedy had become political theater, led by conservatives eager to turn public sympathy for Terri (and her parents) into support for their defense of "moral values." Polls at the time indicated that most Americans found this politicization of the Schiavo case distasteful.[3]

Obscured by such public posturing, though, is the care with which many conservatives argue that euthanasia and related practices erode moral values important to our society. In the Schiavo case, conservatives frequently came off looking opportunistic and somewhat nutty. In reality, many conservatives oppose euthanasia, PAS, and the withdrawal of life-sustaining treatments like feeding tubes on clearly articulated philosophical grounds. Euthanasia is murder, they argue, and murder is wrong, even if it is done with seemingly virtuous intentions. Intentionally to take the life of another person who has done nothing to deserve such capital punishment—even if they request it—is to violate the moral law "do not kill" out of a misguided sense of compassion. Instead of abandoning the sick by killing them, compassion requires that we care for them, be present with them, and do everything we can to make them comfortable. To stand with a dying person is the truly merciful act; by contrast, as the late Jesuit theologian Richard McCormick once put it, euthanasia is a "flight from compassion."[4]

Similarly, PAS is wrong to conservatives because suicide is wrong. Suicide is wrong because it goes against the natural desire of all creatures to live. It is wrong because it reflects a lack of self-respect in the person who sees nothing valuable in her continued existence. It is wrong because it deprives a person's communities from the contributions that person can make to society. For many religious people, suicide is wrong because it usurps God's prerogative as creator to determine when and how we die. Rather than seeking help to end one's life, conservatives implore the dying to face death with patience and courage, knowing that their lives are "valuable" to the human community even as they face their end with dignity. Rather than provide the means by which dying patients may take their own lives, society ought to dedicate itself to managing the pain, discomfort, and isolation that make modern people fear death so much.

As with abortion and gay marriage, conservatives insist that end-of-life choices are not simply private matters. These seemingly personal decisions symbolize (and cumulatively contribute to) our cultural assumptions about life, death, and our obligations to one another. Popular support for PAS and euthanasia betrays a disrespect for the sacredness of life and an obsession with controlling both life and death.

Euthanasia and PAS are attractive options only because our culture has convinced us that the only life worth living is a productive one, and that the only thing we should fear more than death is lingering in a "useless" life. This utilitarian definition of "quality of life" tempts a society like ours to judge as valueless those who cannot contribute in a "meaningful" way—the poor, the sick, the aged, and the mentally handicapped. Once we have bought into that devaluation of these vulnerable members of our society, our arguments for a "right to die" easily become arguments for a "duty to die," a responsibility for those who cannot be "useful" to end their lives in order to yield resources for those of us who can. Thoughtful conservative opposition to assisted suicide and euthanasia, then, stems not from an uncontrollable need to meddle in families' allegedly private decisions. Instead, it comes from a concern for the moral ethos in the United States and a desire to protect the most vulnerable members of our society.

For religious conservatives, opposition to PAS and euthanasia also often derives from understanding death as part of a "bigger picture." In a beautifully written book entitled *Life's Living toward Dying*, Vigen Guroian, a moral theologian in the Orthodox Christian tradition, borrows a term from the title of a Walker Percy novel to describe our simultaneous aversion to and obsession with death in American culture. The "thanatos syndrome" is what he calls our fascination with, often-overwhelming fear of, and need to master death. Guroian thinks that the wane of religious influence on American culture has made us simultaneously obsessed with the finality of death and incapable of dealing with death in a way that can see anything good coming from the processes of death and dying. Death has power over us because we no longer see it in a larger cosmological context, as part of something that gives it meaning.

What causes us so much anxiety about death is the way that it seems pointless, tearing us from the ones we love and the communities of people that give our lives purpose. Our cultural responses to death have actually aggravated the sense of isolation that so frightens us about it. "The ways in which we wage war against death in our society ironically make us accomplices in our own spiritual suicide. Consider our efforts to remove death from the moral sphere of the home and transfer it to the technological environment of the modern hospital, for example. . . . It remains the case that our elaborate technologies often separate people from those whose love they need most of all when they are dying."[5]

In response, Guroian commends the theological traditions and liturgies of the church, which he says urge Christians to practice a "remembrance of death" in a way that does not eliminate our anxiety, but allows us to understand death in a larger context of values. Remembering death through liturgy and religious reflection offers an antidote to the "thanatos syndrome." Rather than epitomizing isolation and the end to meaningful life, death becomes meaningful as an important moment to experience and extend the love and support of community. Rather than being something to resist, death becomes something to embrace, the culmination of a virtuous life. The Christian rituals of death reassure us of our connectedness with human community (and God) even in—especially in—the last moments of our earthly lives. They also remind us that how we die speaks to our values just as much as how we live, and that we should understand our lives as "living toward dying" in ways that exhibit virtue.[6]

Guroian believes that Jesus exemplified what it means to live virtuously toward dying, and for those who would follow his example, the synthesis of purposeful life and meaningful death is symbolized in the liturgy of baptism, when Christians are baptized into the death of Jesus in order that they may live in him as well.[7] The liturgy of anointment also symbolizes the deeper meaning and the connectedness with others we can experience in dying. He does not recommend anointment instead of medical care, but he argues that the liturgy "reveals the telos of medicine," in that it reminds us that the healing arts themselves are most properly understood as means by which we might maintain and enrich our lives with others, and by which our communities assure us that they will not abandon us in our dying.[8] In all these ways, Guroian thinks that the Christian liturgical tradition reminds us that sickness and death are not meaningless ends to our stories, which we should strenuously resist with excessive medical technology or beat to the punch with PAS or euthanasia. Instead, they are occasions in which to celebrate our connectedness with other human beings and with God and to reflect on the extent to which we successfully lived our lives toward "dying well" with virtue.

Guroian recognizes that his perspective on dying may not be immediately translatable to a public that is not immersed in the liturgy and theology of the church, but he does not apologize for the fact that he cannot think of these issues except as an Orthodox theologian. To ignore his voice in the public conversation over euthanasia because it is explicitly theological would be to lose a remarkable perspective on the human struggle with death and dying. His book offers a penetrating critique of common cultural attitudes toward death and dying. It also serves as an invitation for those within and outside the Orthodox tradition to see the resources that Christianity possesses for thinking about the end of life in a different way. The themes he highlights, especially the importance of human community and rituals of remembrance, may hold meaning even for those who do not wish to identify personally with the practices of Guroian's church. His reflections on death also may be read as an invitation to those outside his tradition to adopt, if just for a moment, a worldview drastically different than their own, with the promise that through it they may see new ways to think about our relationship with the cosmos, with death, and with each other.

THE OBLIGATIONS OF COMPASSION

As compelling as conservative opposition may be, however, and contrary to rhetoric sometimes emanating from conservative circles, it is possible to justify euthanasia and PAS from a commitment to moral, indeed religious, values. Religious thinkers who defend euthanasia or PAS are a rare species, but they do exist. These thinkers tend to be less frightened than conservatives of the slippery slope from voluntary euthanasia to involuntary, and are more concerned that restrictions on end-of-life decisions will send other dangerous messages to those who suffer. They may or may not support the *legalization* of PAS and euthanasia, but these thinkers argue that sometimes those measures are *morally* appropriate ways of affirming the dignity and worth of people for whom life has been hijacked by pain and disease.[9]

Rather than signaling our disrespect for the sick and dying, ensuring access to PAS or euthanasia can be seen as an affirmation of human dignity, according to some defenders of the practices. Theologians from the more liberal wings of Christianity and (to a lesser extent) Judaism have argued that what gives human beings dignity and worth is our being created in the image of God, as the book of Genesis says we are. What is a greater reflection of our divine nature than our freedom? Allowing persons to decide for themselves when the burden of living with disease or infirmity outweighs the value of living preserves human freedom in an important context.

Religious defenders of PAS or euthanasia also remind us that, from the perspective of classical Christianity and many other religious traditions, life is not the greatest good, to be defended at all costs. Instead, life is *a* good that may in some circumstances be outweighed by other values. This argument has been used at different moments in history in each of the Western monotheisms to justify martyrdom, but it also can serve a defense of PAS and euthanasia, insofar as a person might judge the continuation of life to be not worth the burdens placed on family members or society. Faced with the high costs of treatment or even palliative care, some dying patients may desire to save their family members from the expense, or may prefer not to occupy resources from the social health network that otherwise might go to treating nonterminal patients. From this point of view, then, the decision to utilize PAS or euthanasia is an act of self-sacrifice for the best interests of others, an act that may not only be permissible but morally praiseworthy.

Other religious defenders of PAS or euthanasia argue that helping the dying to end their lives can be an extraordinary act of compassion, a virtue of supreme importance in many religious traditions. Christian ethicist Karen Lebacqz has argued that support for PAS and euthanasia can be consistent with the compassion Jesus displayed in his healing ministry. Taking seriously possible abuse of the practices, and acknowledging the complicated practical questions that would have to be sorted out regarding who should assist in a patient's death and how we measure which suffering is significant enough to justify euthanasia, Lebacqz nonetheless argues that euthanasia and assisted suicide must be available options for end-of-life care in a society that aims to be compassionate toward those who suffer. "The central moral issue," she argues, "has to do with caring, compassion, and prevention of suffering in the face of death." Sometimes relieving a person's suffering by helping them to accelerate death is an appropriate extension of, not the abandonment of, care.[10]

Ultimately, Lebacqz is convinced that guarded support for euthanasia and assisted suicide makes sense as an extension of Christian charity:

> I love life. I want my parents to live forever. I wish my grandmother had not died. I resist my own aging and the movement toward death. And yet I am also a Christian. I know that death is not the last word, not the greatest evil. Failure to live, to care, to enact justice, to be in proper relationship—those are greater evils. Death can serve evil or it can serve the values of life. As a way of bringing about death, active euthanasia can serve evil or it can serve the values of life. When it serves the values of life, it can be morally justified.[11]

Religious liberals like Lebacqz not only demonstrate the possibility of supporting assisted suicide from a religious perspective. They provide especially compelling moral language to articulate that support and to engage conservatives in conversation. Rather than simply repeating liberalism's buzz words of personal freedom and individuality, thinkers like Lebacqz show how euthanasia can be understood as an extension of the virtues they share with conservatives—compassion, care, respect for human dignity. Conservatives may vehemently disagree with how Lebacqz uses these religious and moral values, but speaking the same language can be a first step in more substantial conversation.

LISTENING TO THE MUDDLED MIDDLE

As with the other "big four" issues, by taking a more careful look at some of the arguments offered by holders of so-called conservative and liberal positions on end-of-life decisions, we can see a couple of things. First, conservative contributors are capable of more thoughtful and nuanced arguments for their positions than the stereotype of conservatism usually assumes. Second, liberal participants in the public debate do not reject a moral politics when they object to conservative positions. Instead, they offer their own moral vision for American society. Granted, the moral values that liberals think are at stake are sometimes very different from what conservatives think are at risk. But sometimes they are not so far apart; we see a different interpretation of principles and circumstances rather than complete disagreement about what is good and right in public morality.

We might make some headway in the debate over euthanasia by recognizing how both sides seem to agree that compassion is a relevant moral norm, even while they disagree over what is the best social expression of compassion toward those in the process of dying. We might be served by recognizing the commitment to human dignity on each side of the debate, even though the obligations of dignity are differently understood. We might make some progress in the debate over abortion and ESCR by taking up Dworkin's observation that just about everyone in the debate seems to be talking about the "sacredness of life," though they mean different things by the term. Our debates over same-sex marriage might be served by pausing to recognize that in fighting for or against same-sex marriages, most Americans are signaling a profound respect for the institution of marriage and the general good it represents. This may not seem like much progress, but given the level of mutual demonization that characterizes the current "moral values debate," acknowledging this initial common ground might be a more significant step than we recognize. At the very least, we can take some optimism for public discourse from the fact that by engaging each other in the debate itself, conservatives and liberals are sharing a common project, advocating for a moral society.

One of the other benefits that comes from complicating our understanding of moral debate is that we put ourselves in a position to discover that a surprising number of Americans do not subscribe to extreme versions of either the right or the left. Many Americans place themselves somewhere between the superliberals and ultraconservatives, while still thinking about these issues in explicitly moral terms. In other words, many Americans—even those who may overall identify with the conservative or liberal camp—are part of a "muddled middle," a majority of more moderate Americans who pick and choose from among conservative and liberal priorities and therefore think about these issues in more complicated ways than the stereotypical extremes seem to do. As this "muddled middle," these folks perhaps represent the best potential for serious and civil conversation across the ideological spectrum.

Some of this moderation is represented by entire traditions within the American religious landscape. Judaism, for instance, offers an interesting angle on the debate over abortion, combining an unapologetically religious interpretation of the issue with a relatively liberal willingness to justify abortion. The majority of the tradition teaches that until forty days after conception an embryo is "like water" and can be aborted when necessary without major moral qualms. Between age forty days and birth, some Jewish authorities talk of the embryo/fetus as a "potential person," and some regard it as part of the woman's body, but few argue that it has rights and interests that compete with the woman's physical or emotional well-being. This is not to say that Judaism allows for cavalier abortions, but the respect the embryo or fetus receives is secondary to the needs of the woman carrying it.[12] Abortion in circumstances when a pregnancy threatens a woman's life is not only permissible; it is often considered obligatory—one cannot sacrifice a person with full moral status (the woman at risk) out of interest in saving an embryo. Abortion in the case of rape or incest is also clearly justified, and in fact many Jewish thinkers entertain liberal justifications for abortion based on the woman's emotional well-being. Despite the constant references by evangelical commentators to our

"Judeo-Christian" moral tradition, Judaism clearly reminds us that not all committed religious citizens walk in step with the moral assumptions held by some conservative Christians, and not all "religious talk" about abortion will wind up at the same conclusion.

Another religious tradition in the American landscape that represents a kind of "muddled middle" is black Protestantism. On some of the "big four," African Americans (especially those with ties to evangelicalism) vote along the same lines as white conservatives. For instance, black Protestants statistically oppose same-sex marriage as vigorously as white evangelicals, and many African Americans bristle at the analogies drawn between the civil rights movement and current efforts for civil equality for gays and lesbians. On the other hand, support for restrictive abortion laws is much lower among black Protestants than white evangelicals. African Americans strongly support parental consent and spousal notification laws, a reflection of the importance of the family in African American culture, but fewer than half of black Protestants in the United States strongly oppose abortion or use of state funding to make abortion available to women.[13] On some issues, black Protestants' voting patterns reflect their historical affinity with American evangelicalism, but the presence of a strong priority on social justice and on family and community distinguish African American Christians in other moral debates. As a group, black Protestants complicate the moral values debate by combining conservative and liberal impulses in creative and coherent ways.

Not only traditions but individual thinkers exhibit this "muddled middle" that I think represents the majority of Americans on the big four moral issues. Karen Lebacqz, for instance, is a liberal thinker. She is a member of one of the most liberal Christian denominations, the United Church of Christ, and her work reflects the influence of social justice and liberationist movements. In her support for embryonic stem-cell research, she denies that embryos are persons with full moral status. At the same time, she insists that if we as a society are going to endorse ESCR, we should do so in a way that respects embryos as the building blocks of human life. She draws analogies between the respect we ought to show animals, plants, and the environment to make her point that the morality of ESCR is not an either-or proposition. We are not caught between either respecting the moral value of the embryo by refraining from research, or denying its value altogether by endorsing the research. We can respect embryos *even while* we permit their occasional destruction for research, by refusing to handle them in cavalier fashion, by appreciating their value apart from what they promise to the research agenda, by speaking about them with respect, by using them only when research requires it, and by minimizing the stress we place on them as we use them.[14] Her rejection of the full personhood of embryos aligns her in the liberal camp on ESCR, but she adopts the language of respect with which conservatives are used to talking about embryos and fetuses. By doing so, she offers at least the possibility of conversation between the moral worldviews of supporters and opponents of this research.

Allen Verhey, a self-identifying evangelical, is another example of this kind of moderate voice. He was educated at evangelical institutions and for many years taught Christian ethics at an evangelical college. His ethical worldview is explicitly Bible based, and his writings normally exhibit heavy use of the New Testament and appeal to the pattern of Jesus. Nonetheless, on the issue of same-sex unions, Verhey's evangelicalism pushes him to speak out against what he calls the homophobia of the church. He comes to this conclusion through a close reading of Christian Scripture, which he argues is a practice that requires not only a commitment to holiness, discipline, and fidelity, but also creativity and discernment.[15] A pious but appropriately creative reading of the Bible reveals that God has certain ideal intentions for human sexuality that must be negotiated with the realities of sin. One example of this kind of negotiation, says Verhey, is that of divorce, where even evangelical Christians recognize the need to "compromise" the Bible's prohibitions on divorce in order to protect marriage partners and the institution itself in a world of unsuccessful relationships.

Analogically, Verhey argues, evangelicals should also recognize that same-sex partnerships can be a "compromise" that furthers God's relational ideals for sexuality—fidelity, mutuality, equality, intimacy, and continuity—even as the form falls short of God's intentions:

> If we allow for divorce in a world like this for the sake of protecting marriage and marriage partners, then we must also consider allowing committed homosexual relationships for the sake of protecting fidelity and mutuality and the homosexual partners. It does not make either divorce or homosexual behavior a good. But it is still not yet the good future of God, and in a fallen world and a fallen sexuality, fidelity and mutuality can be a mark of God's good future.[16]

Appealing to the supreme authority of the evangelical worldview, the Bible, Verhey provides a moderate position on homosexuality, one that does not exactly endorse homosexual behavior, but that is nonetheless prepared to support committed gay and lesbian relationships in the name of preserving the virtues of fidelity and mutuality in an otherwise broken world.

The examples of thinkers like Verhey and Lebacqz, as well as the diversity at home in traditions like Judaism and black Protestantism, represent the promise of conversation and, dare we say, some consensus on these four issues that currently polarize American public debate. This is not to say that the average evangelical will automatically be persuaded by Verhey's read of Christian tradition on sexual issues, or that liberals necessarily will have patience for Lebacqz's talk of respect for the embryo. But if they choose to accept the responsibility, the average conservative and liberal will each have the chance to think deeply on these issues, and to have their worldviews challenged by the encounter with another, because of the mediating rhetoric of religious voices like these. Careful religious perspectives complicate the picture of the so-called moral values debate by revealing the depth of conservative views, by demonstrating the moral commitment in liberal perspectives, and by reminding us of the rich and varied views that exist in the "muddled middle." This picture of the moral debate is messier than the simplistic title fight between extremes that the media constantly serves up to us. But in this case, messier is healthier, because in the mess is the promise for genuine dialogue.

Moral debate gets messier still when we expand the topics of conversation beyond those we have called the big four. To those who argue that other issues entirely are the "values vote" worth talking about, we turn next.

PART THREE

Beyond the Big Four

8
War Is *a Moral Issue*

In the months leading up to the declaration of war in Iraq in 2003, opponents and supporters of armed intervention against Saddam Hussein tussled with each other in the nation's newspapers. Between assertions of national interest and debates over reports of weapons of mass destruction (WMD), many of these pundits argued about the ethics of the war. Progressive evangelical activist Jim Wallis and former president Jimmy Carter appealed to just-war principles to insist that the war in Iraq was morally dubious.[1] Southern Baptist leader Richard Land and political philosopher Jean Bethke Elshtain used that same ethical tradition to argue that the military overthrow of Hussein was not only permissible but necessary.[2] To both critics of the war and many of its defenders, the invasion of Iraq had profound ethical implications.

However, you would not have known that from the way political pundits were talking about "moral values" at about the same time. That 2004 National Election Poll, for instance, when it asked voters to name the most important issue facing the country, pitted "moral values" against war, terrorism, the environment, and the economy. Doing so implied that those other issues had nothing to do with "moral values"; they were topics of political or social importance, but they were not matters of ethics. Self-anointed czars of the "moral values" campaign insisted that the moral fabric of the nation was being ripped by abortion and homosexuality—not by the reality of millions of Americans without health care, signs of human-induced global warming, or evidence that the beacon of democracy in the world employed torture to pursue its national interests. To this day spokespersons for the "values vote" persist in identifying abortion, stem cells, euthanasia, and gay marriage as the moral issues Americans care most about; war, poverty, and the environment are not often on their ethical radar.

But war *is* a profoundly moral issue, just as how we treat the natural world and how we deal with one another in our economic relationships are matters of great moral significance. As we suggested in chapter 1, "moral values" are those norms that help us negotiate what we ought to do and who we ought to be, collectively and individually, both in so-called private issues and public matters. On this definition, the economy, environmentalism, and international conflict are ethical arenas every bit as much as the "big four." In these next three chapters, we will look at the kinds of moral questions that religious perspectives raise about these three issues. By doing so, not only will we see how war, environmentalism, and economic justice clearly count as moral matters; we also will discover that religious perspectives can bring great wisdom and discernment to our public consideration of them.

We begin with a consideration of war. Whether we are talking about Iraq, Iran, North Korea, or the Sudan, our moral values help determine whether armed intervention is unjustified, regrettable but necessary, or justifiable with abandon. Negotiating the relevance of moral values to political realities is a complicated endeavor, but long traditions of philosophical and theological reflection, from pacifism to just-war thinking, have been dedicated to the task of parsing the circumstances in which participation in war may be morally acceptable (if at all). Religious thinkers and traditions have been particularly active in that work, lending voice to a diversity of perspectives and at times even providing the vocabulary for thinking about war's consequences and moral boundaries.

WAR AS MORAL EVIL

Many religious persons think that their faith compels opposition to all war as immoral. Several religions contribute to the growing pacifist voice in the United States. Buddhism is a religious philosophy that emphasizes caring, compassion, and the preciousness of life. The centrality of its precept not to harm others has led many Buddhists (though not all—see Sri Lanka) to adhere to pacifist convictions. Many

Hindus and non-Hindus alike remain deeply attracted to Mahatma Gandhi's pacifist personification of that tradition. Some Muslims consider political pacifism a component of their religious duty to *jihad,* a spiritual striving toward peaceful submission to the will of God.

No pacifist tradition is more prominent in American discourse about war than Christian pacifism. Many Christian pacifists argue that war is wrong because it violates the code of ethics for which Jesus lived and died. Jesus, they say, not only endorsed the Sixth Commandment (NRSV: "You shall not murder"), but he intensified traditional Jewish teaching against unlawful violence to outlaw even hate itself: "You have heard that it was said to those of ancient times, 'You shall not murder'; and 'whoever murders shall be liable to judgment.' But I say to you that if you are angry with a brother or sister, you will be liable to judgment."[3] Rather than responding to his persecutors with violence, Jesus refused to call down the angels of heaven in his defense. He responded to his own abusers with love, peace, and forgiveness, and he insisted that his followers do the same, instructing them to love their enemies and turn their cheeks against those who would assault them. To Christian pacifists, the moral values Jesus taught require a nonviolent response to the violence and injustice of the world.

Stanley Hauerwas, once named "America's best theologian" by *Time*, has said, "I believe that I need to be nonviolent because that's what God was on the cross. That is the ultimate display of how God deals with evil—namely, God dies on the cross to forever undermine the powers of evil."[4] Against the assumption that war is a necessity in our geopolitical reality, Hauerwas insists that Jesus offered a radically different understanding of human politics, of being in community with one another. He thinks that those who would count themselves part of Christ's community must adopt that radical worldview, including its rejection of violence as part of "politics as usual." Christians must be willing to be the body of Christ in the world, says Hauerwas, and part of that task is resisting the cultural baptism of patriotic violence. In that spirit Hauerwas took President Bush to task in 2003 for using the word "evil" to describe Saddam Hussein and to justify his decision to go to war. "Bush's use of the word evil comes close to being evil, to the extent that it gives this war a religious justification (which Christians should resist)."[5] For Hauerwas, Christians are called to reject the co-opting of their religious beliefs for underwriting political decisions, to stand in critical defiance of "politics as usual," and to witness to a better way of understanding human community by modeling the pacifism of Jesus.

Critics have accused Hauerwas of peddling in a naively idealistic interpretation of Christian theology, one that renders Christian witness irrelevant to broader conversations about war and political ethics. In other words, pacifism is too, well, passive to be of any relevance to the international realities in which we live. Hauerwas usually responds by denying that it is the business of the church to say something relevant to the world. The business of the church is to be the body of Christ, regardless of whether or not the world recognizes that witness as "relevant." At the same time, he believes that in embodying Christ's radical politics, the church does have an effect on the world. For Hauerwas, the issue is not what the church has to say to the world. It is that "the church *is* what God has said about war. The church does not have an alternative to war. The church is our alternative to war."[6]

Some pacifists have argued that war is wrong, not only because it violates the teachings of Jesus, but because it will not work. Against the "realist" assumption that armed violence is necessary to defend justice and ensure peace in a violent world, some pacifists insist that violence usually fails to accomplish what realists assume it (and only it) can accomplish. They argue that war normally begets more strife, discourse, and injustice, so that the only surefire way to break the cycle of violence is to commit to peace. Martin Luther King Jr. once said, "The very destructive power of modern weapons of warfare eliminates the possibility that war may any longer serve as a negative good. And so, if we assume that life is worth living, if we assume that mankind has a right to survive, then we must find an alternative to war."[7] King's support of nonviolence was rooted not only in his religious concern for the sacredness of all life, but also in his conviction that nonviolence, and not its opposite, is the only sure method of bringing about global peace.

Some religious thinkers who agree with the pacifist insistence that we must break the cycles of violence in international politics nonetheless fear that traditional pacifism often fails to provide a realistic alternative to war. Among these critics, a movement called "just peacemaking" has gained considerable popularity in recent decades. Just peacemaking argues that the most effective and morally sound response to international strife is neither violence nor passivity. Instead, the way to break the cycles of violence in the world is to attend to the causes of violence. What makes "rogue nations" resort to conflict? What makes terrorism such an attractive option to some people? Just peacemakers argue that social and economic oppression breeds this kind of violence, so that the most effective solution to international conflict is to address these conditions.

Accordingly, just peacemakers call for addressing the economic disparity between industrial and developing nations, in order to minimize the unjust conditions that encourage violence and terrorism. They encourage sustainable economic development, fostering democratic politics, and a dedication to human rights, as ways to minimize the raw ingredients for global violence. They call for strengthening the United Nations, not only to serve as a mediating force between nations in conflict, but also to give greater voice and empowerment to nations whose current disempowerment might tempt them to violent engagement with their neighbors. Just peacemakers argue for the cultivation of diplomacy and other alternative means for negotiating conflicts between nations, so that they are less likely to resort to war. At the same time, they see great value in grassroots campaigns for peacemaking in local communities. Just peacemakers see themselves as carrying through on a theological commitment to pacifism with a more energetic program than most pacifists espouse.[8]

WAR AS INEVITABLE

At the other end of the moral spectrum from pacifists are those religious thinkers who assume that state-sponsored violence is an unavoidable byproduct of global politics in a sinful world. For this so-called realist position, no spokesperson has been more influential than theologian Reinhold Niebuhr (1892–1971). A professor of social ethics at Union Theological Seminary in New York City, Niebuhr was one of the most important voices in American politics in the twentieth century. Political thinkers of no discernible theological commitment found Niebuhr's assessment of the human condition and his understanding of the realities of politics persuasive and useful—so much so that for a time there was a group of intellectuals who identified themselves (somewhat sardonically perhaps) as "atheists for Niebuhr"! His importance in American politics during the middle of the last century is also shown by the fact that *Time* put him on its cover in 1948 and by the attention he garnered from J. Edgar Hoover, whose FBI ran a "loyalty investigation" on him in the early 1950s.[9] For a period of at least twenty years, few public intellectuals had more of an effect on American politics than Reinhold Niebuhr.

As a pastor in Detroit from 1915 to 1928, Niebuhr had a clear view of social conflict. Working on the front lines of the power struggle between American workers and industrial capitalists, he became active in the cause for labor, preaching sermons and writing editorials and eventually joining the Socialist Party for a time. He also became an outspoken critic of mainline Protestantism's response to the economic and geopolitical conflicts of the day. Christian liberalism dominated the churches in Niebuhr's time, but he found it naive and dangerous. Liberals, charged Niebuhr, went light on the doctrine of sin. They assumed that the social problems of the world were largely the product of ignorance and could be solved simply by an increase in education and the spreading of Christian sentiment.

Niebuhr came of age intellectually in the context of the First World War, the brutality of which provided a grave counterexample to liberalism's claim that human history was naturally progressing toward a more civilized age. He suspected that liberals' naiveté derived from the fact that most of them came from the upper classes of American society. He wrote in his book *Moral Man and Immoral Society*, "Evolutionary millennialism is always the hope of comfortable and privileged classes," because they lack the personal experience with life's catastrophes that makes such confidence in the progress of human history seem so unrealistic.[10] To Niebuhr's mind, however, the "kingdom of God" could never be achieved on earth so easily.

By contrast, Niebuhr offered a public theology that took seriously social conflict—between economic classes, racial groups, and nation-states—as an unavoidable facet of the human condition. Contrary to the expectation of liberals, Niebuhr argued that social groups are not "rational," so the solution to their problems cannot rest in the application of reason. They are instead dominated by competing interests and what he called "collective egoism," a preoccupation with the needs of their social group over against other social groups. What keeps these passions and interests in check is not reason, but power. Power is a necessary facet of human society, and the concentration of power is essential to establishing and maintaining order and some semblance of peace. But the concentration of power also leads to the *struggle* for power. Thus social conflict is an inevitable byproduct of the very coercive measures necessary for a society to hold together.

Given this human reality, Niebuhr argued that the best political arrangements we can hope for are those that achieve a balance of power; when that balance is threatened, military action may be necessary. From a theological point of view, Niebuhr argued that the "kingdom of God on earth" was a human impossibility. Rather than heralding in a perfect society of love and peace, the best we can achieve in human history is graded attempts at justice, sometimes backed by the power of the military state.

In his "realist" understanding of politics, Niebuhr believed that both experience and Christian theology were on his side. He was especially fond of Augustine, and he inherited from Augustine his rather pessimistic expectations for a moral society. He followed Augustine in drawing a sharp contrast between the ideals of Christianity and the realities of temporal politics, in which stability and order were the best human beings could hope to achieve. He also borrowed from Christian thought the language of original sin. Niebuhr did not worry too much about trying to root the "original" sin in time; to him, Adam and Eve were not historical figures but symbols of a deep flaw in the human condition. Human beings, he taught, are finite, limited creatures, but we are also transcendent enough to be aware of our finitude and limitations. Awareness of our limits makes us anxious, leading us to deny our limitations by asserting ourselves against one another and attempting to accumulate power. This kind of prideful self-assertion is the root of social conflict and injustice. Niebuhr believed that the theological concept of original sin gave symbolic expression to this human reality, and it made his theology more realistic than the utopian idealism of liberalism.

At the same time, Niebuhr argued that Christian theology was a *hopeful* realism, providing resources to help us understand and act in our moral world in ways that do not simply dissolve into cynical endorsements of coercive politics. Niebuhr thought it a mistake to try to apply the teachings of Jesus directly to politics. In his reading, "The ethic of Jesus does not deal at all with the immediate moral problem of every human life—the problem of arranging some kind of armistice between various contending factions and forces. It has nothing to say about the relativities of politics and economics, nor of the necessary balances of power which exist and must exist in even the most intimate social relationships."[11]

While he thought it impossible to implement perfectly religious ideals in political reality, Niebuhr did think those values were relevant to politics. Human beings may not be able to achieve the perfect "kingdom of God on earth," but the aspirations of the kingdom serve as a standard, a set of ideals, by which we may judge (and judge between) our attempts to arrange a moderately just society. Niebuhr was not willing to simply live with "politics as usual." If we cannot achieve a perfect peace, theological ideals nonetheless should motivate and guide our efforts to lessen the injustice among us.

Niebuhr's realism was quite influential in theological and political circles in the middle of the twentieth century. He spearheaded a philosophical turn from the idealism of Wilsonian politics (best symbolized in Wilson's doomed dream of a peaceful world governed by a League of Nations) to a more realistic accounting of the moral limits to social collectives. He provided theological underwriting to President Roosevelt's concerns with fascism as a threat to democratic civilization, breaking with the strategy of appeasement preferred by leading Christian pacifists of his time. At the advent of the Second World War, Niebuhr rejected pacifist calls for isolation and nonintervention, but he also refused to endorse the "holy war" rhetoric of crusaders for democracy. Instead he reminded Americans that entry into war could never be more than the lesser of two evils, though as such it was still America's moral obligation to fight back fascist aggression.

Similarly, after World War II he helped to make sense of the emerging cold war with the Soviet Union, describing it as an ideological conflict with a "demonic religion" and providing moral language for a generation of anticommunist ideologues. But even in his diatribes against communism, Niebuhr remained a "critic of national innocence,"[12] rejecting the idealistic "religion of democracy" that he thought characterized the America that emerged as a superpower from World War II. Niebuhr believed that a commitment to democracy could be as utopian and dangerous as commitment to any other absolutes, tempting the United States to commit all kinds of atrocities in its zeal to "plant the seeds of democracy" around the world. On all of these fronts, Niebuhr contributed a political vision that spoke in religious terms but was grounded in the practical realities of human politics, resigned to periodic need for violence, but consistently suspicious of zealous commitment to absolutes and ideals, whether those absolutes were theologically conservative or liberal, whether the ideal was fascism, communism, or democracy.

WAR AS REGRETTABLE, BUT JUSTIFIABLE

Reflecting some realist assumptions about the inevitability of conflict in the world, the majority voice through most of Christian history has subscribed to what is known as "just-war theory." Though not exclusively indebted to Christian thought, the history of just-war tradition is deeply rooted in Christianity. Christian just-war thought derives from thinkers like Augustine, Thomas Aquinas, Martin Luther, and John Calvin, and their legacy has had a significant impact on the theological, philosophical, and political evaluation of war in Western culture.

Christian just-war thinking begins with the presumption that killing another human being is normally wrong. It is also based in the acknowledgment that human beings are sinful and therefore will fail to live together peacefully and justly. Human societies will generate conflict with one another; greed will cause nations to try to possess another's resources, and hatred will lead them to oppress others. Occasionally restoring peace and justice will require that antagonistic states be met with violent response, that the prima facie presumption against killing be overridden by more pressing ethical responsibilities. Thus war is periodically an inevitable consequence of the unsurprising conflict between nation-states, and sometimes it is a morally justified response to unjust oppression and violence. Therefore, our moral responsibility is not always to avoid war, but to engage in war only when we are justified to do so.

What justifies a war in the eyes of this tradition? Contrary to the public rhetoric that surrounded the workup to the war in Iraq, there is more to just-war theory than just cause. To be certain, a war can be justified only if it has a just cause, which has been defined in this tradition by three circumstances: (1) self-defense, (2) intervention on behalf of another people to repel an attack on them, or (3) intervention on behalf of another people to restore their human rights and the conditions necessary for decent human existence. Notably absent in this Christian justification of war is religion or ideology as a just cause. In other words, Christian just-war theory does not endorse a war meant to spread Christianity or democracy, but sometimes war is justified in order to protect a nation (including one's own nation) from oppression or attack.

Much of the debate over whether the war in Iraq was justified seemed to stop with the question of just cause, but there is much more to this tradition that this one criterion. Just-war theory has also required that a justified war be initiated only by a legitimate authority (that is, no private grudges), that it be prosecuted with a forthright intention in addition to a legitimate stated cause, that it be engaged in only if there is a reasonable chance for success, and that it be taken up only as a last resort, after all other reasonable options (like diplomacy and sanctions) have failed. No war is justified, says this tradition, if the damage it would inflict is disproportionate to the good that we hope will come from it.

No better encapsulation of the just-war tradition has appeared in the American context than the pastoral letter from the U.S. Conference of Catholic Bishops entitled *The Challenge of Peace*. Known more recently for bungling the clergy-abuse crisis in the Catholic Church, the USCCB has for decades issued well-considered statements for public consumption on major debates over issues like economic injustice, capital punishment, and the attacks of 9/11.[13] The first of its "pastoral letters" to receive a wide reading, and the most impressive, was *The Challenge of Peace: God's Promise and Our Response*, the bishops' critique of the United States' arms race with the Soviet Union.

Published in 1983, *The Challenge of Peace* was a response to early failures to ratify the SALT II treaty between the United States and the Soviet Union, as well as to alarmingly hawkish rhetoric coming from the early Reagan administration. Administration officials had been quoted as having considered the "winnability" of a nuclear exchange, which suggested to the bishops that the American government was actually considering limited nuclear war as a legitimate military option. Concerned that the global catastrophe of a nuclear holocaust was no longer serving as a sufficient deterrent to the actual use of nuclear weapons, the bishops issued *The Challenge of Peace*, a moral evaluation of nuclear escalation and the reality of nuclear war from the perspective of Catholic moral theology.

The bishops began their pastoral letter with a dissertation on peace, as it reflects the ideals of Christian Scripture and the Catholic tradition. With this commitment to peace as their prima facie starting point, they proceeded to illustrate the historical importance of just-war theory to Catholic moral theology, and nicely summarized the criteria commonly invoked by just-war advocates. But based on these standards for justifying war, the bishops eventually implied that no war between nuclear powers could be justified, given the risk of escalation to nuclear exchange. In particular, the bishops were concerned with how nuclear war violated the just-war principle of discrimination, or "noncombatant immunity." Simply put, the principle of discrimination outlaws the intentional targeting of civilians in a military campaign. Acknowledging that no war completely avoids civilian casualties, the bishops drew a distinction between the tragic but unintended killing of nonmilitary personnel in a force-targeting assault and the deliberate targeting of civilian populations. Nuclear weapons are by nature indiscriminate in their range; even if the initial explosion is force-targeted, the long-term effects of the release of nuclear energy would be felt along a wide radius of civilian populations.[14] Because the effects of nuclear weapons are knowingly indiscriminate (indeed, that is a big part of the "fear factor" that makes the threat of nuclear attack such an effective deterrent), the bishops concluded that no use of nuclear weapons could be moral.

In fact, not only did the bishops reject the use of nuclear weapons and any military engagement that would encourage it; they also questioned the morality of even possessing nuclear weapons. Specifically, they were concerned with the "theory of deterrence" that was used at the time to justify nuclear buildup. According to a theory of deterrence, my pointing nuclear weapons at you and your pointing them at me keeps us both from using them. For my having them implies that, if you fire any of yours first, I will retaliate with many of mine. Defenders of nuclear buildup assumed that this kind of mutual threat would actually prevent the use of these weapons, but the bishops were concerned that the intention implied by the threat (or carrying out the "bluff," as it was sometimes called) was itself immoral. While they cautiously accepted deterrence as a short-term justification for possessing nuclear weapons (that is, as a transitional strategy to prevent their use), they insisted on a long-term goal of eliminating the mutual threat and bringing an end to the arms race.

Whether in the hands of Catholic bishops or others, just-war thinking is controversial. Critics argue that the just-war tradition is out of date, that it is a philosophy that matured in an age of conventional war between nation-states, but that it now struggles to respond effectively to a new age of weapons of mass destruction, terrorism, and transnational entities engaged in international conflict. Even among defenders of just-war theory, there is considerable disagreement about the criteria themselves. Some theorists include more than I have cited here, some fewer, and there is widespread debate over how to interpret the standards. There is also disagreement over whether all of the criteria must be satisfied for a war to be considered justified, or whether satisfying most of the criteria would be sufficient for a war to be substantially justified. Those who subscribe to the stricter test (that all criteria must be met) will find few wars that can truly be called justified, while those who argue that only the preponderance of the criteria need be satisfied are acknowledging that no war will be thoroughly defensible. Clearly, there is no consensus on the standards for a just war, their meanings, or their effectiveness in today's world. That disagreement leads some critics to conclude that this tradition has outlived its usefulness.

WAR, RELIGION, AND PUBLIC DEBATE

Despite the critics, however, I think that the just-war tradition still has something helpful to say in the moral evaluation of war in the twenty-first century. While it must adapt to the new features of contemporary warfare, it is capable of doing so. The criterion of legitimate authority, for instance, if taken seriously, could have called renewed attention to Congress's abdication of its role in declaring war in the months before the U.S. invasion of Iraq. The standard of last resort sharpens the debate over whether all reasonable options were exhausted in the run-up to war. The standard of reasonable chance of success forces us to define for ourselves what "success" would mean in a place like Iraq: military conquest, the ability to walk away in a timely fashion, or the construction of a democratic society? Taking seriously the importance of proportionality would have forced us to predict more carefully the consequences of an invasion for our military personnel and Iraqi civilians, and to compare that cost analysis to what we hoped to achieve in Iraq. Acknowledging the need for moral accountability for the means we employ in wartime would have provided additional muscle to beat back the consequentialist arguments employed to justify our use of torture (or "advanced interrogation techniques," as the euphemism goes).[15]

More generally, just-war theory's presence in our culture's political lexicon gives moral shape to our debates over wars and rumors of war, intentionally rebuffing the claims of political realists and some so-called values defenders that morality and war have little to do with each other. It reminds us that war is not only a matter of politics and national security, but also a moral endeavor, one subject to ethical evaluation and judgment. Whether in just-war categories, the assumptions of realism, or the ideals of pacifism, religion has been a primary source of the American moral tradition's vocabulary for ethical discourse over war. Religion could not have this kind of effect if it were incomprehensible to people beyond the communities of faith.

Niebuhr's influence on political discourse in the twentieth century happened, not in spite of his use of religious language and ideas, but arguably because of it. To those who assume that religion acts as a "conversation-stopper" in political debate, Niebuhr exists as a powerful counterexample, for he successfully mined religious language for conceptual categories that a broad political audience found useful. Whether or not they subscribed to his Christian outlook, Niebuhr's fans found something persuasive in his realistic description of political power. Niebuhr himself clearly believed that theology could make some contribution to broader political conversations, by giving expression to both the incredible creativity of the human species and our most destructive passions.

Similarly, it is clear that *The Challenge of Peace* is a Catholic document written by bishops in the authority of church tradition; but while it appeals to Catholic ideals, it also addresses a broader American public, including the nation's political leaders. The bishops specifically targeted their letter to "two distinct but overlapping audiences," the Catholic faithful and "the wider civil community, . . . all people of good will," and they were confident that the letter would speak to all Americans because of the prevalence of just-war theory in Western discussions of war.[16] They also assumed the public would appreciate their argument because its ideals resonated with fundamental values that all Americans—not just Catholics—could recognize as important: peace, justice, and global interdependence.

Their hope for an extended audience was realized, for *The Challenge of Peace* received a wide reading among sympathizers and opponents, generating enormous press and critique. The Reagan administration itself evidently found the letter a compelling contribution to the public debate, because members of the administration saw the need to meet with the bishops as they were finalizing the letter. Among critics of nuclear armament, *The Challenge of Peace* reinvigorated appeals to just-war theory and demonstrated its relevance to a "new moment" in global conflict defined largely by weapons of mass destruction. Even for its most energetic opponents, however, the ability to respond to *The Challenge of Peace* implied that it was at least comprehensible, if not ultimately persuasive, to Catholics and non-Catholics alike.

The work of the Catholic bishops, the legacy of Reinhold Niebuhr, and the contributions of countless religious persons and communities to debates over more recent wars enrich our public moral discourse. They call our attention to the moral implications of and boundaries to the use of violence to settle international disputes, and they provide us vocabulary and worldviews through which to evaluate our decisions to go (or refuse to go) to war. More broadly, in a political climate dominated by debates over abortion and homosexuality, thoughtful religious perspectives remind us that our attitudes toward war also say something about our nation's commitment to moral values.

9
Tree Huggers and Bible-Thumpers Unite!

Environmentalists have struggled for decades to get the broader American public to take their agenda seriously. Then in 2006 Al Gore's documentary *An Inconvenient Truth* raised the profile of climate change and ecological destruction. In that film, the former vice president largely steered clear of partisan politics, insisting that "ultimately [global warming] is really not a political issue so much as a moral issue. If we allow this to happen, it is deeply unethical." What he meant was that our responsibility to the environment—to recognize the negative impact we are having on the earth and to take the necessary steps to reverse the destruction—transcends political differences. If we attend to the overwhelming evidence that virtually all reputable scientists agree is valid, then global warming should appear to us at least as compelling a moral crisis as (and less debatable than) abortion or gay marriage. Our response to the crisis says worlds about our collective sense of ethics; it speaks to the "things we ought to do and the kinds of people we ought to be." Despite its absence from the usual list of issues trumpeted under the banner of "moral values," more and more citizens see climate change as the *ultimate* moral issue, the one ethical responsibility in which our failure to act invites catastrophe.

For some, one of the surprising aspects of the recent surge in popular interest in environmental issues is the growing role of religion. These days religious communities are often the primary sponsors of local environmental activism. Organizations like the National Wildlife

Federation and the Sierra Club find they need religion "liaisons" to connect their groups with the growing interest in ecological causes among persons of faith. Perhaps most surprising to many environmentalists, Christian evangelicals are becoming a powerful voice in the climate-change movement, with leaders like Rick Warren and Richard Cizik leading the charge. More and more Americans recognize that care for the environment is a "moral values" issue with implications at least as great as the "big four," and increasingly religious persons and communities are on the front lines of these battles for environmental responsibility.

It has not always been this way. Some traditions, like Buddhism and Native American religions, are known for the respect for nature they have long encouraged, but the so-called Judeo-Christian tradition has appeared, at best, ambivalent toward the natural world and, at worst, enthusiastic about our destructive habits of consumption. But American Jews and Christians are reinterpreting their traditions' perspectives on ecology, and given their cultural dominance in the United States, the push for "creation care" from these faith communities promises only to raise the prominence of this issue in our collective conscience.

FILL THE EARTH AND SUBDUE IT

Western religion does not have a great track record when it comes to the environment. Historian Lynn White wrote a classic article in the 1960s in which he argued that Christianity was largely responsible for underwriting our disrespect for nature in the West.[1] According to White, our misuse of the environment is a habit that goes back to early modern Europe, when urban development and the evolution of modern economic systems resulted in rates of human consumption that were checked only by our technological resources, at a time when the rate of progress constantly upped the scale on which we could dominate, control, and consume the natural world around us.

White argued that the philosophical justification for such rampant consumption and destruction enjoyed even deeper roots, in medieval Christian theology, which he called "the most anthropocentric religion the world has seen." Christianity encouraged a sharp distinction, even antagonism, between human beings and the rest of the natural world. Human beings were more Godlike than they were like the rest of creation, created to "be fruitful and multiply, and fill the earth and subdue it; and have dominion over the fish of the sea and over the birds of the air and over every living thing that moves upon the earth."[2] Nature was inferior and incomplete, and human beings as the *imago dei* were put on the earth to dominate and domesticate nature, to use it to satisfy our own desires. The exploitation of nature, then, was part of humanity's calling to do God's will on earth, and "dominion theology" provided the worldview that zealously drove the technological rape of the environment that has characterized Western culture since the eighteenth century.

Countless historians and theologians have lined up in support of or opposition to White's implication of Christianity in the ecological crisis, and the essay has been the source of endless debate. Those sympathetic to White's reading of history agree that Christianity's contribution to environmental degradation has been the cultural dominance of its anthropocentrism, or its preoccupation with human beings and insistence on casting them as the center of a Christian cosmology. They argue that biblical theology inordinately focuses on God's relationship with human beings, at the expense of God's relationship with the rest of the created order. Christian orthodoxy prefers the language of God's transcendence beyond nature over talk of divine immanence within it, consistently depicting God as having human features and traits. The ultimate instance of Christian anthropocentrism is the doctrine of incarnation, which represents the pinnacle of God's love through the collapse of the divine into the human.

Some feminist theologians argue that cultural hostility toward women also contributes to the abuse of nature. Christianity perpetuated certain dualisms inherited from Greco-Roman culture: male versus female, reason versus emotion, mind versus body, civilization versus nature. Associating the first items in each pair, men were regarded as the embodiment of right reason and civil order, whereas women and their messy reproductive processes epitomized raw emotion, the "unclean" body, and the untamed natural world. Christian theology insinuated that God was more like the first items than the second; God was malelike if not technically gendered, and was eminently orderly and reasonable. Opposed to this rational, male God was a creation that was disorderly, dirty, feminine, and wild. Fear of the natural and the degradation of women perpetuated one another, leading to a European culture that was as environmentally destructive as it was misogynist.[3]

Other critics of religion charge that our relationship with the natural world is threatened by the hostility toward science that many Protestant conservatives harbor. Suspicion of modern science among evangelicals goes back to the emergence of evolutionary biology in the late nineteenth century. Evangelicals were never categorically hostile to science, but they subscribed to an old school of deductive scientific reasoning that was increasingly pushed aside in the 1880s and 1890s by Darwin's theories of natural selection and by modern attempts to date the earth geologically. This new science was not as compatible with a literal reading of the Bible as the more Baconian scientific worldview had been. Liberal-leaning Protestants responded to modern science by incorporating it; traditional theological claims that seemed to contradict what evolutionary biology taught were jettisoned or revised to reflect better what was known to be scientifically true.

Conservative evangelicals, however, rejected Darwinian science as a challenge to biblical religion; if modern science contradicted something taught by a traditional reading of the Bible, then the scientific claim should be rejected or revised as erroneous, for the Bible is the only reliable and objective source of what is true. The evangelical hostility toward modern science received its most infamous public attention in the Scopes "monkey trial" of 1925, which led to the disgrace of fundamentalism in American culture and the retreat of many evangelicals to a cultural underground that lasted until the 1950s.[4]

Evangelicals then reemerged to become the powerful cultural and political force they remain today, and they brought their suspicion of modern science with them. Hostile toward the scientific establishment because of its association with the teaching of evolution, many evangelicals have waged a kind of culture war against conventional science as a threat to biblical religion and the moral values it represents. (Many in the scientific community have fired back in this culture war, showing open disdain for religion as the enemy to rational reflection and a scientifically informed culture. Among these combatants, Richard Dawkins is currently the noisiest.) One byproduct of this hostility toward science has been the categorical dismissal of scientific claims regarding global warming. Some of that dismissal is the product of conservative politics (the environmental movement is seen as linked to big government and a threat to business interests), but some of it is a reflection of philosophical distrust of the scientific community among conservative American Protestants, a hostility a century in the making.

So when critics charge religion with being an instigator of the current ecological crisis, there is some validity to this charge. "Dominion theology" has been taken as biblical license to see the earth as a storehouse of resources whose only value is their usefulness to us. Anthropocentric theology encourages believers to assume that God loves human beings more than the rest of creation, and that creation was put in place for nothing more than the satisfaction of human desires. When religion has encouraged antagonism between the human and the natural worlds, or between belief and science, this has only aggravated the destructive relationship we have with our ecosystem. Historically, it seems that religion has been largely to blame for the environmental crisis we now face.

THE EARTH IS THE LORD'S, AND ALL THAT IS IN IT

Religion's negative attitudes toward nature are only part of the story, however. As responsible as Judaism and Christianity may have been for theologically underwriting our abuse of the environment, these religions have also been home to voices who clamor for us to take seriously our relationship with the natural world, as a moral responsibility. The Genesis charge to human beings to "have dominion" over creation, the root of so much of our dysfunctional relationship with nature, has also been interpreted not as predatory license but as a calling to responsible stewardship. Human beings are set over creation, which God declared "very good," in order to be its caretakers. God "owns" the natural world and entrusts human beings with the task of managing creation in ways that respect it, not rape and pillage it. "The earth is the Lord's, and all that is in it," and as such it has intrinsic moral value.[5]

The Hebrew psalms testify to this value, while the prophets illustrate nature's dignity by occasionally depicting it as God's ally and witness against human waywardness. The land and its creatures mourn with God at human beings' inability to live in peace with each other and the world. In the New Testament, the apostle Paul takes up that theme, insisting that all of creation mourns as a result of human sin. These allusions suggest something other than hostile dualism between an anthropomorphic God and a deviant nature. They suggest loving intimacy between God and the natural world, standing together against a human species bent on betraying the Divine, in part by abusing the world around it.

As White suggested, there is plenty in Western religion that is anti-ecological, but biblical religions also host great sensitivity for stewardship, the duty to act as trustees of nature, protecting and developing the natural world in line with God's love for it. Especially in the last decade or so, Jewish thinkers have channeled the work of Hans Jonas and the resources of Kabbalah mysticism for rethinking some of the anthropocentrism in biblical religion. Christian history is replete with thinkers who recognized that nonhuman creatures have intrinsic value because of their relationship to God as creator. Examples include Augustine, Basil the Great, John Chrysostom, and of course Francis of Assisi, whom the late Pope John Paul II proclaimed the patron saint of promoters of ecology. One contemporary Christian theologian, Sallie McFague, recommends that we think of the world as God's body, a suggestive metaphor that encourages not only greater respect for the environment, but greater value for our own embodied existence. Bill McKibben, a Methodist and frequent contributor to the mainline Christian newsmagazine the *Christian Century*, has been for decades among the most prominent environmental activists in the country, embodying the potential for rapprochement between religious persons and environmental activism.

The resurgence of these themes and the pressures of the moment have led to a vigorous environmentalism within Judaism and Christianity. Now it is commonplace to see religious people advocating for environmental protections based in part in religious motivations and justification. A delightfully practical example of this leadership within Judaism is a joint effort by the Jewish Council for Public Affairs (JCPA) and the Coalition on the Environment and Jewish Life (COEJL) to launch a campaign called "How Many Jews Does It Take to Change a Light Bulb?" The specific goal of the program is to encourage and underwrite the switch from incandescent to fluorescent bulbs, but the larger agenda is to raise awareness among Jews of the consequences of global warming. The campaign encourages educational efforts, like distributing copies of *An Inconvenient Truth* and coordinating visits by leading scientists to local synagogues. Through their efforts, the JCPA and COEJL call on Jews and their religious communities to get involved in public conversations and concrete actions on behalf of environmental care.[6]

Christian churches too have been active in the environmental movement for decades. They were involved from the beginning with Earth Day, and most mainline denominations have departments dedicated to environmental issues. My own Presbyterian Church (U.S.A.) has an office called the Environmental Justice Ministries, which coordinates educational opportunities for church members to learn more about environmental responsibility and advocacy. The office also works with the PC(USA) Washington Office to lobby for earth-friendly federal legislation, and with the World Council of Churches to address global ecological issues. Similarly, the United Methodists, American Baptists, Evangelical Lutherans, and others have long histories of working on environmental issues. The National Council of Churches has an Eco-Justice Program, with multiple aims to combat pollution, to educate on the benefits of conservation and maintaining biodiversity, and to protect communities vulnerable to environmental hazards. The NCC also teamed up with the Sierra Club to work on a public awareness campaign aimed against drilling for oil in Alaska.[7]

It is not just from the more liberal wing of Christianity that we hear calls for ecological sensibility. As an indication of the seriousness with which the Catholic Church takes global warming, Pope Benedict XVI included pollution in his recent update of the church's list of deadly sins.[8] Before him Pope John Paul II issued a treatise on the ecological crisis in which he developed the themes of stewardship and common responsibility, insisted on the aesthetic value of creation (as opposed to seeing nature as only instrumentally valuable), called for more education on ecological responsibility, and pushed for the recognition of the environmental crisis as an acute moral issue.[9] Reflecting the concerns of the most recent pontiffs, the U.S. Conference of Catholic Bishops promotes its own Environmental Justice Program, an education and activism program that prepares parishes to deal with the issues of justice and responsibility in protecting the earth (and the poor who suffer disproportionately from environmental hazards).

The USCCB in 2001 released its own public statement on the environment, *Global Climate Change: A Plea for Dialogue, Prudence, and the Common Good.* In this paper, the bishops invoke the Catholic concern for the common good to include the entire ecosystem as well as future generations of the human community. Consistent with Catholic social justice, they point out ways that developed nations are disproportionately responsible for the causes of global warming, while developing nations will carry the costs. They call for civility in a public debate over the environment prone to partisan politics and sound bites. They commend to that debate the virtue of prudence, a norm at home in both Catholic theology and moral philosophy, a "practical wisdom" that leads us to seek out the best scientific information on the subject and to initiate deliberate action in response to it.[10]

The Catholic Church's position demonstrates that environmentalism is not just a "moral values" issue for traditionally liberal communities in American religion. It also exemplifies the ability of religious perspectives to offer to the public debate language and arguments that are comprehensible, even useful, to participants beyond their religious communities. Increasingly, religious Americans both conservative and liberal are insisting that the environmental crisis be taken seriously as a matter of moral responsibility, and they are making substantive contributions to that debate.

EVANGELICALS AND "CREATION CARE"

For many observers, the most surprising wind change in the global-warming debate has occurred among evangelical Christians. To be sure, some evangelicals for years have been calling for greater sensitivity to our environmental impact, as an aspect of the responsibilities we have as stewards of God's creation. Jim Wallis's progressive evangelical organization, Sojourners, has advocated "eco-justice" as part of its broader call for global peace and justice. Ronald Sider in 1993 helped form the Evangelical Environmental Network, a group that seeks to educate and mobilize evangelicals to advocate for policies that protect the environment. The EEN's mission is firmly rooted in evangelical principles; its mission statement consists of biblical quotations that root ecological concern in a belief in the lordship of God in Christ, in a respect for the earth as divine gift, in a sense of responsibility that derives from Christian vocation, and in a concern for human sisters and brothers who may suffer from the degradation of the environment. The EEN spearheaded the 2002 campaign that asked "What Would Jesus Drive?"—an effort to highlight the moral significance of driving environmentally friendly vehicles, instead of gas-guzzling SUVs. For the EEN, environmental responsibility is summed up in the catchphrase "creation care," the duty to be good stewards of the world God creates and infuses with intrinsic value.

More surprisingly, prominent *conservative* evangelical leaders have recently joined the fight for environmental protections. Megachurch pastor Rick Warren, best-selling author of *A Purpose-Driven Life*, has labored to expand the "moral values" radar of American evangelicals to include social issues beyond the "big four." Without retreating from his opposition to abortion and gay marriage (opposition that made him a controversial pick for inclusion in the inauguration of President Obama), Warren has been active in combating global poverty and raising awareness of the continuing HIV/AIDS pandemic, especially in

Africa. He also has emphasized the need for evangelical Christians—and Americans more broadly—to take seriously the problem of global warming, commending environmental stewardship as part of the "purpose-driven life."

Richard Cizik, former Washington lobbyist for the National Association of Evangelicals, has been a bold voice of concern over climate change among mainstream evangelicals, despite strong resistance to his message from other evangelical leaders. Citing a conversion to environmentalism akin to his conversion to Christianity, Cizik has worked to elevate global warming on the moral agenda of the evangelical community. He also has reached out energetically to cooperate on environmental issues with nonevangelical organizations. "If we've worked with Free Tibet on religious freedom, the Congressional Black Caucus on slavery, Gloria Steinem and feminists on rape, and the gay and lesbian lobby on AIDS," says Cizik, "why can't we work with environmentalists?"[11]

Warren, Cizik, and other prominent evangelicals made a profound statement in defense of the environment in 2006 when they launched a program called the Evangelical Climate Initiative, a multimedia effort to push federal legislation that would better protect the environment, while trying to convince fellow evangelicals that climate change is a public issue of extreme moral importance. The first stage of the initiative was the release of a statement, "Climate Change: An Evangelical Call to Action," that was signed by eighty-six evangelical leaders, including many megachurch pastors and presidents of several evangelical colleges. The statement asserts that the scientific evidence of human-induced climate change is real, and that the consequences of climate change will be felt throughout the global ecosystem and will negatively affect all members of the human community, but especially the poor.

The statement cites several theological convictions as a basis for evangelicals to act on behalf of the environment. It urges response to climate change, not only out of respect for the Creator of the earth (calling ecological damage "an offense against God Himself") and good stewardship of the gifts God has given us, but also out of a spirit of love for our neighbors. Interestingly, this appeal to neighbor-love implies that nonhuman inhabitants of the earth are to be considered our neighbors, a significant move away from the anthropocentrism of traditional Christian theology, which tends to regard nonhuman life primarily as resources. To be sure, many of the statement's nontheological arguments for environmental awareness reflect the traditional instrumental valuation of nature—the idea that we ought to conserve our ecological resources for the best interests of the human community. But the call also implies the inherent value of the earth as a product of God's creative love, independent of its "usefulness" to us. Equally noteworthy, the statement calls evangelicals to support action from churches and individuals, but also from businesses and government, an important multifaceted approach from a constituency long associated with the Republican Party's aversion to "big government."

The Evangelical Climate Initiative was a remarkable development, coming out of an increasingly vocal caucus of evangelical environmentalists. It is important to acknowledge that many evangelicals are not on board with the concerns over climate change. The statement itself admits that many of its signatories required considerable persuasion to view this issue with the same urgency as abortion or gay marriage. As environmentally concerned evangelicals were preparing the statement, Richard Land of the Southern Baptist Convention, James Dobson of Focus on the Family, and Chuck Colson of Prison Ministries pressured the National Association of Evangelicals to distance itself from the effort, arguing that there is "no consensus" on the science behind climate change.[12] This opposition initially led Cizik, one of the principal forces behind the statement, to withhold his signature, fearing that to sign it would inappropriately imply that the NAE itself had endorsed it.

With time, however, Cizik became bolder in his willingness to advocate publicly for environmental issues, even in the face of intense criticism within evangelicalism. For a while the NAE resisted conservative calls for his dismissal as chief Washington lobbyist, but Dobson, Tony Perkins of the Family Research Council, and others continued in their calls for Cizik to be fired, claiming that his "preoccupation" with climate change was distracting the NAE from attention to "the great moral issues of our time" (by which they meant abortion and gay marriage). Eventually, in late 2008, Cizik's suggestion in an NPR interview that he was open to the idea of civil unions (as opposed to gay marriage) provided the pretext for his removal. Cizik was forced to resign, but that setback has not dampened the enthusiasm for environmentalism among a growing caucus of evangelical moderates.

RELIGION AND ENVIRONMENTAL DISCOURSE

What do these religious perspectives bring to our public discourse? Why should we invite them to the table? The first reason is a bit negative: religious perspectives are important to our conversations over ecological issues precisely because of religion's role in getting us into this mess. The details of Lynn White's reading of history are debatable, but there is some truth to his claim that biblical religion has been a source of substantial philosophical antagonism between human beings and the natural world. Religion has been used to define nature as an "other" that we are commissioned to use, abuse, and subdue. Given the degree to which Western religion has historically underwritten our technological destruction of nature, an antidote to that perspective coming from the same religious traditions is key to ending our unhealthy attitudes. Including religious perspectives in our public discourse reminds us that there are different, healthier ways to interpret Judaism and Christianity on the subjects of nature and environmental responsibility.

More positively, opening public discourse to religious perspective substantially increases the political presence and power of the environmental movement. For despite recent polls that see a drop in religiosity in the United States, this remains a country dominated by citizens who identify themselves as religious and who think about themselves and their obligations at least partially in faith terms. To be sure, the inclusion of religious perspectives means that those who deny the reality of global warming will also get a voice. But the chorus of religious persons who are committed to environmental responsibility is growing exponentially, and growth among evangelicals is especially promising. As long as evangelicals continue to enjoy the substantial power they have in American politics (and although that power would seem to have waned recently, evangelicals are not going away any time soon), their inclusion in these conversations makes it all the likelier that environmentalism will continue its rise up the list of moral issues to which Americans collectively give priority.

Beyond the politics of numbers, though, religious language contributes substantively to our conversation by giving a sense of ultimate moral importance to our concerns for the earth. The poetic force of regard for nature as a reflection of God's creative love may serve as an effective complement to pragmatic and consequentialist appeals that emphasize the effect of global warming on human society. The religious environmentalism we have surveyed here awards the natural world's intrinsic, rather than instrumental, value, and it distinctly (if not uniquely) reminds us that we are part of a greater whole. It emphasizes the moral value of collective responsibility and, as we saw in the Evangelical Climate Initiative, expands the definition of "community" to include nonhuman life. In doing so, contemporary religious voices offer a corrective, not just to the darker moments of their own traditions, but also to the current materialistic culture that deceptively pits environmental protections against economic self-interest. Environmentally conscious religious perspectives remind us that the earth is not just a resource for human consumption, but also a good to preserve in its own right, "kin" to human community.

Finally, theological support for environmentalism promises to bring together otherwise disparate constituents, providing bridges necessary to get conservatives and progressives working with each other. As a result, it encourages a spirit of collaboration, the opportunity for Americans of different starting points—religious and nonreligious—to talk together and discover shared values and concerns for the natural world. Theological commitments can bring religious conservatives and liberals together on the environment, but in the past couple of years we have also seen so-called secular environmental organizations and similarly concerned religious groups awkwardly but enthusiastically exploring prospects for mutual support and cooperation. Arguably environmentalists' current hope for consensus and movement on issues like climate change would not be nearly as realistic if it were not for the political power, theological motivation, and bridge-building potential of the renewed ecological engagement among faith communities.

10
It's the Economy (Again), Stupid!

A popular bumper sticker during the 1992 presidential campaign declared that "It's the Economy, Stupid!" The decal was Democrats' way of dismissing Republican priorities as a distraction from what was weighing most on the minds of voters that fall, namely the specter of economic recession. With apologies for the name-calling, which does not really further the aims of civility, we could break out those bumper stickers all over again in our time. In particular, many Americans concerned with the moral direction of their country would argue that our political preoccupation with abortion and gay marriage misses the mark. It is the economy—again—that most threatens to test our collective commitment to moral values.

THE RIGHTEOUS KNOW THE RIGHTS OF THE POOR

In the United States alone, almost 40 million people live in poverty, almost half of whom are children. Almost 50 million Americans have no health insurance.[1] Throughout the world, the number of people suffering from hunger or poverty is in the neighborhood of 960 million, and 16 million children die every year from malnutrition or insufficient health care.[2] Yet caring for the poor is seldom listed among important "moral values" when the media takes up the subject.

Religious thinkers and communities have had a concern for the poor and disenfranchised for a long time, though, and unsurprisingly much of the leadership on this issue these days comes from more liberal-leaning religious groups, who tend to emphasize social justice among their moral values. The 2006 General Assembly of the Presbyterian Church (U.S.A.) officially called again on Congress to bring the minimum wage in line with actual costs of living, and the National Council of Churches launched a "Let Justice Roll" campaign, dedicated to the same goal. Mainline Protestant denominations like the United Methodist Church pushed for passage of the Global Poverty Act in 2008, which would have required the president to develop a comprehensive strategy to adhere to the Millennium Development Goals that the United Nations adopted in 2000, specifically to cut extreme poverty in half by 2015 through aid, trade, and debt relief. Methodists, Presbyterians, and other Protestant denominations have adopted a common "Social Creed for the Twenty-first Century," in which they commit to combating poverty, working for a living wage, protecting the rights and well-being of laborers, and safeguarding family and leisure time in an economic culture increasingly driven only by "bottom line" concerns.[3] Ecumenical Christian groups like Bread for the World, an organization that has been pressing the federal government on behalf of the poor since 1972, advocate for more aggressive policy to fight domestic and global poverty. Bread for the World is an especially interesting example, not just because it brings together a diverse collection of Christians, but because it enjoys support across the political spectrum as well. Its board of directors has included conservatives like former Republican senators Bob Dole and Chuck Hagel as well as liberals like Clinton administration figures Mike McCurry and Leon Panetta.

Those who view poverty as an acute moral issue include religious groups beyond Protestantism, of course. Jewish thinkers and activists are instrumental in the public discourse and policy debate over economic justice. Immediately after the 2004 presidential election, while everyone was actively talking about the political role of morality, Rabbi David Saperstein, head of the Religious Action Center of Reform Judaism, counseled Democratic members of Congress to think of their antipoverty policy goals in religious and moral terms and to talk about them in that language as well.[4] Synagogues regularly organize petitions and protests to direct state and federal legislators to develop policies that better serve the poor.[5] And in 2008 the Jewish Council for Public Affairs launched a national antipoverty campaign aimed at motivating advocacy for the poor among Jews and raising the importance of economic justice in that year's presidential campaign.

From where does this moral fervor for economic justice derive? For starters, it originates in a biblical worldview in which all of creation, including material wealth, belongs to God. As we saw in the last chapter, the Hebrew Scriptures assert that God alone can claim ultimate ownership of the earth's resources, so that material possessions are best understood as a trust given to us by God. Sometimes wealth can be interpreted as a sign of divine blessing, and sometimes it represents an opportunity for human beings to fulfill social and moral obligations, but in the Hebrew Bible the use of wealth is consistently evaluated in terms of responsible stewardship. What makes for good stewardship is defined by another prominent theme of the Hebrew Bible, economic justice, or more specifically, economic arrangements that promote fairness but that also ensure basic sustenance for the economically disadvantaged in the community.

Throughout the Torah, the Mosaic law dictates measures to safeguard the poor, like restrictions on loan practices (a lender cannot demand as collateral something of basic need, like a coat) and limits to the rights of property owners (a farmer should leave a border of crops around his lands to ensure that there are adequate leftovers in the fields for those who need to scavenge). The prophets routinely blistered political leaders for consolidating power by abusing the poor, and the Hebrew poets and philosophers insisted that wisdom, righteousness, and economic justice were inextricably related: "The righteous know the rights of the poor; the wicked have no such understanding."[6] The Christian New Testament carries on these themes of justice, God's preferential concern for the poor, and our mutual responsibility. Because of these prominent themes in their scriptural worldview, many Jews and Christians insist that providing for the basic needs of all citizens is not just a good political idea, but also a moral imperative.

Lately, health care is one of those basic needs to which religious people are applying their religious and moral fervor in public ways. In June 2009 Christian and Jewish leaders joined representatives from Islam, Hinduism, and a host of other religious traditions at a national interfaith prayer service on behalf of health-care reform. The service took place on Freedom Plaza in Washington, but hundreds of satellite services were held simultaneously in cities across the country, resulting in what has been called the largest faith-inspired mobilization on health-care reform. What brought these different religious citizens together was a shared conviction that the insufficiency of health care in the United States was not only a political problem but an ethical and spiritual crisis as well. One of the prayer service's leaders, Sister Simone Campbell of NETWORK (a Catholic social-justice lobby), called the fact that 50 million Americans lack access to health care "shocking" and a "moral outrage."[7] The result of a shotgun coalition of religious organizations created barely two months before, the "Believe Together: Health Care for All" gathering was meant to call attention to the consensus within American religion that universal, affordable, and accessible health care is a requirement of an ethical society.

Pursuing economic justice has been a long-standing priority for liberal-leaning religious communities, and most of the organizations who signed on to the "Believe Together" prayer service meet this profile. But evangelicals have been increasingly prominent in recent public discussions of poverty, unemployment, and the lack of health insurance too. Tony Campolo, a renegade evangelical and incredibly popular voice among young Christians, has insisted throughout his career as a scholar, preacher, and writer that evangelicalism requires a commitment to social justice. Ronald Sider, founder of Evangelicals for Social Action and author of the now-classic text (among evangelicals, at least), *Rich Christians in an Age of Hunger*, forcefully establishes the biblical imperative for Christians to advocate for the poor.[8]

Campolo and Sider are normally located in the left wing of the evangelical community, but even some more conventional evangelicals have been pushing their religious kin to emphasize social justice as a moral imperative. Before his fall from grace in a sex scandal, megachurch pastor Ted Haggard was increasingly vocal on the need for evangelicals to expand their moral concern beyond abortion and marriage to include the eradication of poverty. Rick Warren, as mentioned earlier, donates much of his time and money to combating the AIDS pandemic in Africa. And Richard Cizik has argued that a commitment to combat global poverty should characterize evangelicalism as much as opposition to abortion.[9] Perhaps the most intriguing recent example of evangelical influence on the public debate over poverty occurred in Alabama in 2003, when Governor Bob Riley attempted to overhaul the state tax system, to shift more responsibility to the wealthy and offer relief to struggling Alabamians—citing his evangelical convictions as motivation.[10] These evangelical voices show that a commitment to economic justice is more than just a liberal mantra. It is part of the biblical mandate and essential to what it means to follow Jesus.[11]

Perhaps the most important religious leader in the fight against poverty these days is Jim Wallis, an evangelical who is equally comfortable in the company of Christians like Rick Warren and liberal activists like U2 front man Bono. He has the ability to join forces with nonevangelical liberals—and in fact to forge deep friendships with them—while at the same time speaking the biblical and theological language of traditional Christianity. He has gained the ear of some of the most important political and moral leaders around the world and participated in groundbreaking global summits on poverty and justice. He participates in these larger conversations, not by muting his religious starting point, but by owning it and commending it as a way to translate the force of the moral imperative to millions of committed Christians.

Wallis's 2008 book *The Great Awakening: Reviving Faith and Politics in a Post-Religious Right America* aims to capture the progressive social-reform spirit of historical evangelicalism and channel it into an address of our most pressing problems.[12] In this book Wallis proposes solutions to racial injustice, the impasse over abortion, and the immorality of war, but his deepest passion is for the poor, both in the United States and throughout the world. Appealing to the Hebrew prophetic tradition, Wallis calls on Americans (especially religious citizens) to live with the poor, to forge a relationship with them that compels a deeper commitment to eradicating poverty in the world. From New Orleans to Africa, Wallis insists that "if our gospel message is not 'good news to the poor,' it is simply not the gospel of Jesus Christ."[13] To this progressive evangelical, poverty is most certainly a moral issue.

ECONOMIC CRISIS AND MORAL MALNUTRITION

In their public insistence on economic justice, religious persons and communities are active in debates over specific issues like health care and world hunger. But they also lend their voices to more fundamental questions. In particular, the economic crisis has caused religious thinkers to join other critics in calling into question the moral axis of American capitalism.

In the summer of 2009, Bill Moyers convened a roundtable of three prominent Christian leaders to discuss a theological reading of the economic crisis.[14] Cornel West, Serene Jones, and Gary Dorrien all represent a progressive Christianity reminiscent of the social gospel from the early twentieth century. Each of them insists that Christianity has something important to lend to our address of the economic crisis. The first thing it offers is language to properly understand "what's going on." West, who teaches at Princeton and is widely regarded as one of the most provocative public theologians of our time, insists that our current predicament reflects a "spiritual crisis, a kind of spiritual malnutrition" that is not immediately apparent from the government's unimaginative address of the problems.

Gary Dorrien, the Reinhold Niebuhr Professor of Social Ethics at Union Seminary in New York, agrees, arguing that our society has "stoked and celebrated greed virtually to the point of self-destruction." We have built an entire economic system on the collective delusion that material acquisition is the path to ultimate fulfillment and that unfettered profit is more important than social solidarity. Our investment in this delusion is so complete, says Dorrien, that we cannot see how our abandonment of mutual accountability and responsibility is the root of our economic problems. Instead, financial and political elites respond to the economic crisis by doing more of the same, excusing individual CEOs and propping up the responsible institutions in a desperate effort to get us back to where we were before. They utterly refuse to critically evaluate our current system and to imaginatively rethink what constitutes a healthy and just economy.

Jones, the president of Union Seminary, believes that the theological language of sin evocatively exposes the kind of delusion under which we have been living. Sin describes the almost intractable temptation to see ourselves or our social group as the center of the universe. It speaks of our inability to live together without making profound errors, as well as the way that injustice takes not only interpersonal but also structural and systemic form. Sin gives name to the inevitability of forces in human community that lead the powerful to gain at the expense of the powerless, an apt description of the roots of the most recent mess in the housing and financial industries.

Of course, one need not subscribe to a Christian doctrine of sin to recognize the kind of deeply rooted injustice to which it speaks. As West put it, "Thucydides understood that power corrupts and absolute power corrupts absolutely . . . [and contemporary Nigerian writer] Wole Soyinka understands the role of greed, selfishness, egoism, narcissism. Neither one of them have a notion of original sin." But the language of sin translates especially well in American democracy, where even our system of checks and balances testifies to the human penchant for greed and abuse of power. Theological language pushes beyond bad luck or individual duplicity for an explanation of social turmoil like this; it reminds us that these kinds of experiences are often instigated by, as Jones put it, a "crisis of value."

Jones, West, and Dorrien insist that recognizing this crisis of value is necessary to ensure true social recovery. Equally essential is changing the vantage point from which we look at our economic problems. Toward this end, Dorrien commends the idea of "economic democracy," which he thinks serves as a "brake on human greed and will to power." He and West expose the tendency of the West's financial and political oligarchy to prop itself up, noting how alarmingly easy it was to come up with billions of dollars to bail out the very financial institutions that precipitated the fall, with little accountability, rather than funneling support directly to the citizens most ruined by the catastrophe. They argue that a theological perspective brings to the table a capacity to see social crisis from the underside. Charging Obama with capitulating to the Wall Street perspective that got us into this mess, West argues that Christianity gives voice to the poor and working class, prophetically demanding that any address of economic problems begins with them. Along with this radical reprioritization of perspective, theology contributes more humane definitions of love and justice as social organizing principles.

Their emphasis on love and justice resonates with another important theological contribution to public debate over the economic crisis, Pope Benedict's encyclical *Caritas in Veritate* (*Love in Truth*). The Catholic Church has a rich tradition of social teachings in which it has long emphasized economic justice and the needs of the poor. The modern Catholic social tradition goes back to 1891, when Pope Leo XIII released *Rerum Novarum*, a groundbreaking pastoral letter that criticized the growing capitalistic culture in the West, demanded economic justice for those on whose backs capitalism was built, and sided (cautiously) with the burgeoning labor movements in Europe and the United States. Supporting both a fundamental right to private property and a commitment to the common good, Pope Leo insisted that capitalism and Christian justice were compatible, but that religion, business, and the state all shared the responsibility to safeguard the working poor, "so that they who contribute so largely to the advantage of the community may themselves share in the benefits they create."[15] He argued for the payment of decent wages, for the right of workers to unionize, for a fair working day, and against child labor. *Rerum Novarum* was the first in a series of modern papal encyclicals, public letters written for the Catholic faithful and (as later encyclicals would put it) for "all men of good will." It was also the beginning of the modern Vatican's long-standing habit of weighing in for the cause of economic justice for the working and extreme poor.

Pope Benedict continued that tradition in *Caritas in Veritate*, issued in July 2009. In it the pope invoked common themes from Catholic social teachings to call for a new perspective on the global economic crisis. He argued that global economic problems had to be understood as one element of a larger moral crisis facing the world, one that had implications not only for the financial sector but for politics, the environment, and science as well. He argued that the root of the problem was a reductionist understanding of human beings and a relativistic regard for truth. A hypercapitalist mentality has tempted us to reduce human fulfillment to individual material acquisition, and to ignore the social, ethical, and spiritual dimensions proper to being human. To this moral malaise, Catholic moral theology has something important to contribute.

The Catholic Church teaches what all "people of good will" recognize as universally true, that genuine justice in our social and economic relations must be characterized by a mutual love for our human brothers and sisters and an attention to the common good of all humanity. That love manifests itself in a respect for the rights and dignity of all human persons, and in a priority on assuring that all persons have their basic needs fulfilled. This means that a just economy strives for food, access to health care, meaningful work, and empowering development for all people. It also means that "development" must be understood as a complex objective for political economy, requiring support for the material and spiritual well-being of members of the human community.

Rejecting the assumption that the economic sphere is somehow immune from moral evaluation, Benedict offered a vision of a healthy economy that is part of a larger global attention to holistic development of peoples:

> The great challenge before us, accentuated by the problems of development in this global era and made even more urgent by the economic and financial crisis, is to demonstrate, in thinking and behaviour, not only that traditional principles of social ethics like transparency, honesty and responsibility cannot be ignored or attenuated, but also that in *commercial relationships* the *principle of gratuitousness* and the logic of gift as an expression of fraternity can

> and must *find their place within normal economic activity*. This is a human demand at the present time, but it is also demanded by economic logic. It is a demand both of charity and of truth.[16]

From the perspective of Catholic social teaching, a healthy economy is a moral economy, one that celebrates the goodness of productivity and profit making within the parameters of social cooperation, mutual respect, and constant concern for the common good—in other words, charity in truth.[17] Often regarded as a conservative voice in American culture because of its very public positions on abortion, stem-cell research, euthanasia, and marriage, the Catholic Church has been consistently progressive in its commitment to social justice for the poor.

RELIGION AND MORAL ECONOMY

Whether liberal, conservative, or something in between, religious persons are increasingly vocal in their call to count economic issues as moral concerns. Jewish and Christian voices in particular draw on theologies of stewardship, interconnectedness, and interdependence to underwrite these priorities. They appeal to the authority of Scripture to make the claim that economic justice has always been an important preoccupation of biblical faith. In doing so, they reflect culturally important traditions that have had a deep history of concern about these issues. For Jews and Christians, the economy is a moral issue, and many other American religious communities also bring powerful resources to bear on questions of economic justice, even though they do not dominate the discussion the way these two traditions do.

How do religious perspectives improve public debate over the economic policies of the United States? For one thing, they bring the potential to substantially elevate these issues as matters of both political and moral priority. They remind us that economics is a matter of moral importance and one that is rightly evaluated by ethical criteria. This may not strike us as a radical contribution until we consider just how "untouchable" capitalism is in American culture. Americans are so ideologically invested in the myth of a free market that any suggestion that appears to be at odds with that free market is quickly labeled as "socialist"—as the recent public debates over health-care reform have made abundantly clear. Americans have deified capitalism to the point that it is no longer just an economic system but a way of life, a moral worldview in itself. As a result, our culture teaches us to judge everything (including religion) with capitalist criteria—everything is a market, everything is evaluated by the conditions of supply and demand. Our love affair with allegedly unfettered market capitalism dulls our moral senses to grave injustices, like those inherent in a system that allows an elite class of CEOs and politicians to play financial roulette with the futures of working people. By contrast, religious voices like the ones we have noted here offer a critical perspective, rousing our collective sense of moral outrage over financial irresponsibility and demanding accountability from those whose greed and mismanagement lead us to the brink of social catastrophe.

In its moral critique of our economic climate, religion invites us to see the larger picture in which our economic decisions and policies should be understood, and commends commitment to the common good as a check on the individualism and hubris that drive abuse of free-market principles. To a culture that worships at the altar of the free market, it may look "un-American" to critique unfettered capitalism, but theological worldviews often remind us that market ideals are not the highest aspirations toward which to strive. They insist that capitalism be affirmed or revised to the degree necessary to conform to the ethical imperatives of a healthy society—mutual respect, solidarity, and a commitment to the basic needs and rights of all human beings.

In putting to rest the notion that morality and money are mutually exclusive topics, religious communities offer leadership in a sometimes radical critique of American capitalism. Religion also has the potential to build bridges between otherwise antagonistic constituencies and therefore accomplish more politically. Commentator David Brooks has pointed to the "natural alliance" between liberals and evangelicals as a partnership with powerful political opportunity, noting how that partnership has already paid dividends in the shared work of liberal rock star and Christian activist Bono and traditional evangelical leaders like Rick Warren, or in the cooperation of former senator Rick Santorum (much-beloved former leader of Washington conservatives) and Jon Corzine on antipoverty legislation. Brooks warns that "we can have a culture war in this country, or we can have a war on poverty, but we can't have both. That is to say, liberals and conservatives can go on bashing each other for being godless hedonists and primitive theocrats, or they can set those differences off to one side and work together to help the needy."[18] Given the spectrum of ideological positions reflected among religious people concerned with poverty, coordination between conservative and liberal Christians on this issue promises to add powerful momentum to the fight for economic justice.

Even if we do not share the particular worldviews offered by these faith communities, the encouragement to be in critical evaluation of our economic policies is a vital contribution. As Pope Benedict put it, religion's place in the public dialogue over our social, political, and economic future is *essential* to our collective well-being:

> Denying the right to profess one's religion in public and the right to bring the truths of faith to bear upon public life has negative consequences for true development. The exclusion of religion from the public square—and, at the other extreme, religious fundamentalism—hinders an encounter between persons and their collaboration for the progress of humanity. Public life is sapped of its motivation and politics takes on a domineering and aggressive character. Human rights risk being ignored either because they are robbed of their transcendent foundation or because personal freedom is not acknowledged. Secularism and fundamentalism exclude the possibility of fruitful dialogue and effective cooperation between reason and religious faith. *Reason always stands in need of being purified by faith*: this also holds true for political reason, which must not consider itself omnipotent. For its part, *religion always needs to be purified by reason* in order to show its authentically human face. Any breach in this dialogue comes only at an enormous price to human development.[19]

11
In Defense of Civility

The end of the 2000 presidential election was especially rancorous, even for the current state of American politics. Both George W. Bush and Al Gore believed they had won the state of Florida and thus had won the presidency. But the actual outcome in Florida was far from clear (and remains so to this day, as we all know), so what followed election night was a month of legal wrangling, as each camp sought to define the recount in a way that would help its candidate. Accompanying the legal maneuvers was an equally zealous contest in the court of public opinion, the tone of which became increasingly snippy, petty, and personal as the month went on. When the Supreme Court ruled in favor of President Bush, and this uniquely protracted election was finally over, we heard both candidates call for a new political tone, a return to civility. In his televised concession, Mr. Gore proposed a renewal in cooperative spirit, insisting that "what remains of partisan rancor must now be put aside." Gore left the political stage by signaling his commitment to civility and by calling "all who stood with [him] to unite behind our next president."[1] Bush accepted Gore's concession with a similar wish for a renewal in political cooperation, suggesting that "we have discussed our differences; now it is time to find common ground and build consensus to make America a beacon" for the world.[2]

Unfortunately, the state of politics in the United States has only grown less civil since that election. Any hope for bipartisan cooperation after 9/11 quickly disappeared with deep divisions over issues like the economy and the war in Iraq, divisions that the political elites on either side look to exploit with venom. More disappointingly, the last two presidential campaigns have been known as much for personal attacks as for a serious engagement with philosophical or policy differences. In fact, the distortion of an opponent's personal record for political gain now has a name—"swiftboating"—thanks to the scurrilous efforts of some G.O.P.-backed veterans to raise questions during the 2004 campaign about Senator John Kerry's combat service in Vietnam. A sign of the power of incivility in American politics, the tactics of Swift Boat Veterans for Truth were successful in making Kerry's military service a liability for his campaign, even though he was running against a president who had initiated a highly unpopular war and whose own military service showed signs of light duty and preferential treatment. Similarly, the 2008 campaign featured more attacks on Barack Obama's patriotism (why doesn't he wear a lapel flag?) and his religion (is he really a Muslim?) than his economic plan.

Television political coverage is especially addicted to incivility. Because conflict makes for sexier news than compromise, the cable news networks naturally gravitate to baser political moments and give them more time than is warranted (just how long did the networks debate whether or not Barack and Michelle Obama engaged in a "terrorist fist jab" at a public event?). But the networks themselves also contribute to the incivility, with uncountable "debate" shows on CNN, MSNBC, and Fox News that feature shouting matches and partisan name-calling instead of actual intellectual discussion. In 2004, comedian Jon Stewart went on the flagship of media incivility, *Crossfire*, to confront its hosts, accusing them of "hurting America" with their "political hackery."[3] *Crossfire* is now off the air, but radio and TV are still filled with the partisan rants of Glenn Beck, Rush Limbaugh, and Bill O'Reilly. And conservatives have no corner on the market of inane political squabble; the unjustifiably pompous Bill Maher is as insufferable as Limbaugh.[4]

Because of the habits of both media and political parties, American politics has grown only harsher in the years since Bush and Gore suggested we come together. But there have been voices in the wilderness, crying for a restoration of civility as an important political virtue. Politicians like President Obama and former Republican Senator John Danforth, public intellectuals like Os Guinness and Alan Wolfe, comedians like Jon Stewart, and an ever-growing number of regular Americans are calling for a healthier model for talking about our differences, one that rejects the mutual demonization so attractive to the extremes, in favor of a public dialogue that is patient, substantive, and subtle. I join the increasing number of Americans calling for this renewed commitment to civility. Only if we commit to civility will our political discourse—and by extension American politics itself—grow stronger.

WHAT IS CIVILITY?

But what do we mean by civility? It may be useful to begin by making clear what I do *not* think is required from a more civil tone in politics. First, civility is not simple passivity, nicety, or acquiescence. It does not require the avoidance of conflict. Indeed, as realists like Reinhold Niebuhr have reminded us, politics *is* conflict; it is the confrontation between opposing interests and worldviews and the norms, values, and priorities that those interests and worldviews commend. Civility does not ask us to pretend that our differences do not exist. It also does not deny that something important may come from the conflict between our different worldviews. Conflict can be constructive; it can be the context in which citizens learn from and about one another. It can be a moment for education and persuasion, the occasion for refining or changing one's views. In other words, contrary to popular opinion, there is such a thing as good conflict. Because of the inevitability of conflict in politics, and the positive potential of some of that conflict, the virtue of civility does not require that we smooth over, ignore, or minimize the differences that exist between us. To do so is as unhealthy as it is unproductive.

Os Guinness suggests that civility in public discourse is much like the importance of sportsmanship to athletics.[5] He draws a comparison with boxing, but enough people regard boxing as mere brutality to strain the analogy, so allow me to use my own favorite sport as an example. Football is a hard, violent, emotionally intense sport. It essentially requires twenty-two men to beat on each other for sixty minutes (a fair description of the play of my favorite team, the Pittsburgh Steelers). Ideally the physical and emotional nature of the contest still leaves room for mutual respect among players. There are rules within which everyone must play, there are boundaries to the physicality that can be inflicted on an opposing player, and most players know the difference between a hard hit and a cheap shot (and those who press the line acquire a corresponding reputation). Most of all, players in the NFL generally respect each other, and many players have close friends on other teams. In fact, after most NFL games it is common to see players on the opposing teams warmly greeting, embracing, and sometimes praying with one another—even at Steelers/Browns games! Likewise, the virtue of civility should act as "rules for the political game," defining what is in bounds and what is out, but the rules of civil discourse do not keep us from playing the game. Civil political debate still may be serious and contentious, and everyone engaged in it still hopes to "win."

Indeed, we should expect participants in public debate to want to win, for they are fighting for values they think are right and true. Commitment to conviction and commitment to civility are compatible, for civility does not require relativism, the belief that all perspectives are equally true, accurate, and valid. Some would argue that the only way to show mutual respect and tolerance for a fellow citizen is to acknowledge that my opponent's views are as valid as my own. What I believe is right and true *for me*, while what my neighbor believes is right and true for her. This is not civility; it is vapid relativism, which does justice neither to the nature of true moral conviction nor to the hard disagreements that characterize much of our political lives together. Most people who hold deep religious or moral values think that those values are important, true, or useful not just for themselves but for others too. It is the nature of moral conviction to believe that certain actions or values are right and good, not just in my own personal circle, but generally.

This is an idea that is particularly difficult for my students at Middlebury College to grasp, raised as they have been in a liberal culture that privatizes morality and equates tolerance with relativism. Every year I teach my introductory course on ethics, I watch students wrestle with the question of why conservatives cannot just believe what they believe without imposing it on others. What my students cannot get their minds around is the idea that a conservative person's beliefs about abortion or homosexuality are not just personal preferences, but instead are rooted in generally applicable moral principles and assumptions about the value of life or the meaning of sexuality.[6] To hold moral beliefs normally means to believe those convictions relevant and true beyond our own lives and experiences.

So tolerance that is built on the assumption that all moral claims are equally valid is only one kind of tolerance, and a rather thin one at that. I can also be tolerant of your views and respect your right to hold and express them, even if I think your views are tragically misguided. This is tolerance too, though it may not resemble tolerance for those who are used to requiring relativism as a prerequisite for mutual respect. Thinking a person is wrong and respecting that person are not mutually exclusive principles. Disagreeing with a neighbor's values and honoring their right to represent them in public conversation are not incompatible priorities. Tolerance and mutual respect can coincide with a zealous commitment to a set of moral values that you think are right and true for everyone, and which (you think) expose the error in others' thinking.

So if civility is not passivity or relativism, then what is it? I like to define civility as the *exercise of patience, integrity, humility, and mutual respect in civil conversation, even (or especially) with those with whom we disagree.* All of the terms in this definition are chosen with some care, so allow me to parse them quickly.

Patience is a key component of the virtue of civility. It pushes us to relate to our ideological opponent as a conversation partner, not simply as an obstacle to getting what we want or a heathen to evangelize. Exhibiting patience in civil conversation leads us to talk with those who disagree with us, but at least as importantly, patience insists that we *listen* to them. Civility requires that we have enough decency to hear our neighbor's position in his or her own terms, and familiarize ourselves with the values and viewpoints that inform it. Patience requires that we take the time to understand our opponent's position, rather than dismissing it out of hand, trivializing it, or attributing to him our own slanted reinterpretation of his beliefs.

Related to this virtue of patience, *integrity* is the commitment to representing our own positions and those of our opponents truthfully. Participants in public debate who lack integrity will misrepresent their motivations or will exhibit hypocrisy in their positions across different public issues. By contrast, integrity requires that we remain consistent and honest in our reasons for advocating our positions. It also prohibits the mischaracterization of our opponents' views, a popular strategy in the current incivility in American public discourse. One of the most egregious examples of this lack of integrity occurred in the last presidential campaign, when Senator John McCain repeatedly claimed "that Senator Obama would rather lose a war in order to win a political campaign" than admit that he was wrong in his Iraq policy.[7] The comment dripped with accusations of treason that should have elicited more outrage than it did, had it not been so ridiculous. It is one thing to regard your opponent's position as foolish, naive, and uninformed; to accuse a fellow presidential candidate of preferring his own victory to ending a war with unacceptable human casualties betrays a stunning lack of integrity from a politician whose reputation was built on this virtue.

The third virtue of civility, *humility*, recommends that we enter every public conversation open to the possibility that we could change our minds, that we could be persuaded to think something different than we believe now. This is not a retreat into that relativism that we earlier rejected. It is instead a nod toward human fallibility, an acknowledgment that even the brightest or most pious does not know, has not seen, has not experienced everything that may be relevant to the issues before us. Even if we enter public debate with a deep commitment to our beliefs, humility keeps us open to the possibility that our beliefs may be refined by what we encounter in those conversations.

Sometimes that refining might be drastic; we may conclude after conversation that we were wrong and our opponent was right, and we may reverse our position. Perhaps our beliefs are informed in more subtle ways by an openness to the position of others. Perhaps we leave the conversation with substantially the same views, but we understand an aspect of the issue better than we did before. Perhaps we sympathize with our opponents and have a greater appreciation for the way our position causes them pain than we did before (even if we ultimately conclude that we cannot conscientiously abandon our views). Even these more incremental changes are accomplishments for healthy public discourse. They are a move toward common understanding, even if they fall short of consensus. They are possible only if citizens engage one another with the humility and openness to be affected by the encounter.

When we take the time to listen patiently to and learn from another, we are in a greater position to exercise *mutual respect* for one another, the fourth component of public civility. Civility requires that in the midst of our most meaningful and intractable disagreements, we still extend the courtesy of respect. This means more than avoiding demonizing one another, as is so common in our public debates. It also means respecting each other's right to represent moral worldviews in public. It means not disqualifying your neighbor from the conversation or dismissing his views as unimportant because he is conservative, or liberal, or religious, or not. Civility requires that, even if I think you are tragically mistaken, I honor your right to participate in the American enterprise of public moral conversation.

Because it does not ignore or whitewash differences, civility cannot guarantee consensus on any issue. Americans will not suddenly come to an agreement over *Roe v. Wade* if they only adopt a more civil tone to their debate. Civility does promise progress, however, because it allows us to better understand one another and helps us learn how to coexist with people with whom we vehemently disagree. As Os Guinness puts it, "What we are looking for [in civility] is not so much truths that can unite us as terms on which we can negotiate and by which we can live with the differences that divide us."[8]

CIVILITY IN AMERICAN HISTORY

If we choose to take up this invitation to greater civility in our public discourse, we will be returning to one of the recurring values in the American moral tradition. A claim that political debate in this country has ever been consistently civil would be naive and a very selective reading of U.S. history, and I am not making that argument here. No better historical evidence of its rarity exists than in the presidential election of 1800, one of the ugliest campaigns in U.S. history. Thomas Jefferson's supporters undermined President Adams's public reputation by characterizing him as bellicose and imperialistic, while Adams's surrogates publicly suggested that Jefferson was a radical atheist, a dangerous infidel, and an unpatriotic friend of the French. The negative campaigning not only contributed to a defeat for the incumbent, but also alienated the two partners in democracy, a strain on a friendship that would not be healed until each man was in his sunset. Sadly, the presidential election of 1800 is evidence that incivility has been a part of American politics since the beginning.

Despite how easy it has been to depart from the ideal, however, civility has been a consistent aspiration for some of our greatest leaders. Perhaps the earliest voice for civility in America was the iconoclastic Puritan Roger Williams. More famous for his defense of religious freedom, Williams worked from a larger vision of public order in which diversity was tolerated, fellow citizens were respected, civil conversation was courteous, and the tasks of living together as a civil community were engaged cooperatively. For Williams, civility was a norm that all persons, religious or not, should be able to exercise. Ideally, it guides the spirit in which public conversation must take place in order to accomplish further consensus on those projects and priorities that constitute a good society. In short, Williams argued, civility enables us to promote the common good. Courteous conversation, listening with integrity and genuineness, showing respect for one's opponent, and refraining from personal insults are among the boundaries he believed civility places on healthy public discourse. By contrast, public debates that are highly argumentative or that include personal attacks or threats genuinely concerned him, for he feared that such disrespect transgresses the civility on which the common good of a society depends.

Williams certainly got a chance to test out his commitment to civility while he was a prominent leader in Rhode Island. In the 1670s, Quaker missionaries began to infiltrate the colony and caused a lot of disruption. The Quakers of the seventeenth century excelled at disruption of the civil order; it was their way of engaging in public protest, calling attention to injustices in society and attracting converts to their cause. Quaker men kept their hair long and refused to greet fellow citizens according to the respectful standards of the day, just to jab at popular conventions. Quakers had a habit of running into public meetings and church services and disrupting them with shouts and protests. On more than one occasion, Quaker men and women were reported to have run naked in the street, just because they claimed the spirit of God led them to do it.

These Quakers came to Rhode Island in the last decade or so of Williams's life, and they caused just this kind of trouble there too. Committed to religious liberty, Williams refused to kick them out of Rhode Island on the basis of their religious belief, but the Quakers' incivility exasperated him. He objected to their habit of interrupting his arguments, shouting him down, attempting to humiliate him personally with name-calling and ridicule, misrepresenting his convictions, and displaying a noted lack of truthfulness in their own arguments. In short, Williams charged that his Quaker antagonists disregarded necessary rules for decorous conversation and deliberation. To do so was, in his words, "against the sober rules of civility and humanity."[9] This behavior was not, as the Quakers insisted, an acceptable exercise of free conscience. Instead it was a moral violation of the basic requirements of civility, and the Quakers concerned Williams so much because their behavior threatened the cultivation of certain shared virtues that he believed were vital to encouraging mutual respect among citizens.[10]

Prominent Americans since Williams have shared his assumption that public virtue is a necessary governor of civil debate. John Adams feared the rise of political parties in the new republic precisely because he thought they would undermine the civility on which the social good depended. In a letter to a prominent Massachusetts politician, Thomas Jefferson lamented the discord that resulted from his controversial election to the presidency. He yearned for a restoration of public civility, insisting that "it will be a great blessing to our country if we can once more restore harmony and social love among its citizens. I confess, as to myself, it is almost the first object of my heart, and one to which I would sacrifice everything but principle."[11] Two hundred years later, George W. Bush referred to Jefferson's letter in his own public appeal for a restoration of common regard after a contentious election. And Vice President Gore conceded with reference to the words of Senator Stephen Douglas, who ended his hotly contested battle with Abraham Lincoln in the 1860 presidential campaign with an olive branch and the promise that "partisan feeling must yield to patriotism."

Indeed, Abraham Lincoln was the embodiment of civility, prosecuting a civil war with saintly combination of conviction and humility, always prioritizing the restoration of national kinship and reaching out to his bitterest political enemies (even giving some of them cabinet posts in his administration). A century later, in an important speech delivered at American University, President John F. Kennedy commended civility as a pathway to domestic and global peace:

> So let us not be blind to our differences, but let us also direct attention to our common interests and the means by which those differences can be resolved. And if we cannot end now our differences, at least we can help make the world safe for diversity. For in the final analysis, our most basic common link is that we all inhabit this small planet. We all breathe the same air. We all cherish our children's futures. And we are all mortal.[12]

Despite the rancorous nature of political debate in American history, our greatest leaders have still held out the hope for greater civility. Indeed, civility is rooted in our founding principles.

IT STARTS WITH US

Given the importance of civility as an American ideal, how do we make it a reality? Commitment to this virtue starts with each one of us. The first thing we can do is demand it from our political leaders. We should require of our political candidates and leaders that they demonstrate their commitment to civility by representing differences and similarities between them and their opponents clearly and accurately, by treating their opponents with respect, and by telling us the truth (and not just what they think we want to hear). We should assure them that we want political campaigns to be about the important issues that preoccupy us, and that we are turned off by the distortion of records and by baseless or irrelevant personal attacks. We should make a commitment to the common good, not just an appeal to our baser self-interests, our litmus test for civil leadership. How do we get this message across to our politicians? By participating in the political process and voting along our commitment to civility. When we reward with our votes those candidates who exhibit these virtues, and penalize with our votes those who insist on perpetuating "politics as usual," politicians will hear the call for civility's renewal.

The rejuvenation of civility also requires a commitment from the media, and here too ordinary citizens can make a difference. The media operate on market principles; they package what they think we want to watch, and they ignore what they think will fail to attract viewers. If we make clear and public that our "viewer preferences" include a fondness for civil discourse, the media will respond accordingly. With our viewing habits, our phone calls, and our e-mails, we can signal to media outlets that we take it personally when they insult our intelligence, when they reduce the complexities of important issues into sound bites that distort what is at stake, and when they refuse to cover important substantive issues in favor of more titillating items of little public importance. We can show them that we prefer news and analysis over sensationalism and banter, and we can assure them that stories of depth about consensus and progress will sell airtime as much as features on division and conflict. If we demand more sophistication and fairness from our news media, they will comply, if only out of a desire to grow their market audience. By being better informed by the media presentation of the important issues of our day, we will be in a better position to understand their complexity and participate in public discourse over them.

Surely this is another front on which ordinary citizens can have a profound effect on the level of civility in American public life. We can affect civility by being active in public discourse and by conducting our own debates respectfully. Whether debating before the local school board, participating in state elections, or volunteering in a national campaign, we can lead the way in prioritizing the virtues of patience, understanding, mutual respect, and humility. Letters to the editor of the local newspaper are an occasion to exercise civility, as are contributions to online discourse. With the advent of Web sites, blogs, and chat rooms, the Internet has made the old adage "all politics are local" truer than ever (in the sense that they facilitate more ground-level discourse), but the anonymous nature of much of this online conversation has made this medium particularly susceptible to meanness and disrespect. Citizens committed to civility can challenge the tenor of these virtual exchanges by modeling respectful behavior with their own contributions.

Besides working within the new media for civil discourse, however, we might consider resurrecting an older one. In my home state of Vermont, we still have something called Town Meeting Day. Recent presidential elections have featured televised "town hall" sessions, but in reality these events were photo ops with audiences stacked in the candidates' favor. What we have in Vermont are *actual* town meetings, an opportunity before our local elections each year for residents to gather together and have conversation, face to face. Of course, most of these town meetings are preoccupied with budgetary matters, but as we know full well, budget debates are often a form of talking about social priorities. In Vermont at least, town meetings are about not just the budget but other local, national, and global matters of concern to citizens. Our town meetings might feature a conversation about environmental responsibility, the threat of "big box" stores, same-sex marriage, or the war in Iraq.[13] These conversations are unscripted, messy, sometimes productive, sometimes frustrating, but, more often than not, civil. After all, the conversations are among citizens who are also neighbors, who work, live, worship, and educate their children together in the midst of their differences. Of course, town meetings still work in Vermont because we have virtually more cows than people in our state. But the idea of local conversation is, I think, a model that works even in communities and subcommunities in more populated areas—in churches, synagogues, mosques, social clubs, reading groups, and bowling alleys. The idea is to get citizens talking with others in their neighborhoods, struggling over important issues and sometimes intense disagreements with a commitment to mutual respect and patience—borne of the fact that they are talking to people with whom they also must live.[14]

RELIGIOUS COMMUNITIES AS MODELS OF CIVIL DISCOURSE

It is particularly promising to encourage this kind of civil conversation among our worshiping communities, for they have potential for leading us in the return to civility. Again, we do not want to be naive; religious communities often are as uncivil in their conversation as the culture at large, though I suspect that is true because they model their conversation on the culture. In my own denomination, we have debated without end the permissibility of blessing same-sex unions and the appropriateness of ordaining openly gay or lesbian people. These debates have been hurtful, lacking in mutual respect, and high on ad hominem attacks on both sides. We even have our own unofficial denominational tabloid that specializes in mean and divisive "journalism." When one is in the midst of one of these perennial debates over homosexuality, it is sometimes hard to imagine how religious communities can serve the cause of civility in public life.

But the same religious communities that historically have found it difficult to practice civility nonetheless have rich traditions for thinking about moral conversation in better terms. Disagreement and conversation are part of the modus operandi for Judaism, for instance. In many ways, the rabbinic tradition is a template for moral discourse with its dialogical nature, its appeal to tradition while remaining sensitive to changes in historical circumstances, and its avoidance of the heavy authoritarianism that characterizes other religious traditions. Buddhism teaches that one of the requirements in the movement toward spiritual enlightenment is "right speech," which in its modern interpretation includes an openness to learning through dialogue rather than seeking only to win an argument.[15] Protestant Christianity from its beginnings has had to grapple with diversity within its ranks. While in darker moments Protestants have responded to difference with wars and persecution, more often than not they have dealt with their differences through negotiation and dialogue. In the first generations of the Reformation, there was a lot of conversation among Protestants on theological matters, and the last couple of decades have seen a rejuvenation of that ecumenical spirit, as churches have worked together on issues as wide ranging as the Eucharist and climate change. In fact, dialogue between the Roman Catholic Church and Protestant churches has grown more amicable and productive in recent years.

In recent years Presbyterians have begun to talk about the divisive issue of homosexuality in ways that do not automatically threaten a split in the denomination. Conservatives and liberals have sat in the same room together at the denomination's highest governing body, debating and voting on various proposals for the church's stance on ordination of gays with decorum and patience. In one remarkable expression of ecclesial civility, the Presbyterian Church (U.S.A.) commissioned a

"Theological Task Force on Peace, Unity, and Purity of the Church" to study this and other issues. The task force consisted of members who identified with diametrically opposed theological positions, and they were instructed to meet to help guide the larger church through the impasse. Not only did they talk; they engaged in prayer and Bible study together and formed wonderful friendships across ideological lines. The result of their time together was an experience of personal growth and a proposal for a church wrought with division over important theological and ethical matters. In their final report, the task force came to no unified position on any of the issues. They insisted that it was neither realistic nor theologically necessary that everyone in the church agree. What they did recommend was a more civil and loving way of "being together," of listening to and respecting one another, insisting that "the quality of our life together . . . is compelling testimony to the truth and power of the gospel we proclaim."[16]

Religious communities like my own discover the resources for respectful dialogue in their own theological traditions. Acknowledgment of the limits to human understanding encourages a certain level of humility and openness to learning from others. A doctrine of sin (or some correlate) compels the religious person to take seriously the likelihood that she could be wrong about one or more aspects of a moral question, and that self-interest might be driving her position in ways inconsistent with the greater good. An appreciation for the grandness of God reminds us that God's moral intentions for the world are likely larger than we can fathom from our limited vantage point, another reason to adopt a spirit of humility in our conversations. Seeing our fellow human beings as children of God encourages believers to respect even those with whom they disagree, and compels us to maintain this respect and a modicum of patience as we talk about tough matters. A commitment to the common good, an especially strong emphasis in Roman Catholicism, gives theological importance to the struggle to find shared ground and seek progress on the issues that most perplex us.

Yes, religious communities have fallen tragically short of their own theological aspirations for constructive and civil moral conversation, and the history of religion's missteps is quick off the tongues of its cultured despisers. But religious communities also possess the theological resources to host healthier moral dialogue, and in doing so they just might offer a model for moral conversation to the rest of the culture. Theologian James Gustafson was fond of speaking of "the church as a community of moral discourse," and the idea could certainly be extended to other religious communities as well.[17] What he meant by this is that a religious community is "a gathering of people with the explicit intention to survey and critically discuss their personal and social responsibilities in the light of moral convictions about which there is some consensus and to which there is some loyalty." In other words, one of the chief tasks of the religious community, a reason for its being, is to provide the setting for its members to confront together the moral issues that vie for their attention in the context of a basic worldview they all share. Gustafson was not naive about the level of theological and moral disagreement that can exist within religious communities, but he also recognized a commitment to a basic set of beliefs, a sense of internal authority and tradition, that brings people to a religious "family" and keeps them together. Some basic agreement on the origins, identity, and mission of the community forms the basis—and provides the imperative—to talk with one another about important moral responsibilities.

If the religious community's shared beliefs make moral discourse *possible*, the complexity of the issues before us makes it *necessary*. Gone are the days when religious communities confidently deferred to the judgments of ministers on moral questions, if they ever did. These days, tackling the tough issues before us requires leadership not only from those trained in ethical deliberation (like ministers, theologians, and philosophers), but also from those trained in the fields of economics, law, health care, and politics. No single person has the technical expertise to decide for herself what is right in circumstances as varied as stem-cell research and humanitarian intervention. As Gustafson put it, "The specialization of knowledge makes moral *discourse* all the more necessary."[18] Furthermore, the increased diversity within religious communities and in the larger society compels the inclusion of people with different backgrounds, values, and loyalties. This broad participation makes for a richer and healthier conversation, a pattern of civility for the larger culture.

Ultimately, the habits of civil discourse that religious communities encourage are the real gifts they give to American public life. In many ways, those habits of civil conversation are more important than any consensus we might hope to achieve on heretofore divisive issues. Gustafson was sure that promoting *conversation*, not necessarily *agreement*, was religious communities' most important moral achievement. He argued that "participation in a serious moral dialogue moving toward consensus is more important than the consensus itself," because "participation in moral discourse deepens, broadens, and extends [people's] capacity to make responsible moral judgments" themselves.[19] Striving for healthier, more respectful conversation will yield fruit, not just because it will move us toward mutual understanding and possibly substantial agreement, but because *it will teach us how to think ethically*, as individuals and as a society.

Without the resources of religion, American civil discourse loses out on rich intellectual traditions that promise profound contributions to our moral deliberations. Without religion, the voice of a large segment of the American middle is effectively ruled out of the conversation. Without religion, American politics is ruled by the extremes, and a politics governed by excess will never value civility. However, when we open wide the doors of public moral discourse, when we extend civility and respect to all citizens and demand it from them as well, we lay the groundwork for an enriched public discourse that just might make some progress, some move toward greater understanding on the issues that most divide us. When we open our conversations to good-faith reasons of any kind, we make real the possibility of a "moral values" debate that is intelligent, civil, open, respectful, and fruitful.

Notes

Preface

1. James Dobson, "The Values Test," *New York Times*, 4 October 2007.

2. As quoted in *CQ Weekly*, 7 March 2005.

Chapter 1: At War over Values (Allegedly)

1. David R. Jones, "Why Bush Won," CBS.com, 3 November 2004: http://www.cbsnews.com/stories/2004/11/03/politics/main653238.shtml.

2. CNN's *Crossfire*, 5 November 2004; Rick Hampton, "Few See Conciliation on Bush's Agenda," *USA Today*, 4 November 2004.

3. Joe Klein, "The Values Gap," *Time*, 22 November 2004, 29.

4. http://www.cnn.com/ELECTION/2004/pages/results/states/US/P/00/epolls.0.html.

5. William J. Bennett, "The Great Relearning," *National Review*, 3 November 2004.

6. Erik Gorski, "Dobson: GOP Abandoned Us," *Denver Post*, 9 November 2006. Whether Dobson was right about the importance of some disillusionment among "moral values" voters to the GOP's failure to hold on to Congress is a matter of debate. It may be true that moral values played some part in the GOP's troubles in 2006, but the moral issues that received the most scrutiny in that election cycle weren't Bush's record on abortion and same-sex marriages. At least as damaging to the Republicans may have been the souring situation in Iraq, the missteps of Republican Senator Mark Foley and Speaker of the House Tom DeLay, and the increasingly villainous role in which Vice President Cheney was cast by his public detractors.

7. As reported in Dick Meyer, "How Did One Exit Poll Answer Become the Story of How Bush Won?" *Washington Post*, 5 December 2004.

8. Richard Reeves, as reported in "Moral Values: A Decisive Issue?" CBS.com, 3 November 2004.

9. See Gary Langer and John Cohen, "Voters and Values in the 2004 Election," *Public Opinion Quarterly* 69, no. 5 (Special Issue 2005): 744–59. After the election, many political analysts pointed out the shortcomings of those postelection polls and suggested that "moral values" did not play nearly the decisive role in President Bush's reelection that they were credited with

playing. See also David Brooks, "The Values-Vote Myth," *New York Times*, 6 November 2004.

10. William Raspberry, "Rewarding the 'Values' Crowd," *Washington Post*, 8 November 2004.

11. Even the most scripturally bound Christian fundamentalist must acknowledge that the Bible itself occasionally assumes a divinely endowed natural human capacity to distinguish good from evil. In the first two chapters of his Letter to the Romans, for instance, the apostle Paul accepts that Gentiles who do not know God may nonetheless "do instinctively what the law requires" because "what the law requires is written on their hearts, to which their own conscience also bears witness" (2:14–15). Paul also cites this natural conscience as a basis on which to judge all human beings as having fallen short of the law. This biblical endorsement of natural morality must be acceptable to even the most conservative Christian, coming as it does in a section of Scripture particularly associated with conservative denouncements of homosexuality.

12. Babylonian Talmud, Erubin 100b, as quoted in Louis E. Newman, *An Introduction to Jewish Ethics* (Upper Saddle River, NJ: Pearson Prentice Hall, 2005), 120.

13. Admittedly, the theological school most open to the idea of a natural morality based in reason, the Muᶜtazilites, is a minority perspective in contemporary Islam. The majority of Muslim clerics subscribe to the Ashᶜarite school and insist that divine command defines what is morally good and bad. From this perspective, less integrity is granted to the phenomenon of moral performance outside the influence of Islamic teachings. Nonetheless, I want to argue that the fact that this debate exists within Islamic theology testifies to an implicit acknowledgment that some kind of universal moral capability exists to be explained.

14. We should note that my example is simplistic in a lot of ways, not the least being that it implies one and only one source for our friend's worldview. In truth, our committed Christian's reading of reality is likely influenced not only by her immersion in a religious tradition but also by her location in the United States and her identification as an American. It also is surely affected by her socioeconomic status, gender, ethnicity, and race. Together these experiences create for her a moral perspective through which she interprets her world.

15. We see both positive and negative moral rules at work in the Ten Commandments. The negative rules get most of the press (e.g., "You shall not murder"), but the Ten Commandments also commend actions as obligatory or commendable (e.g., "Remember the sabbath day" and "Honor your father and your mother").

16. Patrick J. Buchanan, "1992 Republican National Convention Speech," http://www.buchanan.org/pa-92-0817-rnc.html. Interestingly, the strident rhetoric in Buchanan's speech was subsequently blamed for contributing to President G. H. W. Bush's failed bid for reelection.

17. For instance, sociologist Alan Wolfe conducted extensive interviews with middle-class Americans that led him to conclude that most of us are moderate

and pragmatic in our approach to moral questions, sharing commitment to a wide spectrum of values, in contrast to the strident rhetoric featured in the media. See Alan Wolfe, *One Nation after All* (New York: Viking, 1998).

Chapter 2: Aren't We a Christian Nation?

1. Jerry Falwell, *Listen, America!* (New York: Doubleday, 1980), 29.

2. Pat Robertson, *Courting Disaster: How the Supreme Court Is Usurping the Power of Congress and the People* (Nashville: Integrity Publishers, 2004), 45.

3. David Barton, a leader in the Texas Republican Party and vocal advocate for emphasizing this side of American history, observes that "we have all been trained to recognize the two least religious founding fathers," but that focus on Thomas Jefferson and Benjamin Franklin leads to an inaccurate reading of religion's importance to the formation of the new republic. He too claims that most of the founders were traditional Christians, and that even Jefferson and Franklin would have welcomed the label. Recognizing the religious convictions of the founders is crucial to understanding the proper role of religion in American politics, he says, because "if we are arguing off the premise that we have to be secular today because we have always been secular, then we are arguing off the wrong premise." See David K. Kirkpatrick, "Putting God Back into American History," *New York Times*, 27 February 2005.

4. Falwell, 33. Falwell's reading of the Puritans fails to account for the fact that some of them from the beginning were calling for a society that respected religious freedom and the separation of religion and government. In other words, Puritan Christianity produced not only the apologies for religious uniformity Falwell found attractive, but also a defense of religious liberty best represented by Roger Williams. For more on this disagreement within Puritan culture, see my introduction in *On Religious Liberty: Selections from the Works of Roger Williams* (Cambridge: Harvard University Press, 2008).

5. Falwell, 54.

6. Ibid., 53.

7. Robertson, xxii.

8. Ibid., xxi.

9. Ibid., 103.

10. Foreword to John Eidsmoe, *Christianity and the Constitution: The Faith of Our Founding Fathers* (Grand Rapids: Baker Books, 1987), 9–10.

11. As quoted in Jane Lampman, "For Evangelicals, a Bid to 'Reclaim America,'" *Christian Science Monitor*, 16 March 2005.

12. Robertson, xxiii.

13. As sociologist Christian Smith has made clear in his research, Robertson's and Falwell's impulse to "reclaim America for Christianity" is not necessarily indicative of the average evangelical's understanding of the relationship between

Christianity and American politics. See Christian Smith, *Christian America? What Evangelicals Really Want* (Berkeley: University of California Press, 2000).

14. As quoted in Jon Meacham, *American Gospel: God, the Founding Fathers, and the Making of a Nation* (New York: Random House, 2006), 261.

15. Letter to Zabdiel Adams, as quoted in Edwin S. Gaustad, *Neither King nor Prelate: Religion and the New Nation, 1776–1826* (Grand Rapids: Eerdmans, 1993), 92.

16. See John Witte Jr., "'A most mild and equitable establishment of religion': John Adams and the Massachusetts Experiment," *Journal of Church and State* 41, no. 2 (Spring 1999).

17. As quoted in Frank Lambert, *The Founding Fathers and the Place of Religion in America* (Princeton, NJ: Princeton University Press, 2003), 276–77.

18. Gaustad, *Neither King nor Prelate*, 96.

19. Derek H. Davis, *Religion and the Continental Congress, 1774–1789: Contributions to Original Intent* (New York: Oxford University Press, 2000), 97.

20. Ibid., 198.

21. Ibid., 69–70. Adams seems to have opposed ministers in political office both because of the possible encroachment of religious authority on the political sphere and because he observed that ministers were often insufficiently prepared for the realities of public office: "The Clergy are universally too little acquainted with the World, and the Modes of Business, to engage in civil affairs with any Advantage," he wrote to his wife in September 1775.

22. Edwin S. Gaustad, *Sworn on the Altar of God: A Religious Biography of Thomas Jefferson* (Grand Rapids: Eerdmans, 1996), 138–40.

23. Ibid., 134.

24. Derek H. Davis, *Religion and Continental Congress*, 84–88.

25. Ibid., 87.

26. Ibid., 73–74.

27. In Madison's words, "The establishment of the chaplainship to Congress is a palpable violation of equal rights, as well as of Constitutional principles. The tenets of the chaplains elected [by the majority] shut the door of worship against the member whose creeds and consciences forbid a participation in that of the majority" (Derek Davis, 77–78).

28. Derek H. Davis, *Religion and Continental Congress*, 91–93.

29. Falwell, 265.

30. Ibid., 20.

31. Washington's Farewell Address, as quoted in Derek H. Davis, *Religion and Continental Congress*, 210.

32. Madison followed up on his objections in the "Memorial and Remonstrance" by reintroducing "A Bill Establishing Religious Freedom," an act written by Jefferson and first introduced in the Virginia legislature in 1777. Henry's legislation was defeated, and Jefferson's bill was adopted in 1786.

Chapter 3: But What about the Separation of Church and State?

1. The last state-established church to fall was the Congregational Church in Massachusetts, which finally dissolved its religious establishment in 1833.

2. *On Religious Liberty: Selections from the Works of Roger Williams*, ed. James Calvin Davis (Cambridge: Harvard University Press, 2008), 70.

3. The term "Puritan" represents a large tent in seventeenth-century English Protestantism, which included a variety of (mostly Calvinist) theological perspectives that all shared a profound dissatisfaction with the teachings and practices of the English church of the time. That large family had some offshoots—estranged cousins, so to speak—Protestant communities that took Puritan ideals and radicalized them in ways that the "orthodox" Puritans largely rejected. One of those cousin communities was the Baptists. The Baptists exaggerated the Puritans' emphasis on a pure Christian community to the point where they rejected infant baptism, preferring instead to construct churches of people who were baptized as adults after a distinct conversion experience and confession of faith. After his expulsion from Massachusetts and in his quest for a pure religious community, Williams took up with a group of Baptists in Providence. They formed a church there, and as a result Williams is considered one of the fathers of Baptists in America. But Williams stayed with the Baptists only a couple of months before deciding that they too failed to live up to his vision of pure Christianity. By contrast, Williams never retreated from the core Calvinist principles that marked him in most things as a conventional Calvinist, and in fact many of those Calvinist convictions formed the foundation for his apology for religious freedom (see James Calvin Davis, *The Moral Theology of Roger Williams* [Louisville, KY: Westminster John Knox Press, 2004]). For this reason Williams, while he was a temporary Baptist, should be understood as fundamentally a Puritan.

4. My discussion of the evolving popularity of the "separation of church and state" in the nineteenth and twentieth centuries is indebted to Philip Hamburger's fine book *The Separation of Church and State* (Cambridge: Harvard University Press, 2004).

5. *Everson v. Board of Education*, as printed in Robert S. Alley, ed. *The Constitution and Religion: Leading Supreme Court Cases on Church and State* (Amherst, NY: Prometheus Books, 1999), 52–54.

6. For instance, see Hamburger, *Separation of Church and State*, 422–63; Daniel Dreisbach, *Thomas Jefferson and the Wall of Separation between Church and State* (New York: New York University Press, 2003), 225n33.

7. Michael J. Perry makes just this argument, that restriction on the right of religious citizens to political participation is itself an unconstitutional act of discrimination. See *Under God? Religious Faith and Liberal Democracy* (Cambridge: Cambridge University Press, 2003), 28–34.

8. David Bebbington, *Evangelicalism in Britain: A History from the 1730s to the 1980s* (London: Unwin Hyman, 1989), 2–17.

9. Sydney E. Ahlstrom, *A Religious History of the American People* (New Haven, CT: Yale University Press, 1972), 637.

10. "Slaveholding Not Sinful" (1855), in Edwin S. Gaustad, ed., *A Documentary History of Religion in America to the Civil War*, 2nd ed. (Grand Rapids: Eerdmans, 1993), 488–91.

11. Quoted in Mark A. Noll, *The Civil War as a Theological Crisis* (Chapel Hill: University of North Carolina Press, 2006), 2.

12. The Works of the Right Reverend John England, in Gaustad, *A Documentary History*, 488.

13. "Conscience and the Constitution," as quoted in Noll, *Civil War*, 38–39.

14. Quoted in Noll, *Civil War*, 2.

15. Memoir of the Rev. Elijah Lovejoy, in Gaustad, *Documentary History*, 479.

16. Albert Barnes, "The Church and Slavery," in Gaustad, *Documentary History*, 497–500.

17. When Stowe had the occasion to meet President Lincoln at the White House, Lincoln, one story goes, said to her: "So this is the little lady who started this big war." While historians dispute whether Lincoln actually said this to Stowe, the legend testifies to the importance of *Uncle Tom's Cabin* to the elevated public sentiments that led to the Civil War.

18. Ed. Charles M. Wiltse, rev. ed. with an introduction by Sean Wilentz (New York: Hill & Wang, 1995).

19. Noll, *Civil War*, 65.

20. R. Marie Griffith, ed., *American Religions: A Documentary History* (New York: Oxford University Press, 2008), 216.

21. The rhetoric of radical abolitionists like William Lloyd Garrison, for instance, had proved relatively ineffective in persuading the average citizen that slavery was a terrible evil, because such radicals refused to ground their arguments in religion, and in general they demonstrated little regard for what the Bible said about it. Garrison's antibiblical stance only reinforced the position of proslavery theologians who depicted abolitionists as anti-Christian. See Noll, *Civil War*, 36.

22. Ahlstrom, *Religious History*, 673. Mark Noll recently has argued that the religious arguments of abolitionists did relatively little to resolve the stalemate over slavery. He calls the Civil War a "theological crisis," arguing that "while voluntary reliance on the Bible had contributed greatly to the creation of American national culture, that same voluntary reliance on Scripture led only to deadlock over what should be done about slavery" (*The Civil War as Theological Crisis*, 159). Noll himself admits, however, that religion helped "to provoke the war and greatly increase its intensity," but he thinks it showed itself "ineffective for shaping public policy in the public arena" (161). Considering the degree to which religious sentiment kept up the pressure for Lincoln's Republicans to prosecute

the war and end slavery in America, though, it would seem that religion contributed significantly to the political resolution to the crisis.

23. Walter Rauschenbusch, *Christianity and the Social Crisis* (1907; repr., 1991; with a foreword by Douglas F. Ottati, Louisville, KY: Westminster John Knox Press), 65.

24. Ibid., 71.

25. Ibid., 77.

26. Gary Dorrien, *The Making of American Liberal Theology: Idealism, Realism, and Modernity 1900–1950* (Louisville, KY: Westminster John Knox Press, 2003), 86.

27. Josiah Strong, a prominent leader of the movement, has been especially criticized for peddling the racial superiority of whites over blacks, and even Rauschenbusch was occasionally known to appeal to such racism.

28. Rauschenbusch, *Christianizing the Social Order* (New York: Macmillan, 1912), 125 (emphasis mine).

29. Presbyterians and others articulated their commitment to social justice in the Social Creed of 1908.

Chapter 4: Isn't Religion a Conversation Stopper?

1. Richard Rorty, "Religion as Conversation-stopper," in *Philosophy and Social Hope* (London: Penguin Books, 1999), 168–74.

2. It is not clear to me why Rorty calls this Jeffersonian perspective a "compromise," because that term implies that neither party gets everything it wants. What devotees of the Enlightenment give up in the so-called Jeffersonian "compromise" is not at all evident; as Rorty describes it, religious believers have made the principal concessions—unless you interpret Enlightenment toleration of us believers as a significant concession. But in a democracy, toleration is not a compromise; it *is* democracy.

3. This is a fair rendition of Rorty's classic stance, but late in his career he added a bit of nuance to his hostility toward religious reasons in public discourse, in response to critiques from philosophers Nicholas Wolterstorff and Jeffrey Stout. See Richard Rorty, "Religion in the Public Square: A Reconsideration," *Journal of Religious Ethics* 31, no. 1 (2003): 141–49.

4. Richard Dawkins, *The God Delusion* (Boston: Houghton Mifflin Co., 2006), 5.

5. John Rawls, *Political Liberalism* (New York: Columbia University Press, 1995), 226.

6. Ibid., 13.

7. Rawls's political philosophy is, of course, more complicated than I have portrayed here. Strict exclusionism remained Rawls's ideal, but in response to critics Rawls did adjust his position to allow for public arguments that appealed to comprehensive views. In *Political Liberalism*, Rawls imagined that appeals to

justice from within comprehensive views might occasionally be required in societies that are not "well ordered," that is, societies in which political justice is so dysfunctional that it needs a prophetic jump start. Lincoln's Second Inaugural and the public rhetoric of King struck Rawls as classic examples of warranted violations of "public reason." Eventually, Rawls modified his view further to allow for regular inclusion of comprehensive views in public debates, as long as those who offered them could articulate a public reason for their positions when required (when this would be required, Rawls never said). For this development in Rawls's position, see his essay "The Idea of Public Reason Revisited" in *University of Chicago Law Review* 64, no. 3 (1997): 765–807. Despite this evolution in Rawls's thought and nuanced "exclusionist" positions among other political philosophers (e.g., Robert Audi), Rawls's original position remains typical of many exclusionists in the popular debate over religion in American politics.

8. Thomas Nagel, *The View from Nowhere* (New York: Oxford University Press, 1986).

9. Ronald F. Thiemann, *Religion in Public Life: A Dilemma for Democracy* (Washington, DC: Georgetown University Press, 1996), 74.

10. Jeffrey Stout, *Democracy and Tradition* (Princeton, NJ: Princeton University Press, 2004), 64.

11. On this point, I am reminded of the Religious Right's support of "stealth candidates" in recent local elections across the country. These candidates do not campaign on a platform that makes their religious convictions and intentions plain, but once they are elected, they essentially seek to become arms of the Religious Right's control of local school boards and community councils. In these cases, voters may be surprised to discover the real motivations of those whom they elected, and they may rightly feel manipulated or "duped." Defenders of such stealth candidates seem to take as given that religious convictions will be unpersuasive to their public constituency, so they circumvent the democratic process, encouraging deception in the name of "good politics." By asking religious citizens to pretend they are something else in order to qualify for public conversation, opponents of religion similarly undermine mutual respect and the open exchange of ideas. For more on the use of stealth candidates in Religious Right campaigning, see Clyde Wilcox and Carin Larson, *Onward Christian Soldiers? The Religious Right in American Politics*, 3rd ed. (Boulder, CO: Westview Press, 2006), 47–48, 102–4.

12. See, for instance, Jim Wallis, *God's Politics: Why the Right Gets It Wrong and the Left Doesn't Get It* (San Francisco: Harper San Francisco, 2005), 110–22.

13. Lisa Sowle Cahill, *Love Your Enemies: Discipleship, Pacifism, and Just War Theory* (Minneapolis: Fortress Press, 1994), 73.

14. J. Daryl Charles, *Between Pacifism and Jihad: Just War and the Christian Tradition* (Downers Grove, IL: InterVarsity Press, 2005), 65.

15. Reinhold Niebuhr, *The Irony of American History* (New York: Charles Scribner's Sons, 1952), 143.

16. Of course, religion (particularly Christianity) is also implicated in this environmentally threatening shortsightedness. For a classic example of the charge that theology underwrites a destructive attitude toward the environment, see Lynn White, "The Historical Roots of Our Ecological Crisis," *Science* 155 (1967): 1203–7.

17. Rawls's own understanding of religion in politics eventually made room for these events, but as exceptions to a general rule against appeals to "comprehensive doctrines" like religion. See note 7 of this chapter. But to regard Lincoln's address or King's public witness as exceptional does injustice to the importance of religious contributions to American public discourse throughout our history.

18. Thiemann, *Religion in Public Life*, 72.

19. Ibid., 135.

20. Ibid.

21. Ibid., 136.

22. Ibid., 121.

23. Ibid., 140.

Chapter 5: Abortion and Stem Cells

1. Judaism and Islam are more complicated in their judgment of when personhood begins, but a large segment of both traditions assigns significant moral worth to the fetus by forty days after conception (though Jewish thinkers normally do not claim that the fetus is a full moral "person" until birth).

2. Recently there has been some movement on this restriction, however. As I am writing, there have been reports of scientists being able to "reprogram" somatic cells so that they revert to a less differentiated state, making them more broadly useful as substitutes for embryonic stem cells. Opponents of ESCR have hailed this development, of course, under the assumption that it renders the destruction of embryos unnecessary.

3. As examples of this unjustified optimism in the scientific community, opponents of ESCR often refer to fetal tissue research and gene therapy, two arenas that were supposed to usher in new ages of rapid medical advancement, but both of which have failed to deliver on the ambitious predictions scientists made for them.

4. Adult stem cells, more properly called somatic stem cells, are stem cells that are more differentiated than embryonic cells. As a result, to this point adult cells may be useful in regenerating tissue of the type from which they derive, but they cannot be programmed beyond those specific tissue types, thus limiting their applications.

5. Traditional Catholic moral theology can imagine circumstances in which an abortion might occur as a secondary consequence to a medical procedure and not be condemnable. For instance, in the case of an ectopic pregnancy, Catholic moral theology would allow for the removal of the woman's fallopian tube as a therapeutic measure, even though that procedure would also result in the termination of the

pregnancy. A case such as this one, however, does not represent so much an exception to the rule that intentional abortion is wrong, as a case in which the abortion is unintended—foreseen as a likely consequence of the other action (that is, the removal of the fallopian tube), but not wished for in itself by those involved.

6. See John Paul II, *The Gospel of Life* [*Evangelium Vitae*] (New York: Random House, 1995), §60.

7. What counts as "significant development" is an important debate too. A rudimentary brain stem has developed by the second month of pregnancy, but of course there is no cognitive ability. By the seventh month, brain waves similar to those of adults are detectable. But anything we could call cognitive capability in the human brain does not develop until late in pregnancy, arguably after birth.

8. The possibility of twinning has compelled some conservative thinkers to locate the beginning of personhood not at fertilization but after the twinning stage has passed. While still very early, this move already opens the door to justifying early abortion (for instance, the use of the "morning after pill") and ESCR (since the embryos used are seldom more than a week old), a consequence many conservatives would find hard to swallow.

9. Rabbi Elliot Dorff identifies as a "major principle" of Jewish medical ethics that "for Judaism the body is as much the creation of God as the mind, the will, the emotions, and the spirit are." So Dorff argues that from a Jewish ethical perspective "the body is morally neutral and potentially good." See Elliot N. Dorff, "Jewish Views on Technology in Health Care," in *Claiming Power over Life: Religion and Biotechnology Policy*, ed. Mark J. Hanson (Washington, DC: Georgetown University Press, 2001), 194.

10. Laurie Zoloth, "The Ethics of the Eighth Day: Jewish Bioethics and Research on Human Embryonic Stem Cells," in *The Human Embryonic Stem Cell Debate: Science, Ethics, and Public Policy*, ed. Suzanne Holland et al. (Cambridge, MA: MIT Press, 2001), 100.

11. Dorff, "Jewish Views," 195. The three commandments that cannot be overridden in the name of saving a life are idolatry, incest, and murder (Babylonian Talmud: *Tractate Sanhedrin*, 74a).

12. See Ted Peters, *Playing God? Genetic Determinism and Human Freedom*, 2nd ed. (New York: Routledge, 2003).

13. Those risks can include the side effects of the hormone injections and risks associated with overstimulation of the ovaries to release multiple eggs.

14. Suzanne Holland, "Beyond the Embryo: A Feminist Appraisal of the Embryonic Stem Cell Debate," in *The Human Embryonic Stem Cell Debate*, 80.

15. Ibid., 83.

16. Ibid.

17. See Ronald Dworkin, *Life's Dominion: An Argument about Abortion, Euthanasia, and Individual Freedom* (New York: Vintage Books, 1994).

18. Ibid., 71.

Chapter 6: The End of Marriage as We Know It?

1. Massachusetts opened gay marriage to nonresident couples in the summer of 2008 when it abolished its "evasion law," a 1913 statute that prohibited nonresidents to marry in Massachusetts if their marriage would be illegal in their home state. Critics had resurrected attention to the law out of concern that legalized gay marriage would encourage droves of gay and lesbian couples to flock to Massachusetts. The abolition of the evasion law was likely motivated as much by the recognition of the fiscal benefits to inviting nonresidents to marry in Massachusetts as it was by concerns for equal protection.

2. Maine's support of gay marriage was short lived, for Mainers overturned the decision by popular vote in the 2009 general election.

3. David Novak, "Some Aspects of Sex, Society, and God in Judaism," in *Contemporary Jewish Ethics and Morality*, ed. Elliot Dorff and Louis Newman (New York: Oxford University Press, 1995), 282.

4. Ibid., 275.

5. Ibid.

6. Ibid., 276.

7. Ibid.

8. Ibid., 277.

9. Stanley J. Grenz, *Welcoming but Not Affirming: An Evangelical Response to Homosexuality* (Louisville, KY: Westminster John Knox Press, 1998), 104.

10. Ibid., 106.

11. Ibid., 111.

12. Ibid., 113.

13. *Catechism of the Catholic Church* (New York: Doubleday, 2003), §2357.

14. Congregation for the Doctrine of the Faith, *Letter to the Bishops of the Catholic Church on the Pastoral Care of Homosexual Persons* (1986), §7. Found on Vatican's Web site: www.vatican.va/roman_curia/congregations/cfaith/documents/rc_con_cfaith_doc_19861001_homosexual-persons_en.html.

15. Arthur Waskow, "Down-to-Earth Judaism: Sexuality," in *Contemporary Jewish Ethics and Morality*, 299.

16. Daniel C. Maguire, "A Catholic Defense of Same-Sex Marriage," on the Web site of the Religious Consultation on Population, Reproductive Health, and Ethics: www.religiousconsultation.org/Catholic_defense_of_same_sex_marriage.htm#5.

17. Martha A. Ackelsberg, "Jewish Family Ethics in a Post-*halakhic* Age," in *Contemporary Jewish Ethics and Morality*, 307.

18. See Marvin M. Ellison, "Beyond Same-Sex Marriage: Continuing the Reformation of Protestant Christianity," in *Heterosexism in Contemporary World Religion: Problem and Prospect* (Cleveland: Pilgrim Press, 2007), 37–68. For a helpful summation of the concerns on all sides of the same-sex marriage debate,

see also Marvin M. Ellison, *Same-Sex Marriage? A Christian Ethical Analysis* (Cleveland: Pilgrim Press, 2004).

19. See Margaret A. Farley, *Just Love: A Framework for Christian Sexual Ethics* (New York: Continuum, 2006), 26–56; John Witte, *From Sacrament to Contract: Marriage, Religion, and Law in the Western Tradition* (Louisville, KY: Westminster John Knox Press, 1997).

20. In 2004 the American Psychological Association publicly opposed discrimination against gays and lesbians in access to marriage and parenting opportunities. The position was partially based on the APA's professional conviction that children of gay or lesbian parents tend to be as psychologically healthy as children of heterosexual couples. The resolution can be viewed at http://www.apa.org/pi/lgbc/policy/parentschildren.pdf.

Chapter 7: Living and Dying Well

1. Sometimes the term "euthanasia" is used as an umbrella to refer to all cases of deliberately ending the life of a patient suffering a terminal illness or some other intolerable condition. Strictly speaking, though, the term "euthanasia" refers to those cases in which a third party (for instance, a doctor) commits the act by which a patient's life is ended (by administering high doses of pain medication, for example). By contrast, "physician-assisted suicide" refers to those cases in which a patient gets help from a third party (for instance, getting a doctor's prescription) but herself commits the act that brings about her death.

2. See Mike Allen, "Counsel to GOP Senator Wrote Memo on Schiavo," *Washington Post*, 7 April 2005.

3. See the Harris poll from 15 April 2005, at http://harrisinteractive.com/harris_poll/index.asp?PID=558.

4. Richard McCormick, "Physician-Assisted Suicide: Flight from Compassion," in *Arguing Euthanasia: The Controversy over Mercy Killing, Assisted Suicide, and the "Right to Die,"* ed. Jonathan D. Moreno (New York: Simon & Schuster, 1995), 133–39.

5. Vigen Guroian, *Life's Living toward Dying* (Grand Rapids: Eerdmans, 1996), 29.

6. Reportedly one reason Pope John Paul II never "retired" from the papacy during his terminal struggle with Parkinson's and other ailments was because he wanted his public suffering and death to be this kind of moral lesson. By suffering publicly, he hoped to exemplify Christian dying, just as he had patterned Christian living, in contrast to what he considered the easy outs the "culture of death" commends in PAS and euthanasia.

7. Guroian, *Life's Living*, 35.

8. Ibid., 56.

9. Some who defend PAS and euthanasia on moral grounds argue nonetheless that the practices should *not* be legal. They suggest that keeping PAS and

euthanasia illegal, even if the judicial system turns a blind eye to the occasional use of them, prevents society from being too cavalier about the premature termination of a life. By contrast, the legalization of PAS and euthanasia risks making their use widespread, complicating regulation of them, and making it easier to justify the extension to nonvoluntary (euthanizing unconscious or incompetent persons) or even involuntary euthanasia. See Tom L. Beauchamp and James F. Childress, *Principles of Biomedical Ethics*, 6th ed. (New York: Oxford University Press, 2001), 144–46.

10. Karen Lebacqz, "Reflection," in *On Moral Medicine: Theological Perspectives in Medical Ethics* (Grant Rapids: Eerdmans, 1998), 666–67.

11. Ibid., 667.

12. According to Orthodox Jewish ethicist Laurie Zoloth, "After infants are born, their moral status is still in a process of development, albeit of a less dramatic nature. Children are not named or admitted to community (public) membership until the eighth day of life, and if a child dies before the thirtieth day of life, the necessary rituals of death are not performed (*shiva* is not observed, and the *kaddish* is not said for the requisite year of mourning)" (from "The Ethics of the Eighth Day: Jewish Bioethics and Research on Human Embryonic Stem Cells," in *The Human Embryonic Stem Cell Debate: Science, Ethics, and Public Policy*, ed. Suzanne Holland et al. [Cambridge, MA: MIT Press, 2001], 100).

13. Kenneth D. Wald and Allison Calhoun-Brown, *Religion and Politics in the United States*, 5th ed. (Lanham, MD: Rowman & Littlefield, 2007), 289–91.

14. Karen Lebacqz, "On the Elusive Nature of Respect," in *The Human Embryonic Stem Cell Debate: Science, Ethics, and Public Policy*, 149–62.

15. Allen Verhey, "The Holy Bible and Sanctified Sexuality: An Evangelical Approach to Scripture and Sexual Ethics," *Interpretation* 49, no. 1 (January 1995): 31–45.

16. Ibid., 44. See also Verhey, *Remembering Jesus: Christian Community, Scripture, and the Moral Life* (Grand Rapids: Eerdmans, 2002), 238–39.

Chapter 8: War *Is* a Moral Issue

1. See Jim Wallis, "Is Bush Deaf to Church Doubts on Iraq War?" *Boston Globe*, 9 December 2002; Jimmy Carter, "Just War—or a Just War?" *New York Times*, 9 March 2003.

2. Richard Land, "This Is Not Vietnam," Web site of the Ethics and Religious Liberty Commission of the Southern Baptist Convention (http://erlc.com/article/this-is-not-vietnam), 19 March 2003; Jean Bethke Elshtain, "A Just War?" *Boston Sunday Globe*, 6 October 2002.

3. Matthew 5:21–22 (NRSV).

4. *Religion and Ethics Newsweekly*, 19 October 2001: http://www.pbs.org/wnet/religionandethics/week507/feature.html.

5. Stanley Hauerwas, "No, This War Would Not Be Moral," *Time*, 23 February 2003.

6. Hauerwas, *Against the Nations: War and Survival in a Liberal Society* (South Bend, IN: Notre Dame Press, 1992), 16.

7. Martin Luther King, "A Christmas Sermon on Peace," in *A Testament of Hope: The Essential Writings and Speeches of Martin Luther King, Jr.*, ed. James M. Washington (San Francisco: HarperSanFrancisco, 1986), 253.

8. A good summary of "just peacemaking" can be found in Susan Brooks Thistlethwaite, "New Wars, Old Wineskins," in Jon L. Berquist, ed., *Strike Terror No More: Theology, Ethics, and the New War* (St. Louis: Chalice Press, 2002), 264–77.

9. The association of Niebuhr with communism was ironic, given his vocal attacks on suspected communist sympathizers and his contributions to the intellectual and political rejection of communist ideology in the 1950s.

10. Reinhold Niebuhr, *Moral Man and Immoral Society* (New York: Charles Scribner's Sons, 1932), 62.

11. Niebuhr, *An Interpretation of Christian Ethics* (New York: Meridian Books, 1958), 45.

12. Arthur Schlesinger Jr. "Forgetting Reinhold Niebuhr," *New York Times*, 18 September 2005.

13. What is currently known as the U.S. Conference of Catholic Bishops before 2001 was two separate working committees, the National Conference of Catholic Bishops (NCCB) and the United States Catholic Conference (USCC). See the USCCB Web site (http://www.usccb.org/whoweare.shtml) for a brief history of the Conference and its predecessor organizations.

14. By this criterion, of course, the U.S. bombing of two Japanese cities in World War II should be considered unambiguously immoral, despite the celebratory way the events were portrayed in my high school textbooks, even as late as the 1980s.

15. By "consequentialist argument" I mean the claim that the end of protecting American lives justifies the use of these interrogation techniques. I think opponents of torture do a disservice when they rely so much on arguing against these claims of effectiveness. More important, it seems to me, is the argument that a decent society would not employ torture *even if* it were effective, because it violates widely shared moral minimums for the treatment of other human beings.

16. National Conference of Catholic Bishops, *The Challenge of Peace* (Washington, DC: United States Catholic Conference, 1983), §16.

Chapter 9: Tree Huggers and Bible-Thumpers Unite

1. Lynn White, "The Historical Roots of Our Ecological Crisis," *Science* 155 (1967): 1203–7.

2. Genesis 1:28 (NRSV).

3. See, for example, Rosemary Radford Ruether, "Ecofeminism: Symbolic and Social Connections of the Oppression of Women and the Domination of Nature," in *Moral Issues: Philosophical and Religious Perspectives*, ed. Gabriel Palmer-Fernandez (Upper Saddle River, NJ: Prentice-Hall, 1996), 452–59.

4. For a thorough discussion of the conflict between fundamentalism and evolutionary biology in the late nineteenth and early twentieth centuries, see George M. Marsden, *Fundamentalism and American Culture*, 2nd ed. (New York: Oxford University Press, 2006).

5. Psalm 24:1 (NRSV).

6. For more information on this effort, see the COEJL Web site: http://www.coejl.org/climatechange/cc_cfl.php.

7. Robert Booth Fowler's book, *The Greening of Protestant Thought* (Chapel Hill: University of North Carolina Press, 1995), helpfully explores the evolution of environmentalism among modern American Protestants, mainline and evangelical.

8. David Willey, "Fewer Confessions and New Sins," *BBC News* (http://news.bbc.co.uk/2/hi/europe/7287071.stm), posted 10 March 2008. It is important to note that the pope also included embryonic stem-cell research and other biotechnology on the list.

9. *The Ecological Crisis: A Common Responsibility* (1990). Found on Vatican Web site: www.vatican.va/holy_father/john_paul_ii/messages/peace/documents/hf_jp-ii_mes_19891208_xxiii-world-day-for-peace_en.html.

10. Also apparent in this document is sensitivity around the issue of population control, which the Vatican sees as a moral euphemism for legalized abortion. Critics cite the hostility toward population control as a sign of troubling limits to the Catholic Church's commitment to ecological responsibility.

11. Amanda Little, "Cizik Matters: An Interview with Green Evangelical Leader Richard Cizik," on the *Grist* Web site, http://www.grist.org/article/cizik/, posted 5 October 2005.

12. Dobson and his supporters also released their own statement on the environment, in which they acknowledge that environmental stewardship is a biblical responsibility but voice their belief that the climate-change movement is based on faulty claims of "speculative dangers" based in disputed science. See Cara Degette, "As Cizik Crusades for Creation Care, James Dobson Insists 'We Get It!'" *Colorado Independent*, 15 June 2008: http://coloradoindependent.com/view/as-cizik-crusades.

Chapter 10: It's the Economy (Again), Stupid!

1. Domestic poverty and health insurance figures are taken from U.S. Census Bureau, *Income, Poverty, and Health Insurance Coverage in the United States: 2008* (report issued September 2009), 13 and 20.

2. Global hunger statistics are courtesy of Bread for the World, an ecumenical group that combats global and domestic hunger. See their Web site, http://www.bread.org/learn/hunger-basics/.

3. The creed can be found on the Web site of the National Council of Churches: http://www.ncccusa.org/news/ga2007.socialcreed.html.

4. See John Leland, "One More 'Moral Value': Fighting Poverty," *New York Times*, 30 January 2005.

5. For just one example, see the story of local religious groups working for universal health-care coverage in Massachusetts. See Eileen McNamara, "Healthy Support," *Boston Globe*, 5 October 2005.

6. Proverbs 29:7 (NRSV).

7. See Bob Abernathy's interview with Sister Campbell on the PBS program *Religion and Ethics Newsweekly*, 26 June 2009—http://www.pbs.org/wnet/religionandethics/episodes/june-26-2009/religion-and-health-care-reform/3377/.

8. Ronald J. Sider, *Rich Christians in an Age of Hunger*, 3rd ed. (Dallas: Word Publishing, 1997).

9. See Holly Lebowitz Rossi, "Poverty is Rick Warren's Passionate New Purpose" (RNS), on the Pew Forum on Religion and Public Life Web site: http://pewforum.org/news/display.php?NewsID=4938.

10. Riley's proposal was rejected by Alabama voters in the fall of 2003. See Bob Smietana, "Alabama Governor Says Faith Drives Tax Hike" (RNS), on Beliefnet Web site: http://www.beliefnet.com/story/129/story_12980_1.html.

11. This is not to say that evangelicals who advocate for the poor are not feeling a push-back from their religious brothers and sisters who would prefer that evangelicals stay focused on abortion and gay marriage. As one spokesperson for Dobson's Focus on the Family put it, "It's not a question of the poor not being important. . . . But whether or not a baby is killed in the seventh or eighth month of pregnancy, that is less important than help for the poor? We would respectfully disagree with that." While they grant that helping the poor is a biblical priority, many evangelical leaders claim it is of secondary importance to saving unborn children, and is a responsibility better entrusted with churches and charity than the government. See Jonathan Weismann and Alan Cooperman, "A Religious Protest Largely from the Left," *Washington Post*, 14 December 2005.

12. Jim Wallis, *The Great Awakening: Reviving Faith and Politics in a Post–Religious Right America* (New York: HarperOne, 2008).

13. Ibid., 133.

14. Quotes from the program are included in the paragraphs that follow. For a transcript of the interview on the 3 July 2009 episode of *Bill Moyers' Journal*, see the Web site: http://www.pbs.org/moyers/journal/07032009/transcript1.html.

15. *Rerum Novarum*, §27, in David J. O'Brien and Thomas A. Shannon, eds., *Catholic Social Thought: The Documentary Heritage* (Maryknoll, NY: Orbis Books, 2001), 27.

16. Pope Benedict XVI, *Caritas in Veritate* (2009), §36. Found on Web site of U.S. Conference of Catholic Bishops: www.usccb.org/jphd/caritasinveritate/.

17. In the United States, the Conference of Catholic Bishops has been the voice for Catholic moral theology in the public response to the economic crisis, reflecting major themes of Benedict's address and standing faithfully in the long tradition of Catholic social justice. As early as January 2008, the American bishops began peppering Congress with appeals on behalf of the poor and unemployed. As the federal government was considering various economic stimulus packages, the bishops pleaded for protection of programs like food stamps and the Low Income Home Energy Assistance Program, arguing that prioritizing low-income citizens was both morally appropriate and a good economic strategy. They insisted on accountability and responsibility on the part of those in the financial and political arenas who were responsible for the mess. Even before the release of Benedict's encyclical, they were reminding Congress that the economic woes were part of a larger moral disease, to which social solidarity and attention to the global common good were the only reliable antidotes. For examples of the bishops' petitions, see various letters to the U.S. Congress and Treasury at http://www.usccb.org/sdwp/national/economic-justice.shtml.

18. David Brooks, "A Natural Alliance," *New York Times*, 26 May 2005.

19. *Caritas in Veritate*, §56.

Chapter 11: In Defense of Civility

1. Gore's concession speech can be found at http://www.americanrhetoric.com/speeches/algore2000concessionspeech.html.

2. George W. Bush's election victory speech can be found at http://www.americanrhetoric.com/speeches/gwbush2000victoryspeech.htm.

3. It should be noted that Stewart's exasperation with *Crossfire*'s Tucker Carlson led him to express his concerns in ways that were themselves uncivil (including calling Carlson a vulgar name). That aside, Stewart's objection to the show was a refreshing public protest against media incivility, one that, according to CNN president Jonathan Klein, contributed to the decision to cancel that show.

4. Some examples of healthier political discourse on television do exist, of course. PBS's *Washington Week* with Gwen Ifill doesn't have the bells and whistles of cable news, but it offers some of the most substantive political analysis on television. Of course, part of the tragedy of Tim Russert's passing in 2008 was that it deprived the public of his leadership on *Meet the Press*, a show that took its dual priorities on accountability and respect from the character of its late host.

5. Os Guinness, *The Case for Civility: And Why Our Future Depends on It* (New York: HarperCollins, 2008), 152.

6. My students also fail to recognize the extent to which they hold similar "universal" convictions. For instance, relativists' assumption that all moral values are equally valid is itself a universal claim that justifies their judgment of conservatives.

7. Dana Bash, "With Spotlight on Obama, McCain Steps Up Attacks," CNN.com, 22 July 2008: http://www.cnn.com/2008/POLITICS/07/22/mccain/index.html?iref=newssearch.

8. Guinness, *Case for Civility*, 149.

9. Roger Williams, "George Fox Digg'd out of His Burrowes," in *On Religious Liberty: Selections from the Works of Roger Williams*, ed. James Calvin Davis (Cambridge, MA: Harvard University Press, 2008), 262.

10. For more on Roger Williams's vision of civility, see Timothy L. Hall, *Separating Church and State: Roger Williams and Religious Liberty* (Urbana: University of Illinois Press, 1998), chap. 4; James Calvin Davis, "A Return to Civility: Roger Williams and Public Discourse in America," *Journal of Church and State* 43, no. 4 (2001): 689–707; James Calvin Davis, *The Moral Theology of Roger Williams: Christian Conviction and Public Ethics* (Louisville, KY: Westminster John Knox Press, 2004), chap. 5.

11. Thomas Jefferson to Elbridge Gerry (a letter also known as "Reconciliation and Reform"), the Electronic Text Library of the University of Virginia, 1089: http://etext.virginia.edu/etcbin/toccer-new2?id=JefLett.sgm&images=images/modeng&data=/texts/english/modeng/parsed&tag=public&part=138&division=div1.

12. John F. Kennedy, American University Commencement Address, 10 June 1963. The speech can be found at http://www.americanrhetoric.com/speeches/jfkamericanuniversityaddress.html.

13. During George W. Bush's presidency, several Vermont towns debated whether he should be impeached over his handling of the war. More amusingly, perhaps, in 2008 two towns also voted to arrest Bush and Vice President Cheney for war crimes and obstruction of justice if the two should venture into the towns' jurisdiction.

14. My faith in the town meeting was tested in August 2009, when opponents to health-care reform planted activists in public meetings across the country with instruction to shout down public officials with charges of "socialism." Fortunately, the absurdity of these displays—and their incompatibility with the virtues of civility and public discourse—soon turned popular sentiment against them, and the tactic seems to have fallen out of favor.

15. *Religion and Public Discourse: Principles and Guidelines for Religious Participants* (Chicago: Park Ridge Center, 1998), 11.

16. For a copy of the task force's report, see http://www.pcusa.org/peaceunitypurity/finalreport/final-report-revised-english.pdf.

17. See James M. Gustafson, "The Church: A Community of Moral Discourse," in *The Church as Moral Decision-Maker* (Cleveland: Pilgrim Press, 1970), 83–95.

18. Ibid., 92 (emphasis mine).

19. Ibid., 93.

Index

abortion
  Catholic opposition to, 79
  as contest over human rights and interests, 77
  contributing to debate about when we become persons, 79–80
  discussion of, as part of consistent ethic of life, 70
  Judaism's approach to, 111–12
  justifications for, 87
  no exceptions to prohibition of, 79
  as public and private issue, 15
  thinness of debate over, 76–77
abortion rights, 9–10
absolutes, 12–13, 124
Ackelsburg, Martha, 96
Adams, John, 25, 26, 27–28, 33, 161, 162
Adams, Samuel, 29, 30
adult stem-cell research, 78
Ahlstrom, Sydney, 44, 49
America, calls to Christianize, 51–52
American Psychological Association, 182n20
Americans, in the ideological middle, 67, 111–14
American Values, 5
anointment, liturgy of, 107
anthropocentrism, 132–33, 134–35, 139
Appeal, in Four Articles; Together with a Preamble, to the Coloured Citizens of the World . . . (Walker), 46–47
Aquinas, Thomas. *See* Thomas Aquinas
Aristotle, 13
Ashʿarites, 172n13
assisted reproductive technologies, 92–93, 96
Augustine, 64, 123, 125, 136

Baptists, 38, 40, 175n3
Barnes, Albert, 45
Barton, David, 173n3
Basil the Great, 136
Beck, Glenn, 156
Beecher, Henry Ward, 45
believers, across the political spectrum, 7
"Believe Together: Health Care for All," 146
Benedict XVI, 137, 149, 150–51, 153
Bennett, William, 5, 13
Bernardin, Joseph, 70
big four of American moral conservatism, 3–4
Bill Establishing a Provision for Teachers of the Christian Religion, 33–34
black Protestantism, in the muddled middle, 112
Black, Hugo, 40–41
Bono, 147, 152
Bread for the World, 144
Brooks, David, 152
Buchanan, Pat, 16, 172n16
Buddhism, 13, 65, 118, 166

Bush, George H. W., 172n16
Bush, George W., 3, 4–5, 104, 120, 155, 163, 188n13
Bush, Jeb, 104
Bush administration (George W.), preventative war policy of, 64

Calvin, John, 83, 125
Campbell, Simone, 146
Campolo, Tony, 146
capitalism
  deification of, 151–52
  effects of, 49–51
Caritas in Veritate (*Love in Truth*) (Benedict XVI), 149, 150–51
Carlson, Tucker, 4, 187n3
Carter, Jimmy, 3, 117
Catechism of the Catholic Church, 93
Catholic Church
  addressing environmental issues, 137–38
  on homosexuality, 93
  opposition of, to abortion, 79
  on sex and marriage, 92–93
  social teachings of, 149–51
Catholicism, American, growth in, 40
Challenge of Peace, The (U.S. Conference of Catholic Bishops), 126–27, 129
Channing, William Ellery, 43
Cheney, Dick, 171n6, 188n13
Christian doctrine, 11
Christianity
  as a comprehensive doctrine, 58
  encouraging antagonism between humans and nature, 132–33
  environmentalism within, 136–37
  pacifist tradition in, 119–20
  theology of, hopeful realism of, 123
Christianity and the Social Crisis (Rauschenbusch), 50–53
Christian liberalism, 122
Christian nation
  advocates of, 21–24
  America as, historical evidence relating to, 24–31
Christian Right, assuming that morality requires religion, 32
Chrysostom, John, 136
civility
  in American history, 161–63
  commitment to, 156–58, 163–65
  defining, 159–61
  rediscovering, 67
civil unions. *See also* same-sex marriage
  as unsatisfactory compromise, 96–97
  Vermont as first state to allow, 89
Civil War, as theological crisis, 176–77n22
Cizik, Richard, 132, 139, 140, 146
climate change. *See* global warming
"Climate Change: An Evangelical Call to Action," 139–40
Clinton, Bill, 3, 89
Coalition on the Environment and Jewish Life, 136
Cohen, Jon, 6
collective egoism, 122
collective responsibility, 141–42
Colson, Chuck, 140
compassion, 83, 109, 110
comprehensive doctrines, 58–59
conflict, potential value of, 157
Congregationalism, establishment of, 27, 33
Congress, chaplains for, 30
connectedness, 65
conscience, freedom of, 83
conservatives, liberals' views of, 18
consistent ethic of life, 70
Continental Congress, 30
contraception, 92–93
Coral Ridge Presbyterian Church, 23
Corzine, Jon, 152

creation care, 138
Crossfire (CNN), 156, 187n3
culture wars, ix–x
  moving beyond, 16–19
  reality of, for "Christian nation" advocates, 24
Cushing, Thomas, 30

Danbury (CT) Baptists Association, 37–38, 39–40
Danforth, John, 156
Darwinian science, 134
Davis, Derek, 28, 30–31
Dawkins, Richard, 57, 134
death
  obsession with, 106
  remembrance of, 107
death penalty, 70
Defense of Marriage Act, 89
DeLay, Tom, 171n6
deliberation, private and public, 59
democracy, virtues of, 68
deterrence, theory of, 127
divorce, 113
Dobson, James, ix, 5–6, 140, 185n12
Dole, Bob, 144
dominion theology, 133, 134
Dorff, Elliot, 83, 180n9
Dorrien, Gary, 147–49
Douglas, Stephen, 163
Douglass, Frederick, 47
Dworkin, Ronald, 86–88, 110

Eco-Justice Program, 137
economic democracy, 149
economic justice
  as moral issue, 118, 143–53
  scriptural approach to, 145
economy, as moral issue, 10
ectopic pregnancy, 179–80n5
eggs, donation of, for ESCR, 84
Ellison, Marvin, 97–98
Elshtain, Jean Bethke, 117
Ely, Richard, 50
embryo
  considered human at point of conception, 77
  as potential person, 111
embryonic stem-cell research, 9, 10, 112–13
  conservative opposition to, 77–78
  obligation to engage in, 83–84
  requiring destruction of embryos, 78
  thinness of debate over, 76–77
end-of-life issues, 103–13
England, John, 44–45
Enlightenment, the, 24–25, 26, 29
enthusiastic religion, 42–43
environmentalism
  as moral issue, 118, 131–42
  theological support for, 141–42
Environmental Justice Ministries, 136–37
Environmental Justice Program, 137
ESCR. *See* embryonic stem-cell research
euthanasia, 9, 10, 105–6, 182n1
  discussion of, as part of consistent ethic of life, 70
  as public and private issue, 15
  religious defense of, 108–10
Evangelical Climate Initiative, 139–40, 141
Evangelical Environmental Network, 138
evangelicals
  cultural and political force of, 134
  growing interest of, in social justice issues, 146–47
  involvement of, in global warming debate, 132, 138–40, 141
  role of, in developing American moral traditions, 43
  suspicion of, toward modern science, 133–34

evasion law (Massachusetts), 181n1
Everson v. Board of Education, 40–41
exclusionist perspective, 57–58, 60
extramarital sex, 92

faith, as a worldview, 61–62
fallibility, 160
Falwell, Jerry, 173n4
  on America as a Christian nation, 21–23, 24
  assuming that morality requires religion, 32
  blaming 9/11 on American support for the homosexual agenda, 56
family, reimagining the definition of, 96
Family Research Council, 5
family values, disagreements about, 3
feminist theology, on abuse of nature, 133
fetus
  determining the personhood of, 79–82
  as potential person, 111
Focus on the Family, 5
Foley, Mark, 171n6
founders
  religion among, 24–31
  suspicious of talk about America as a Christian nation, 35
Francis of Assisi, 136
Franklin, Benjamin, 25, 26, 173n3
Frist, Bill, 104

Garrison, William Lloyd, 176n21
gay marriage. *See* civil unions; same-sex marriage
gender complementarity, 91–92
Gibbons, James, 50
Gladden, Washington, 50
Global Climate Change (U.S. Conference of Catholic Bishops), 137
Global Poverty Act, 144
global warming
  dismissing of scientific claims about, 134
  evangelicals' interest in, 138–40
  as moral issue, 131
God Delusion, The (Dawkins), 57
Gore, Al, 131, 155, 163
Graham, Franklin, 56
Great Awakening, The: Reviving Faith and Politics in a Post-Religious Right America (Wallis), 147
Grenz, Stanley, 91–92, 94
Grotius, Hugo, 64
Guinness, Os, 156, 157, 161
Gurorian, Vigen, 106–8
Gustafson, James, 167–69

Hagel, Chuck, 144
Haggard, Ted, 146
Hamburger, Philip, 39
Hauerwas, Stanley, 119–20
healing, importance of, 83–84
health care, as moral issue, 10, 145–46
Healy, Brian, 6
Henry, Patrick, 33–35
heterosexuality, correcting human tendency toward self-absorption, 91
heterosexual sex, theological meaning of, 92
Hinduism, 65, 119
Holland, Suzanne, 84
homophobia, 94
homosexuality, 113–14
  Catholic Church's outlook on, 93
  conversation about, needing to move beyond biblical one-liners, 90
  Presbyterian discussion on, 166–67
  running counter to human nature and divine intention, 90–94
Hoover, J. Edgar, 121
How, Samuel, 44
human consumption, 132

human dignity, 108
humans, embodied nature of, 82–83
humility, 160
Hussein, Saddam, 120
hyperindividualism, 65

Ifill, Gwen, 187n3
imago dei, 86, 92, 108, 133
incarnation, 133
Inconvenient Truth, An (Guggenheim, dir.), 131, 136
individuality, 80
industrialization, 49
integrity, 70, 159–60
interconnectedness, 65, 151
interdependence, 65, 151
Iraq war, 64
  debate over, 125–26
  ethics of, 117
  run-up to, 117
Islam, 8, 119
isolationism, 65

Jay, John, 30
Jefferson, Thomas, 25–30, 161–63, 173n3
  hoping for demise of "enthusiastic religion," 42
  invoking the wall of separation, 37–39
  suspicious of public religion, 39–40
Jeffersonian compromise, 56
Jesus
  death of, 107
  nonviolent responses of, 119
Jewish Council for Public Affairs, 136, 144–45
John Paul II, 80, 136, 137, 182n6
Jonas, Hans, 136
Jones, David R., 4
Jones, Serene, 147–49
Judaism
  on abortion, 111–12
  emphasizing healing, 83–84
  environmentalism within, 136
  involvement of, in economic justice issues, 144–45
  on moral status of infants, 183n12
  rabbinic tradition in, dialogical nature of, 166
  recognizing natural capacity for moral achievement, 8
  sexual ethic of, 95
Judeo-Christian tradition, 132, 135–36
just peacemaking, 120–21
just war, 64, 124–28

Kabbalah, 136
karma, 65
Kennedy, D. James, 23
Kennedy, John F., 163
Kerry, John, 4, 156
killing, prohibition against, 14
King, Martin Luther, Jr., 66, 120
Klein, Joe, 4
Klein, Jonathan, 187n3

labor movement, 149
labor unions, 49–50
Land, Richard, 117, 140
Langer, Gary, 6
Lebacqz, Karen, 109–10, 112–13, 114
Leo XIII, 149
"Let Justice Roll," 144
Lewinsky, Monica, 3
liberal Christians, role of, in developing American moral traditions, 43
liberals, conservatives' views of, 18
life, sacredness of, 86–88
"Life and Morals of Jesus of Nazareth, The" (Jefferson), 29
Life's Living toward Dying (Gurorian), 106–8
Limbaugh, Rush, 156

Lincoln, Abraham, 47–48, 66, 163, 176n17
Listen, America! (Falwell), 22–23
love, related to social justice, 149–50
Lovejoy, Elijah, 45
Luther, Martin, 125

Madison, James, 30, 34–35, 174n32
Maguire, Daniel, 95–96
Maher, Bill, 156
Maimonides, Moses, 13
marriage
  institution of, injustices surrounding, 97
  as political and religious institution, 99–100
  rejecting, as religious and legal institution, 97–98
  serving to further God's intentions for people and society, 91
  shaped by historical circumstances, 99
  theological significance of, 92
Martinez, Mel, 104
McCain, John, 159–60
McCormick, Richard, 105
McCurry, Mike, 144
McFague, Sallie, 136
McGuffey Readers, 43
McKibben, Bill, 136
Meet the Press (NBC), 187n3
"Memorial and Remonstrance" (Madison), 34
Millennium Development Goals, 144
moderation, in approach to moral issues, 111–12
moral
  defining, 10–11
  related to the political, 63
moral agendas, debate between, 7
moral discourse, 18–19, 168
morality
  defining, 14–15
  as part of political discourse, 63
  religion and, 32–33
Moral Majority, 22, 32
Moral Man and Immoral Society (Niebuhr), 122
moral values
  assumptions about, ix, 9–10
  broadening the sense of, 7–12
  debate over, recognizing common ground in, 110–11
  defining the issues related to, 117–18
  disagreements about, 3, 6–7
  many faces of, 12–15
  nonreligious, 8
  not needing to be absolute, 12–13
  private-public distinction relating to, 14–15
  recovering an expansive view of, 16–19
  relationship of, to one's worldview, 10–12
  restrictive and descriptive approaches to, 14
  role of, in 2004 presidential election, 4–7
  taking the form of rules, 13
  underlying views on many issues, 15
moral worldviews, political positions derived from, 8
Moyers, Bill, 147
muddled middle, 111–14
Muʿtazilites, 172n13
mutual respect, 69–70
myth of neutrality, 62
myths, of the Religious Right and the secular left, 75–76

Narrative of the Life of an American Slave (Douglass), 47
National Association of Evangelicals, 140

National Council of Churches, 137, 144
National Election Pool (NEP) Exit Poll, 4, 6, 14, 117
National Wildlife Federation, 131–32
Native American religions, 65
natural morality, biblical endorsement of, 172n11
nature, intrinsic moral value of, 135–36
NEP Poll. *See* National Election Pool (NEP) Exit Poll
Niebuhr, Reinhold, 64, 121–24, 128–29, 157
Noll, Mark, 46, 176–77n22
nonbelievers, commitment of, to moral worldviews, 7
noncombatant immunity, 126–27
nonviolence, 118–20
norms of plausibility, 68–71
Novak, David, 90–91, 94
nuclear weapons, 126–27

Obama, Barack, 3–4, 149, 156
Obama, Michelle, 156
office holders, prohibiting religious tests for, 35
O'Reilly, Bill, 156
original intent, determining, 21–31
original sin, 123

pacifism, 118–20
Paine, Tom, 30
Panetta, Leon, 144
PAS. *See* physician-assisted suicide
patience, 159
Perkins, Tony, 140
Perry, Michael J., 175n7
personhood, beginning of, 79–82, 179n1
Peters, Ted, 83–84
Pew Research Center, 6
physician-assisted suicide, 105–6, 108–10, 182n1
political, related to the moral, 63
Political Liberalism (Rawls), 58
political positions, consistency in, 70
politics
  based in conflict, 157
  different understandings of, in 18th and 21st centuries, 31
  governed by excess, 169
population control, 185n10
poverty, as moral issue, 143–45
power, as necessary facet of human society, 122
Presbyterian Church (U.S.A.), 136–37
  addressing issues relating to homosexuality, 166–67
  addressing the minimum wage, 144
preventative war, 64
prima facie norms, 13
prophetic witness, 66
Protestant Christianity, dealing with diversity of opinions, 166
public debate
  determining worthiness of, 68–69
  moving away from extremes in, 17–18
  mutual respect in, 62
  rethinking, 17
public discourse
  circumventing the objectives of, 71
  civility in, 72
  welcoming participation in, 68
public policy, religious grounds for, effects of, 55–56
public reasons, 58, 59, 66
public religion, role of, x–xi
Puritans, 38, 173n4, 175n3

Quakers, 162
quiet middle, giving voice to, 66–67

rabbinic dialogue, 67
Raspberry, William, 7, 8
rationality, as distinguishing characteristic of personhood, 80, 81
rational theism, 26, 29
Rauschenbusch, Walter, 50–53
Rawls, John, 57–59, 61, 66, 177–78n7
Reagan, Ronald, 3
Reagan administration, 126, 129
relativism, 158–59
religion
  contribution of, to political discourse, 19
  as conversation stopper, 56–57, 60
  different understandings of, in 18th and 21st centuries, 31
  environmental discourse and, 140–42
  government support of, 33–36
  growing role of, in environmental issues, 131–32
  improving debate over U.S. economic policies, 151–52
  linked with morality, 32–33
  as moral tradition, 26
  political divisiveness of, 55–56
  portrayal of, as a pathology, 57
  positive contributions of, 63–67
  promoting incivility and intolerance, 67
  role in American public life, 42–43
  role in America's ethical discourse over war, 128–29
  role in debate over slavery, 44–49, 55
  role in public dialogue, 153
  society's inability to determine which is "right," 57–58
  within public debate, 68–72
religious arguments
  reasonableness and accessibility of, 60–61
  responding to, 56–57
  secular liberals' mistake regarding, 60
  understood by nonbelievers, 61
religious bigotry, 40, 41, 56
religious communities, as models of civil discourse, 165–69
religious displays, on government property, 41–42
religious education, 33–34
religious freedom, as mantra of the new United States, 26–27
religious language, usefulness of, 66
religious perspectives
  attempting to understand, reasons for, 85–86
  enriching public discourse, 9
Religious Right, myth of, 75
religious traditions, contributing to moral values debates, 8–9
Rerum Novarum (Leo XIII), 149
respect, 160
resurrection, doctrine of, 82–83
Rich Christians in an Age of Hunger (Sider), 146
Riley, Bob, 146
Robertson, Pat, 22, 23, 24
Roosevelt, Franklin Delano, 124
Rorty, Richard, 56–57
rules, moral values in form of, 13
Russert, Tim, 187n3
Rutledge, John, 30

sacredness of life, 66, 86–88, 110
same-sex marriage, 9, 10, 113. *See also* civil unions
  debate over, as gauge of culture's moral direction, 90
  declared legal, 89–90
  issue of, as debate over moral values, 98–99
  as public and private issue, 15
  raising children within, 100

as social justice issue, 96–97
support for, 94–98
Santorum, Rick, 152
Saperstein, David, 144
Schiavo, Michael, 103–4
Schiavo, Terry, 103–5
schools, Bible readings and prayers at, 41
science, modern, responses to, 133–34
Scudder, Vida, 50
Second Great Awakening, 42–43
secular left, myth of, 75–76
separation of church and state, ix, 9
Adams's advocacy for, 28
coming from the courts, 40–42
gaining steam in the 19th century, 40
Jefferson invoking the concept of, 37–39
not in the Constitution or the Bill of Rights, 37
overstating the concept of, 36
sex, unitive and procreative functions of, 92–96
sexual compatibility, 92–93
sexual relationships, as feature of human sociality, 95
Sider, Ronald, 138, 146
Sierra Club, 132, 137
sin, 123, 148–49
slavery, debate over, religion's role in, 44–49, 55
Smith, Christian, 173–74n4
social conflict, unavoidability of, 122
"Social Creed for the Twenty-first Century," 144
social gospel, 50–53
social justice
as element of ESCR debate, 84
grounded in Scripture, 98–99
as moral value, 98–99
same-sex marriage as issue of, 96–97
social nature, humans', as distinguishing characteristic of personhood, 80–81
social reform, beginnings of, related to religious beliefs, 43–44
Sojourners, 138
somatic stem cells, 179nn2, 4
Soviet Union, cold war with, 124
Soyinka, Wole, 148
sportsmanship, 157–58
states, established churches in, 38
stealth candidates, 178n11
stem cells, undifferentiated, pluripotent, and immortal, 77–78. *See also* embryonic stem-cell research
stewardship, 135, 145, 151
Stewart, Jon, 156, 187n3
Stout, Jeffrey, 62
Stowe, Harriet Beecher, 45–46, 176n17
Strong, Josiah, 177n27
Stuart, Moses, 45
suicide, 105
swiftboating, 156

television, political coverage on, 156
thanatos syndrome, 106–7
"Theological Task Force on Peace, Unity, and Purity of the Church" (Presbyterian Church (U.S.A.)), 166–67
Thiemann, Ronald, 68–72
Thomas Aquinas, 13, 125
Thornwell, James Henley, 44
Thucydides, 148
tolerance, 158–59
torture, 128
Town Meeting Day (Vermont), 165

Uncle Tom's Cabin (Stowe), 45–46, 176n17
Unitarianism, 42
United Methodist Church, 144

United States, politics in, growing less civil, 155–56
USA Today, 4
U.S. Conference of Catholic Bishops, 126–27, 129, 137, 184n13, 187n17
U.S. congressional elections, 2006, 171n6
U.S. Constitution
  establishing societal framework based on equality, liberty, and toleration, 68
  lacking reference to God or religious authority, 35
U.S. presidential elections
  1800, 27–28, 39, 161, 162–63
  1860, 163
  2000, 155
  2004, 4–7, 156, 171–72n9
  2008, 156
U.S. Supreme Court, on church-state separation, 40–41
utilitarianism, 58

values vote, ix, 118
values voters
  identification of, x, 6
  role of, in 2004 presidential election, 4, 6–7
veil of ignorance, 59
Verhey, Allen, 113, 114
Virginia, religious freedom in, 33–36

Walker, David, 46–47
Wallis, Jim, 13, 117, 138, 147
wall of separation. *See* separation of church and state
war
  civilian casualties in, 126–27
  ethics of, 64–65
  inevitability of, 121–24
  just cause for, 125
  moral evaluation of, 128
  as moral evil, 118–21
  as moral issue, 10, 118
  as regrettable but justifiable, 124–27
Warren, Rick, 132, 138–39, 146, 147, 152
Washington, George, 22–23, 25–27, 32–33
Washington Week (PBS), 187n3
Waskow, Arthur, 95
Welcoming but Not Affirming (Grenz), 91–92
West, Cornel, 147–49
Western religion, history of, on environmental issues, 132–33, 141
White, Lynn, 132–33, 141
Willard, Frances, 44
Williams, Roger, 38–39, 67, 161–62, 173n4, 175n3
Wilson, Woodrow, 124
Witherspoon, John, 29, 30
Wolfe, Alan, 156, 172–73n17
Woman's Christian Temperance Union, 44
women
  concerns of, 43–44
  cultural hostility toward, 133
  health of, concern for, 82–83
World Council of Churches, 137
worldview, 10–11, 61–62

Zoloth, Laurie, 83, 84